# IS OVER THE ROAD TRUCKING FOR YOU?

# IS OVER THE ROAD TRUCKING FOR YOU?

## SECOND EDITION

### *EARN SIX FIGURES WITH NO INVESTMENT*

What you need to know about truck driver schools

GORDON J. KNAPP

authorHOUSE®

*AuthorHouse™*
*1663 Liberty Drive*
*Bloomington, IN 47403*
*www.authorhouse.com*
*Phone: 1-800-839-8640*

*First published by AuthorHouse    05/10/2011*

*ISBN: 978-1-4634-0333-1 (sc)*
*ISBN: 978-1-4634-0332-4 (ebk)*

*Printed in the United States of America*

*Any people depicted in stock imagery provided by Thinkstock are models, and such images are being used for illustrative purposes only.*

*Certain stock imagery © Thinkstock.*

*This book is printed on acid-free paper.*

*Because of the dynamic nature of the Internet, any web addresses or links contained in this book may have changed since publication and may no longer be valid. The views expressed in this work are solely those of the author and do not necessarily reflect the views of the publisher, and the publisher hereby disclaims any responsibility for them.*

# CONTENTS

This book is not intended as a substitute for legal, accounting or other professional services. It has been written by a lifelong trucker to inform, instruct, teach and guide. If expert service is required, the services of a competent professional should be sought. The author does not accept any responsibility for loss or damage that may be caused, directly or indirectly, by the information and opinions contained in this book. Any goods or services that are recommended are not the responsibility of the author or publisher. The ideas and opinions expressed in this writing are a result of information gathered through the author's experience and observation as well as the opinions and ideas of his peers. Some information is a result of media facts, comments and articles that have been paraphrased from memory. Any possible errors of facts due to hearsay are unintentional. Acknowledgements in most cases would be nearly impossible because of the many sources and overlapping information through the years from government and private publications as well as from radio and television. Please understand, the author's primary career was in trucking rather than journalism.

This writing has to do with the many inequities of long haul OVER THE ROAD trucking, of which there are many. Undoubtedly, some of the viewpoints expressed in this writing are not going to be very popular with some of those who are profiting most in these times from this phase of the transportation industry at the expense of those who are committing their time and effort to a profession that has gone from chaotic origins back in the Thirties to well-paid, organized labor in the Fifties through the Seventies and then in the Eighties back again to an unstable, sometimes unacceptable career in many cases, that sometimes does not even meet federal minimum wage and hours of service requirements for the major players.

In loving memory of my mother,

Ellen Elizabeth Knapp

Many thanks to my lifelong friend James Warren and his wife Carol for their helpful criticism and positive comments after reading my manuscript. As successful independent owner-operators, their opinions were very helpful in editing this writing.

I also want to express appreciation for the helpful comments from the many students that listened to me read from the unfinished manuscript and interjected their thoughts and opinions as we traveled about the country.

Author may be contacted by e-mail at *gordonknapp@comcast.net*, or facebook address is *gordonknapp68@yahoo.com* or call 435-817-0545.

# INTRODUCTION

In using the term OVER THE ROAD truck driver, I am referring to those who are gone away from home for at least a week and even up to several months at a time, with little control of when or where they go. It is these drivers that are badly in need of a major pay and benefits package overhaul, especially if this is their primary or only source of income. They number into the millions.

I do want to thank the many trainees that listened to me read from my manuscript as this writing progressed, for their input and encouragement to continue on and finish the book. There were many times that I became skeptical as to whether or not I should expose so much of the inner workings of this profession since it has been such a large segment of my lifelong career and one dislikes to be too openly critical of their own field of endeavor. The questions are, *how can we change things if we do not have the weapon of information? How much pain, suffering and death on the nation's highways must we endure before we have the courage and resolve to change the system causing these things?* Although a livable income can usually be earned, there are many conditions that need to be improved upon if OVER THE ROAD truck driving is to again become the respected and professional career it used to be. Newcomers feel as I do; that these things need to be told so that those affected by them can make intelligent decisions *before* jumping into this intriguing but troubled profession. It is hoped to assist those that can influence positive changes to do so.

The nation's highways are continually being flooded with new entrants into the field of OVER THE ROAD trucking who are inexperienced, timid and unsure of what it is all about, handling enormous equipment into areas they have never been before, in all kinds of traffic and adverse weather conditions. Contrary to what seems to be a popular belief, OVER THE ROAD trucking is not a 'one size fits all' career. These folks and anybody else taking on the responsibility and commitment of OVER THE ROAD trucking, certainly deserve more than what it has to offer them at this time. As they tolerate and endure the inequities of this 'profession', constantly keeping the country supplied with the basics of life every day, the arrogance and lack of compassion toward them by those who are ignorant of this field, and many who are not, is remarkable.

Before deregulation, Teamsters Union truck drivers used to dominate the highways and courtesy and respect existed to the highest degree. Compensation was as it should be. Benefits were excellent. Entry was difficult. Even the owner-operators and so-called 'gypsies' were more professional in their driving habits, as was the general driving public. It was contagious! Far more trucking took place during the nighttime hours while the public slept in safety. Since deregulation, everything has changed!

Millions of lives are affected daily by this profession, some in a positive way and others not positive. Most trucking now takes place in the daytime hours resulting in highway congestion being a major safety issue. This writing is intended to bring a more thorough understanding of what has happened to this profession in hopes that everyone may benefit in the end. Additionally, this book should be read by the spouse of anybody that drives a truck OVER THE ROAD so that they will more fully understand many of their partners functions and problems, whether it is the husband or wife of the other.

This is the second edition of this book and has been edited and condensed to make it easier for the reader to understand and find things of interest. Much of the first edition has been edited out because of duplication and 'too much information'.

Hopefully, this a much easier read for those interested in OVER THE ROAD trucking as a career.

# PREFACE

This material is an accumulation of thoughts, ideas and opinions from a lifelong trucker who experienced **over twenty years of city delivery and then another twenty-five years and more of OVER THE ROAD trucking.** I have been an owner of trucks and co-owner of distribution warehouses and manager of Teamster Union drivers. Additionally, I have experienced OVER THE ROAD trucking as a solo driver, team driver and as a truck driver trainer in OVER THE ROAD non-union trucking.

There are presently many thousands of people continually flooding into this field that have little or no idea of what OVER THE ROAD trucking is all about. It needs to be thoroughly understood up front that those in training could be gone several months during the initial training period, *probably with no physical contact with family or friends!* Upon completion of training, a week or so at home may be possible and after that they may regularly be gone three or four weeks or more at a time, depending on who they choose to work for.

Unlike other transportation industries that are periodically bailed out by government subsidies, that is planes, trains and buses, trucking has had to stand on its own merit and was doing so nicely until deregulated by the government, seemingly to disorganize and reduce the cost of most of the organized labor that ground transportation depends on; the OVER THE ROAD truck driver.

The good news for the public is that much of the money saved by not having to be concerned about fair wage and labor laws has been utilized to enhance and improve the overall service of the transportation industry as a whole. Many huge non-union trucking companies have been developed that can satisfy the transportation demands of the manufacturing and distribution industries to the fullest at tremendous cost savings.

The bad news is that this cost savings has ultimately caused the reduction or demise of millions of high-paying professional driving positions and replaced them with jobs of less than acceptable conditions, filled many times with undesirables. This has resulted in an unsafe and unprofessional attitude to develop in a major labor force (OVER THE ROAD truck drivers) due to the fact that most OVER THE ROAD truckers commit themselves to their job 24 hours a day for weeks, sometimes months at a time, and many times cannot even meet their monthly financial obligations due to inadequate compensation. Subdued anger and frustration are prevalent, sometimes explosive. Safety on the nation's highways, or lack of it, has now become a major issue.

Basically, there are two types of OVER THE ROAD trucking; regular and irregular route. This writing is mostly about the latter.

**After reading and understanding this writing, there should be little doubt as to whether or not OVER THE ROAD trucking is suitable for someone and their family.**

While at first glance it may seem very simple and intriguing to do this, the truth of the matter is that OVER THE ROAD trucking is very complex and not suited to most who pursue it for any prolonged length of time due to the various high risks and excessive time away from home, much of which is uncompensated for. This career is generally not conducive to most home life styles, *especially those with young families!* However, many unemployed people utilize it as a way to survive financially until they can return to something they are more comfortable with. Others choose it as a long-term career or stepping stone to local employment in trucking or related careers. Many older folks enjoy it as a second career after they retire from their primary profession.

Let me make one thing clear up front. I love trucking! Trucking has been my life! I thank the good Lord that I have been able to perform in a career that has placed such a variety of demands on a man's physical and mental talents and skills. It is a grass roots business. There is nothing else like it. Getting out on the highway in a big truck in the early morning hours is refreshing, invigorating and makes you feel good to be alive!

From the time I was a little boy, I have been fascinated with trucks. My father bought a tiny trucking company in the year of my birth (1940) that consisted of a pickup truck with only two wheels and a six-wheeler with only four wheels. His hired hand had to take two wheels from his car every day and put them on the pickup before he could start the workday, and then replace them to his car to go home at night. Times were tough in those years after the depression and during the WWII era.

I can remember riding on the truck with my dad as a boy and being thoroughly engrossed with all the ongoing activity. To me, truck drivers were important and very real people. I looked upon them as very special and viewed those who owned trucks with the utmost respect. For me, there has always seemed to be a certain intrigue or mystery about anything to do with trucking. Truck drivers worked hard and accomplished a lot in a day's time, moving goods from one customer to another. Nearly all other businesses depend on trucks to keep them functioning, one way or another. It was exciting to see how happy the customers were to get their shipments. Truck drivers were treated with great respect by those people, almost like heroes! That was local and short haul, city delivery. It was the real world for me and when I was old enough to drive a truck, my dad showed me the ropes. I looked forward to every day with great anticipation. Each day was another challenge and it was up to me to make it happen. It is much the same today with most types of trucking. Trucking is interesting, challenging, adventurous and educational. It is a fascinating business!

My dad always said 'a bitching truck driver is happy truck driver.' If that is still true today, there sure are a lot of happy truck drivers in this country! As far as I am concerned, it sure beats punching a time clock. However, there *is* much to complain about and rightly so. Most of those complaints are in this book.

Yes, trucking can still be a wonderful profession and fulfilling occupation. There seems to be something for everybody that is adequately prepared to pursue it. Besides providing jobs as company drivers, there may sometimes be opportunities to start a business for those with an entrepreneurial spirit. *Great caution is advised here!*

There is far more to OVER THE ROAD trucking than driving from point A to point B. Even the media has recognized that long haul trucking is the toughest and one of the most dangerous of all professions. *Do not take this lightly!*

My first book, "*All About Trucking and Becoming A Driver Trainer*" was an introduction to trucking in general. This writing is a more in-depth look at OVER THE ROAD irregular route trucking, with emphasis on safety and driver compensation as well as challenging working conditions and professionalism, or lack of it.

# IS OVER THE ROAD TRUCKING FOR YOU?

I have been doing this type of trucking for well over twenty-five years. It is this kind of trucking that everybody seems to be most interested in and wants to know more about. It is also here that most present day entry-level truck drivers get started and then may move on to other more local or regular route truck driving careers. To emphasize the importance of the distinction between all other trucking careers and OVER THE ROAD trucking, I have capitalized these three words (OVER THE ROAD) throughout this book. This writing has been carefully edited for maximum understanding by the reader. I suggest reading it at a relaxed pace for maximum comprehension rather than simply plowing through from start to finish. I also recommend using a bright yellow highlighter for items of interest to you. Repetition is prominent throughout for emphasis.

I am going to recap and expand on a few of the more pertinent thoughts presented in my first book because of overlapping with this writing. It will help in understanding some of the things presented in this book.

From OVER THE ROAD irregular route trucking a driver can transfer into almost any other type of trucking after he or she has gained adequate experience in handling a big rig and acquired the trucker's mentality or way of thinking, if you will. The 'feel' of trucking is important to a person. You can feel good about it and welcome the challenge or it can be drudgery and therefore become work. Equipment size is formidable! Variety of customers is unlimited. Traveling around the country in an eighteen-wheeler can be very enjoyable and adventurous. Every day is different and the scenic views can be awesome! Wildlife can be viewed that most people only see in magazine pictures or on television.

Due to the massive turnover in truck drivers, there are always positions open for new entrants into the field of OVER THE ROAD trucking. It is impossible to write a book that pinpoints *all* the endless demands and circumstances involved in OVER THE ROAD trucking and I do not claim to do that. I am simply trying to pass on what I have experienced in *my* lifetime as a trucker as well as what I have read about and talked about with other truck drivers. If some of the facts are in error, I apologize. It can be difficult to research facts while traveling border-to-border and coast-to-coast.

As co-owner of a small family trucking and distribution warehousing company many years ago, I feel that many of the present day OVER THE ROAD trucking companies are doing the best they can under the circumstances to satisfy their drivers needs and demands with the limited revenue available. However, some of these companies far surpass the rest in compensation and treatment of drivers. These will be the companies that will most probably survive the growing pains of this industry and will emerge as winners, along with their drivers.

Additionally, as a previous trucking company executive and then an OVER THE ROAD truck driver trainer, I feel it is necessary to present the career of OVER THE ROAD truck drivers from my viewpoint. Since I was exposed to both sides of the fence and then became a long-time driver trainer, I feel I have a considerable amount of first-hand information to offer new entrants constantly coming into the field, then leaving abruptly as reality sets in. This 'revolving door' is one of the main things that inspired my writings.

Having said that, the fact is that there are many times when an OVER THE ROAD truck driver can feel wonderful about his profession. Successfully handling heavy equipment sometimes is it's own reward. Each day is different and the freedom, traveling and sightseeing can be looked upon as a bonus. Few jobs offer as much variety. There is freedom to stop whenever and wherever you choose, even to sightsee and/or shop, as long as there are no local truck restrictions and you can meet your schedule.

*Having good common sense is mandatory!* This writing includes many of the day-to-day chores and driving situations and my ideas on how to deal with them. It is important to realize that there are as many opinions about OVER THE ROAD trucking as there are OVER THE ROAD truck drivers and this writing simply presents a viewpoint of the profession as *I* see it.

Usually, you must have a flexible attitude about when and where you travel because you must go where the freight is going rather than where you think you want to go. This is called 'forced dispatch' in 'irregular route' trucking operations and is commonplace, as opposed to always going to the same locations as in a 'regular route' trucking operation.

For those who are stuck in dead end careers and think they need a major change in their lives, trucking can do it. If you are changing careers due to the many layoffs and downsizing of many companies, trucking may also work for you. Many retirees are coming into this profession. There *is* a good income to be made as an OVER THE ROAD truck driver but it is *not* the simple profession most people believe it to be. Contrary to popular belief, not just anybody can do it! It is very important to realize this up front and find out as much as you can about it *before* getting involved in it.

In my first book I also described many different circumstances and conditions an OVER THE ROAD truck driver must be prepared to deal with and offered my ideas on how to best handle them. As I pointed out in that book, everybody has their own way of doing things. However, in this profession as well as many others, there are only so many options and some of them can lead to disaster. My choices were made based on the many years of experiences I had and the safe results of the solutions I chose. I would like to think that my thoughts will be helpful to those considering coming into this field and save them some heartache or assist them in their endeavor should they go ahead with OVER THE ROAD trucking as a career. Several trainees that read the manuscript as I was working on my first book said that they wished they had read it before they had obligated themselves to do this as a profession. Some said they would not have gotten involved in trucking and others said they would like to use that book as a manual. *This was the exact purpose of that writing!*

This book tells it like it is and how I think it should be, *with competent, experienced drivers being thought of and treated as valuable major players* instead of mindless pawns. *Every competent truck driver with experience has developed special skills and routines that are valuable* not only to him or her, but to those they do business with and the general public at large. It is mostly the multitudes of incompetent and inexperienced newcomers that are constantly creating problems. *While experience may be the best teacher, thorough initial training and schooling are mandatory* to provide drivers with the basic information necessary for them to comply with the various government regulations and company requirements. A couple of weeks in a driver training school and a few more weeks with a driver trainer are merely the *tip of the iceberg!* Far more time spent training and acquiring experience than is presently being done are necessary before someone can truly be considered a *competent, professional truck driver. Most present training is insufficient!* It is a matter of life or death!

In some cases, becoming an OVER THE ROAD trucker may be made to order for those that want to escape the humdrum of the eight to five segment of society and travel around the country, *if they can accept and meet all the requirements!* Especially if someone is already somewhat financially independent and simply would like to experience being a truck driver while riding around the beautiful United States of America and get in some sightseeing. I do not know of any eight to five job where you can pull into a rest stop in New Mexico and many other states and go over and pat the horses on the neck as the horse haulers are exercising them. Truly, we are 'commercial tourists' and more! This career can be a good option for those and OVER THE ROAD trucking has much to offer in this regard. There are many retired military folks that have come into this field for this reason and enjoy it very much.

This should *not* be construed to mean that the enjoyable aspect of trucking should be utilized or considered as partial compensation, as it is sometimes presented to newcomers. For comparison, the feeling of flying a Boeing 747 must be almost godlike to a pilot but he still gets *professional compensation and full benefits, paid for by the employer!*

There can also be times when a trucker wishes he never saw a truck. Hopefully, not too many of those! However, it is this aspect of the business that has caused much of the tremendous 'driver turnover', resulting in the ongoing so-called 'driver shortage'. In my opinion, if OVER THE ROAD truck drivers were professionally compensated, if nothing more than for the time he or she must be 'on the job' and away from home for weeks or months at a time under questionable living conditions, *much of the 'driver turnover' and 'driver shortage' would disappear.* It all comes down to time and money! If a person is deprived of being with family and friends because of his career, he should be fairly compensated for it and is in most other major professions. Additionally, some of the fines and penalties for forgetting or failing to comply with some of the local, state and federal regulations would stagger a millionaire! Earning capability of truck drivers does not justify such horrendous fines.

Due to the great numbers of new entrants constantly flooding into this field that are unfamiliar with the laws, rules and regulations of trucking, *millions of dollars in fines are continually being collected from them* by local, state and federal law enforcement officials! It seems as if everybody is preying on these 'greenhorns' to generate revenue in the guise of safety and compliance. Infractions by unsuspecting newcomers not only jeopardize the driver's commercial driver's license (CDL), but should they lose their CDL and not be able to continue with their new OVER THE ROAD trucking career, they also cannot return to driving their own car at another career because *they will have no driver's license. Double jeopardy!*

Additionally, *each individual trucking company has it's own set of rules and compliance requirements that must also be adhered to by their drivers.* Failure to do so can result in termination. Trucking companies tend to be very demanding of their drivers, most of the time with little consideration for the drivers' personal needs. In return, there are *no guarantees to drivers that they will acquire even enough miles to meet a minimum amount of income as compensation for their time, efforts and skills. It is this that is extremely one-sided in favor of the companies.* Minimum wage does not exist!

The brutal truth is, should there not be enough work for the driver to acquire adequate mileage pay or the truck breaks down resulting in unpaid waiting time, the driver's bills may not get paid, even though he was constantly on the job, available for work and far away from home, friends and family. *Again, it is important to understand that there are no guarantees of earnings!* This is a major shortcoming that has resulted in up to 300 percent driver turnover in some trucking companies and ultimately a serious driver shortage!

Over-hiring, inadequate scheduling and poor dispatching has a lot to do with this. Since a driver's time generally costs trucking companies nothing, there seems to be little or *no incentive for management* in most trucking companies *to be efficient in driver utilization.* Many times, to compound the problem, you cannot even get anybody in management to answer the phone or respond to sat-com (satellite) messages of inquiry that are sent to them, on a timely basis, if at all. *Voice messaging and telephone on-hold buttons can sometimes cause a brick wall* when drivers attempt to communicate with those that control their activity, or lack of it. Additionally, it becomes obvious that messages sent by the driver via sat-com are not even being read when specific questions that have already been answered by the driver continue to be asked by those on the other end. *This is a direct result of drivers being paid only by the mile rather than hourly, with no minimum wage provision!*

Should this be brought to the attention of their manager's supervisors, vindictive dispatchers have been known to make life on the road miserable and even more unprofitable for the (justifiably) complaining OVER THE ROAD truck driver. For the most part, there seems to be *no system of checks and balances* in regard to a dispatcher's performance and/or treatment of the drivers he is directing.

Many OVER THE ROAD truck drivers rationalize things to make this career more acceptable to them. Looking at the pay annually instead of hourly, daily, weekly or monthly, the picture may look somewhat brighter. What a driver does not earn during lean periods can many times be partially re-cooped later, although this may require a bit of 'creative' logbook work. It can ultimately result in a decent overall income by the end of the year. This is what keeps most seasoned drivers somewhat satisfied with their income but it does not justify being paid less than fair compensation and certainly compromises safety. *This is simply the way things are at this time, like it or not! More than a career, this is a lifestyle!* Computerized logging and/or on-board recorders would eventually eliminate this option. No more 'creative' logging! However, it would and should result in more realistic pay and conditions for drivers.

Anybody that can tolerate the lifestyle of an OVER THE ROAD trucker should be amply rewarded with *at least* enough income to afford a decent place for his family to live and a guaranteed pension after twenty years or so. Under present conditions, many retired OVER THE ROAD truckers are destined to live in sub-standard housing and depend solely on Social Security as retirement income. The financial rewards are sadly lacking! The demands are beyond any other career!

What we are dealing with here is a situation that requires that the driver actually live in the truck as if it were an RV (recreational vehicle) rather than staying in motels, although occasionally that is certainly an option, usually at the driver's own expense. There are some exceptions, such as driving for private corporations and union oriented companies. These companies generally pay better and cover motel expenses, sometimes with daily meal allowances, in a more organized and professional atmosphere.

If you are a self-starter, responsible, dependable and have good common sense, you have a good start. You must also be flexible in your thinking and be able to sort things out to your advantage on a daily basis. To be successful as an OVER THE ROAD truck driver, you have to develop basic routines related to the daily activity pertinent to keeping your truck in good condition to reduce or avoid the many problems that can occur. While it is understood that while everyone does things in order of their own personal priority, if the basics are neglected, overlooked or forgotten, they can become not only a priority, but also a necessity. Regular equipment inspections can prevent breakdowns and accidents from happening later. If you are mechanically inclined, it can be an advantage but is not required. However, *regular preventive maintenance by a qualified mechanic is mandatory!* If you have an eight to five mentality, forget it! This is not for you!

The effects of deregulation were the result of many years of political plans for reducing transportation costs and therefore went virtually unnoticed and were accepted by everyone, even somewhat by the truck drivers, who had no say in the matter. Millions of truck drivers ultimately suffered dramatic loss of earnings while those causing this loss profited from it, and still are.

To those in management who are truly concerned about ending the 'driver shortage' and are genuinely interested in correcting the conditions causing it, this writing may be very helpful and informative in helping to solve some of the many problems. Trucking is a very high-cost industry and driver compensation is one of the highest cost factors, as is the labor cost in most other industries. The thing to keep in mind is that without drivers willing and able to get behind the wheel and move product throughout the country, nothing else can happen and nobody else would get paid because there would be no revenue. Good, dependable, responsible and safe drivers are crucial to the success of all trucking companies and can better be retained through adequate compensation, home time when needed, and acceptable working conditions.

# TRAINEE COMMENTS RE: AUTHOR'S FIRST BOOK, "ALL ABOUT TRUCKING AND BECOMING A DRIVER TRAINER".

My name is Danny Harris. I am twenty-four years old and training to be an over the road truck driver. I am married and we have a three-year-old son. I wish I had read Gordon Knapp's book *ALL ABOUT TRUCKING AND BECOMING A DRIVER TRAINER* before I went and spent all this money on two weeks of driver training for $7,500.00 plus 19 % interest which brought it to over $17,000.00 over ten years.

Especially since I graduated from the school after only eight days and got no refund for the motels I didn't use or the time not spent to comply with the trucking companies' requirement of 140 hours schooling. My school gave me an appropriate certificate even though I was only there 80 hours.

Because I was excited about getting into a new high paying career, I didn't consider how emotional my wife and three year old son would be without their husband and daddy home for weeks at a time, and of course, they didn't either.

Since Gordon Knapp's book gets into the details involved with this type trucking, I would have definitely taken more time to think things out and done things a lot different, even though I would have still gone ahead with trucking as a career.

That book has far more practical and useable information than the $7500.00 school presented to me and I recommend it to anybody that wants to know what long haul trucking is all about.

I know that the other students that attended my school would have benefited from that book.

Something should be done about these schools ripping off people like me that can't afford to lose this kind of money in good faith.

This is a 'must read' for anyone interested in trucking of any kind as a career.

---

The last time I heard about Danny, he was doing fine as an OVER THE ROAD truck driver

Another trainee:

My name is Roosevelt Owens. Why did I come into this field? I felt there were a lot of job opportunities and I could move around to different companies, if necessary, to find the right job for me.

It hasn't turned out like I expected because now that I'm here I find out there are few benefits and no paid holidays or other things I had in my previous career.

I am glad to get my CDL [commercial driver's license] so now I can find a local job and be home regular and still make a good living that includes being with my family.

At first it seemed exciting traveling around the country but now, after being here a few weeks, that has worn off and I need to be with my family. I have a wife and two sons, eight and fifteen, that need their Dad around. This kind of life style is not for me.

If I had the information in Gordon Knapp's book I could have done things differently by making different choices.

Anyone coming into this field needs to do a lot of research, one way or another.

---

I have no idea what happened to Mr. Owens or hundreds of other trainees of my acquaintance.

# PURPOSE OF THIS BOOK

The purpose of this book is to provide information, advice and opinions about OVER THE ROAD trucking that may be helpful to anyone interested in trucking as a career. It is hoped that by pointing out the many realistic aspects and demands of the transportation industry in advance of entry into it that *those who are serious about it will be encouraged and those that are not will refrain from getting in the way. There are already too many inexperienced and unsafe truck drivers on the highways!* The results can be observed constantly. It is also hoped that by pointing out the problems relating to this profession, it will create a dialog to influence those that can effect changes, to do so as time and circumstances allow. Without such dialog, nothing is likely to improve any time soon.

This writing is intended to *help everybody understand* some of the many different aspects associated with big trucks so that *all* may benefit, one way or another. Presently, there is a gross lack of understanding by nearly everyone about OVER THE ROAD trucking, as well as trucking in general. *This includes the general population, which is badly in need of knowledge about safely sharing the nation's highways with big commercial trucks.* It also includes shippers, receivers, those in transportation management, lawmakers, law enforcement and safety organizations as well as many others in transportation related industries and endeavors. *Safety on the highways is a key issue to everybody!*

It basically comes down to the *pay and conditions. It's all about money, or lack of it!* Undoubtedly, this is a major factor that causes OVER THE ROAD truck drivers to always be in a hurry, *driving over-aggressively.*

Over-aggressive driving frequently ends in disaster! It may be difficult for some people to realize that *there are up to fifty-five thousand fatalities a year due to traffic accidents!* The stark reality of this hits you when you come upon an accident and see *people's bodies being covered up* and others being taken away in ambulances or helicopters. *Knowing how to deal with or avoid many of these circumstances is important to everyone!*

An important fact to consider is that *trucking has had one of the highest fatality rates of any profession!* Accidents caused by inexperience, poor judgment, other traffic and hazardous road conditions can many times be fatal. Statistics on trucking accidents and the resulting fatality rates of truck drivers seem to be sketchy, possibly *so it will not discourage badly needed newcomers from coming into the field* due to the already *immense driver turnover and driver shortage problem.* It seems as if only *after* trainees have made a non-refundable *financial* commitment are they exposed to the many great dangers involved in the transportation industry.

I urge great caution to newcomers before obligating to a private truck driving school as opposed to a training school operated by an OVER THE ROAD trucking company. Of course, there are many acceptable private schools but I feel that most potential students would have a difficult time sorting out the good from the mediocre or those mainly interested in taking the student's money for minimal training, whereas *trucking companies need good drivers for their trucks.*

**Throughout this writing are circumstances that I feel need improvement to enhance the profession of OVER THE ROAD trucking for drivers, management and the safety of the driving public at large. They will be mentioned whenever deemed necessary, for emphasis.** Many of the different shortcomings are connected to the same problems that are causing them and those things will be repeated.

While there are many things that need to be improved, it is noteworthy that there have also been several positive steps taken over the past two decades since deregulation, among which are *newer, upgraded equipment* to drive and massive *truck stop improvement*. *Satellite technology* has also been introduced which provides instant communication almost anywhere. Additionally, whereas years ago non-union trucking companies specializing in OVER THE ROAD transportation operated out of sub-standard facilities consisting many times of ghetto office buildings or broken down house trailers, there are now *premium terminal facilities* and new office buildings with *first-class accommodations for their drivers.* Many companies provide big-screen TV rooms, laptop hookups for personal computers, exercise rooms, free laundry facilities and showers. Clearly, these improvements have been accomplished with the drivers' well being in mind, *albeit at the driver's expense,* as will be explained later.

**Among advanced technologies that have been forthcoming is the often-feared 'black box' on-board computer that could and should entirely replace logbooks while at the same time change driver compensation from pay per mile to pay per hour. This one major change in the world of trucking could completely revolutionize transportation and at last get drivers a 'fair days pay for a fair days time and effort'.**

Let us hope it happens sooner rather than later. These hard working people need help now!

I challenge anybody to tell me things are not as I describe in this book with few if any exceptions! Once again, as in my first book, although there are many very qualified women truckers too, we will use the male gender in referring to truck drivers for the sake of simplicity. To think I am promoting a union would be a mistake but these drivers do need some help regarding industry wide representation.

# 1.

# IS OVER THE ROAD TRUCKING FOR YOU?

Still interested? OVER THE ROAD trucking has taken a real beating in this writing so far and we are just beginning. Being fairly paid is clearly the biggest shortcoming. The lifestyle is also a major problem. Only families with the strongest of relationships can survive OVER THE ROAD trucking as a long time career! The divorce rate for truckers is high. Very high!

## 1.  OVER THE ROAD TRUCKING IS A STARTING POINT

Many people try *OVER THE ROAD* trucking as a starting point but eventually give it up after a short time. Some come back to it later, others go on to other endeavors, never to return. Most find local trucking positions that allow them to be home regularly. Others may go into management positions in trucking, such as dispatchers, fleet managers or maintenance positions. There is definitely a lot of opportunity in the transportation field, one way or another. One big advantage as a driver over many other professions is the flexibility to move anywhere in the country and not have to be concerned about a job. Trucking is everywhere. An old trucker saying is, "Once a truck driver, always a truck driver".

## 2.  GETTING STARTED

If you are going to become an OVER THE ROAD company driver you must have a starting point. *There are as many different pay and benefit packages as there are carriers.* Some of these companies start new drivers out at less than desirable rates of pay and take years to get to the top rate, which can soon discourage a sole breadwinner trying to support a family. Others have moderate rates of pay to start and quickly increase the rate to top level so that drivers with proven track records will stay on as valued long-term employees. Obviously the latter is a better choice.

The unwary apprentice drivers that are unlucky enough to get with a company that pays five or ten CPM (cents per mile) less than others for the same work are actually subsidizing those companies with their cheap labor. Let us take a quick look at this. Ten CPM for driving 100,000 miles in a year comes to $10,000 and most experienced drivers average 150,000 miles in a year that would bring it to $15,000.

To my way of thinking, *anything less than thirty cents per mile (CPM) to operate an 18-wheeler is not a realistic rate for even a beginner to make an acceptable income at this time.* I realize that many people without advanced education are coming into trucking from other jobs and may be used to earning meager incomes of four and five hundred dollars a week, so if they can earn six or seven hundred dollars a week at twenty-five CPM, they are satisfied. This may be all right for a short time but when they begin looking around at other driver pay packages after they have 'gotten their feet wet', so to speak, it then becomes obvious to them that they have chosen the wrong company to work for. Especially, when they realize their rate will escalate very slowly to what other new drivers are making from the start working for other companies and that those drivers' pay will soon go to a higher rate of forty CPM and up. Meanwhile, the under-paid new driver has spent time and effort developing relationships with dispatchers and other company personnel that may be difficult to leave behind. Good people to work with in any company are hard to find. It can take a long time for you to 'prove' yourself to the point of being respected as an experienced or 'favored' driver, if you will.

The main point I am trying to make here is that you need to check out as many options as possible and go with one of the leaders rather losing a lot of time and effort having to change jobs later because of undesirable pay and conditions.

Companies that are paying up to 40 CPM and higher are finally increasing. To my way of thinking, new drivers would be doing themselves a big favor to check into these companies sooner rather than later. Starting pay for new drivers with these companies is usually over 30 CPM. Such companies are setting the pace. Other incentives and bonuses may be included that make working for less just not feasible. Medical and life insurance, paid vacation time and holidays figure prominently here, as well as conditions.

Advantages of working with a small trucking company might be:

1. Fancy, made to order truck.
2. Fast truck.
3. Home regular (maybe).
4. Better personal relationship with dispatch.
5. Better recognition for a job well done.
6. More flexible routes and fuel stop selection.
7. Feeling of freedom and independence, similar to an owner-operator, without being one.
8. More logbook flexibility.

Disadvantages can be:

1. Financial instability, resulting in loss of pay in case of a business failure.
2. Few or no benefits.
3. No trailer pools for drop/hook operation.
4. Favoritism.
5. Speeding tickets.
6. Wrecks due to fatigue and high speed.
7. No holiday pay.
8. No vacation pay.

Going into a terminal facility of a large trucking company can be confining since most companies do not allow their drivers bob-tailing out and using the truck cab as a taxi. Once you enter the terminal facility, if you do not have a personal vehicle there, you are basically trapped unless you are within walking distance of the outside world. Of course, you can always call a cab and some companies provide limited shuttle services. Some drivers are buying mini-bikes with lawnmower size engines and attach them to the back of their cab so when they get somewhere and they have to wait they will have their own transportation. That could be a little hairy in the winter or in bad weather. Keeping an expensive item such as this from being damaged or stolen might also be a challenge.

## 3. FIND A COMPANY IN THE RIGHT LOCATION

This is why it is important that you choose a company that is located near where you live or has heavy traffic lanes through there so you can stop by the house on the way to your deliveries. Your lifestyle must be altered to fit the job, rather than vice verse. All members of your household will be affected one way or another. Knowing and accepting this upfront is imperative. Being unable to get home on a timely basis is a major concern. Most companies recognize this and are doing the best they can to improve this situation. Some do not seem to care. Where you live can make all the difference in how often you get home.

## 4. LIVING IN A TRUCK

As an OVER THE ROAD trucker, be prepared to live in a truck for long periods of time and to drive thousands of miles (hopefully} each week on interstate highways as well as on lesser U.S., state and county roads, in all kinds of weather. Having a truck for a home is mentioned casually but *is a major part of this profession!* Realization of this alone can be reason enough for some to pack it in. It is a 'hurry up and wait' business, usually without motels or other accommodations while waiting unless the driver pays for them himself.

Most companies allow drivers to take their truck home during a few days off. However, if you want to take a week or so of prolonged time-off you may be required to turn your truck in for someone else to use (live in). This equipment is very expensive and must produce regular income to justify the expenditure and maintain profitability for the company. What this means is that you must remove all your belongings from the truck and store them somewhere until you are ready to return to work, at which time you will be assigned another truck. This can be quite an inconvenience should you live more than a couple of hours away from one of your company's facilities and do not have your car available to use. You may have to find storage for your things either at a company location or rental facility and then find a way home, probably at your own expense. Because of this aspect most drivers do not take extended time off so that they will not have to endure this hassle. The drivers seem to be prisoners to their trucks that in turn can result in drivers quitting.

## 5. REALITY

Reading or hearing about doing something is one thing but actually doing it is quite another, especially in this career. It can be real easy to think, "Oh, I can do this, no problem." However, the reality of full participation will not be forthcoming until you actually get involved and behind the wheel as an OVER THE ROAD truck driver.

Handling the heavy over-sized equipment efficiently is one thing but accepting the lifestyle is quite another. Being gone away from home for several weeks at a time in all kinds of weather while accepting responsibility for an over-sized behemoth that most of the general public does not want around anyway, does not enhance the profession.

I have heard it said many times that 'anybody can drive a truck'. While this may or may not be true, there is a world of difference between someone who can drive a truck and a truly professional truck driver. It does not matter that 'anybody' can drive a truck. It *matters* that they do it *safely!* It *matters* that *they are away from home for weeks at a time!* It *matters* that they *receive realistic and fair pay and benefits!* It *matters* that *they be treated with dignity and respect!* In truth, just anybody *cannot* drive a truck! The reasons are obvious.

OVER THE ROAD trucking equipment is very expensive. Properly maintained trucks that continually travel nationwide must constantly be in top condition to avoid breakdowns and accidents. So must those that drive them! It is the responsibility of these professional truck drivers to realize that most of the general public simply lacks the knowledge of just how dangerous it can be to share the nation's highways with OVER THE ROAD trucks and drive accordingly. In addition to the fact that these truckers are expected to meet all schedules on a timely basis, they must nevertheless be knowledgeable in safety and accident prevention to the highest degree to compensate for the ignorance of others that simply do not realize or understand what trucking is all about. Patience and understanding are mandatory! The forward momentum of this heavy equipment moving at highway speeds is formidable! *Truck drivers must hurry, slowly!*

## 6. NO MILES, NO PAYCHECK

There are many variables beyond a driver's control that constantly affect his daily mileage and therefore, his earnings. O*ne of the toughest parts of this career is being on the job and waiting around for hour after hour sometimes days without pay to get dispatched for a load!* I think I speak for all OVER THE ROAD truck drivers that have experienced this and there are many. Nobody works for nothing! *Except* present day OVER THE ROAD truck drivers!

## 7. WORK BY THE H0UR BUT PAY BY THE MILE

Additionally, since compensation for this profession is based almost solely on the *number of miles driven* it can result in a very meager paycheck if the truck does not move for some reason, of which there are many. *Again, the OVER THE ROAD truck driver's time is of minimal or no consideration!* Why should this be? What about minimum wage? What about the labor laws governing overtime? What about the welfare of the trucker's family? What about the age-old adage, "Time is money!" *What about the safety of the motoring public?*

It would seem that *freight rates are simply too low* to adequately provide professional compensation that is comparable to other highly demanding careers. There does not seem to be enough revenue to go around. Significantly, various shippers and receivers have commented that *they too,* do not understand how freight rates have not increased appreciably from what they were *thirty years ago* since the cost of fuel, trucks, maintenance, insurance and other costs *have* kept up with inflation! The fact that apprentice OVER THE ROAD truck drivers are earning *less than half what truck drivers used to make* might have something to do with it among other things such as *having to pay for their own benefits and those of their families out of their already somewhat meager earnings.*

Time and money are two of the most precious things in life but both are being deprived of most OVER THE ROAD truckers. This deprivation not only results in unprofessional and unsafe driving methods but also affects each and every family member of each and every OVER THE ROAD truck driver.

I am not going to pretend that I know all there is to know about trucking. Only a fool would do that! Transportation is such a wide field that the many people and industries affected by it are virtually unlimited. However, I was involved in not only trucking but also warehousing and distribution. Therefore, I am able to look at things from the other side of the fence, if you will. Following are just a few of the issues you will have to deal with.

It seems that every business involved in material handling and transportation is continually struggling to maintain a profit any way possible and one way to do it these days is to get the employees to perform many duties with little or no cost to the company.

The big one in trucking of course is waiting time! This can be very costly if an employer has to pay his drivers by the hour! *Hence, the modern day OVER THE ROAD truck driver had better be prepared to spend a lot of time waiting without pay for many things that he is expected to do because he will be paid strictly by the mile!* These things include equipment maintenance and repair, waiting to get dispatched, loaded and unloaded and countless other duties. Once the truck driver realizes that this is expected of him and feels he can accept it he just might make it!

I think the following story explains the difference very well. Years ago, there was a blizzard in the northeast so severe that it completely closed down all highways for hundreds of miles. Since it was obvious that it would take several days to open highways up after the storm, some of the trucking companies that employed union drivers for such delays sent helicopters in to retrieve their drivers and get them 'off the clock'. Everyone else had to wait it out!

## 8. NEGLECTED REPAIRS

Because of most drivers getting paid little or nothing for waiting time of any kind, it has resulted in many drivers failing to report needed repairs on trailers they are dropping somewhere. Taking these deficient trailers to a repair shop and/or waiting for the repairs to be done requires plenty of time, all without pay. They simply leave it for the next driver, who then must take the trailer to a shop for repairs before going to his pickup or delivery, possibly causing him to miss an appointment, resulting in another delay. Flat tires are the most common problem I have found regarding this situation. Broken springs, missing lights and malfunctioning landing gear can also be a problem. Thorough inspections should be made when picking up trailers, especially if you are getting an empty trailer and have more than one to choose from. Long delays at customers to get loaded or unloaded are also commonplace.

This situation will never be resolved until people in management positions at shippers and receivers are made to realize that a delay in the loading or unloading of trucks servicing their account will cost their company money by having to pay detention charges (to drivers) for this time. This is one of the key problems that contribute to truck drivers being inconsiderate of each other in all other areas. It has resulted in rude drivers crowding ahead of each other whenever possible. The pressure to get as many miles as possible for maximum earnings is tremendous and continuous!

Presently, there are only a few trucking companies that will charge shippers or receivers detention for delaying their truck and driver. This is because trucking companies fear losing the business to another carrier that will tolerate this nonsense. *This is a very cutthroat business!*

## 9. TIME IS MONEY

*Time is money!* Unless you are an OVER THE ROAD truck driver! It is not uncommon for OVER THE ROAD truck drivers to sit around all day waiting for a load, only to get dispatched just before the day office shift goes home, even though the loads may have been available many hours sooner that same day. The problem is that many drivers cannot sleep during the daytime and therefore busy themselves with various activities, waiting for a load that may not come until late in the day or early evening. This causes driving during the nighttime hours in a tired condition, most probably with a bad attitude since it can be very difficult to get any sleep during the daytime due to anticipating a load and/or interruptions of one kind or another, resulting in *broken sleep or unfinished naps.* To make a point of comparison, waking prisoners of war from a deep sleep is a form of torture used by the military to extract information. Additionally, a driver has no way of knowing whether or not there even *are* any loads and may therefore waste away the daytime hours trying to entertain himself rather than resting or sleeping in preparation for a later dispatch that may not happen.

This can cause some drivers to look to over the counter or even illegal drugs that will assist in keeping them awake. *This is never a good idea!*

An exception to this unscheduled dispatching might be those on dedicated runs that have regular routes and routines on a weekly schedule. This is how most trucking used to be and would most likely be now, had it not been for *deregulation of trucking!*

## 10. NO PAY FOR EXTRA DUTIES

In addition to no pay for *time* lost, there is *no pay to the driver for minor or major chores,* such as installing chains on the tires in winter and mountain conditions or taking the chains back off. However, *licensed chain installers on location are paid well for this service.* Other time consuming duties performed without compensation include weighing the load, sliding the trailer axles or 5th wheel for legal weight distribution, fueling, getting tires repaired or replaced, truck washes, sweeping out the trailer, drop and hooks, breakdowns, vehicle inspections, and routine maintenance. If you pull a refrigerated trailer, there are trailer washouts and examination of the temperature control units that need to be serviced before loading to assure proper temperature. This can require taking the trailer many miles out of the way to a facility/ dealer that specializes in this. Picking up or taking pallets to storage depots can also be very time consuming. Additionally, should you pick up a heavy load that may be over-gross on weight and there is no nearby public scale, you may have to drive to a scale twenty or thirty miles away and if you are overweight you must return to the shipper and have enough weight removed to become legal, usually without compensation to the driver. This can take several hours to do these things, which can use up your logbook time, all *without pay,* if you record it as required by law. Few drivers do.

## 11. GUARANTEED DAILY COMPENSATION IS NEEDED

Of course, I am not advocating that a solo *OVER THE ROAD* truck driver should have a starting pay of over $200,000.00 a year or even close! However, if their productivity is acceptable they should at least be realistically compensated for their time every day they are away from home and on the job, regardless of whether or not their company can provide them with a load. *One commitment deserves another, just as in all other professions!* This would require efficiency of operations, something sadly lacking in most companies at this time.

When an OVER THE ROAD truck driver is available for dispatch early in the morning and does not get assigned to a load until that night or the next day through no fault of his own, there is no way he can make up for that lost day. If this happens two or three times a week, which is possible, the end result is a sorry paycheck and a very unhappy driver and wife at home with no way to pay the bills. Presently, most companies provide only twenty or thirty dollars layover pay *after* sitting idle twenty-four hours. This is hardly enough to provide an incentive to the company to be very concerned about keeping the truck moving. It certainly falls short of adequate compensation for a *professional's* time. Additionally, if the driver gets dispatched *before* being idle twenty-four hours, he then does not qualify for even that small amount of compensation and of course, *this is how many companies play the game* because it saves them money!

## 12. DRIVER FATIGUE

Driver fatigue has become a major concern in OVER THE ROAD trucking by various safety groups. If these groups read this book and fully comprehend what is presented, *most of the causes and prevention of driver fatigue are here!* Put simply, there was a far better handle on driver fatigue before deregulation than there is now. Realistic rest conditions were written into the national union contract and adhered to the letter by drivers and management. *Those in management were forced to become efficient in the use of drivers rather than the gross abuse of driver's time prevalent today.*

*When a driver's time costs the company nothing, little is going to take place in regard to efficiency in driver utilization!* In fact, presently there is practically no concern at all on the part of management as to whether a driver is driving or not, *unless or until he is needed!* Then, he had better be prepared to drive, almost at a moment's notice or lose his load to another driver and risk being charged with a service failure that could result with termination.

An entirely new category of OVER THE ROAD truck drivers has emerged along with an entirely new type of truckload carrier. These companies and drivers have certainly changed the routines of long haul trucking in the United States dramatically, not necessarily for the better!

One of the major differences I have observed that directly affects safety is that most of present-day OVER THE ROAD truck drivers park their trucks at night and sleep until morning whereas before deregulation, most of the trucks traveled at night which relieved congestion with other traffic during the daytime hours. *The result has been to jam the highways with trucks and cars all day and have nearly empty highways at night.* Could this be a safety issue?

# 2.

# WHY SUCH AN ONGOING DRIVER TURNOVER?

Boot camp in the military is a sort of filter or preparation to see if the recruit can meet up to the standard and be there for his comrades when needed at a split second's notice without even thinking about it. Lives depend on it! Learning to drive a big truck is similar but *a truck driver's unknowing 'comrades' are the general population and in most cases ignorant of the fact that close proximity to big trucks on the highway can be dangerous or fatal!* I fear some of the truck driver training schools are not adequately getting this point across. *All* driving schools should put more emphasis on this fact.

## 1. PREPARATION

*Trainees may be stranded away from home for as long as three months or more* from the time they start school until they achieve solo status and are issued a truck. The pay during this time is minimal. Unless they have prepared in advance, their bills may go unpaid and other personal business left unfinished until the training is completed. Once the student is assigned to a trainer, communication from the company to the trainee is almost non-existent. Students regularly complain that they feel like less than a part of things since they are expected to fall in line with their trainer's way of doing things, good or bad. However, they usually have the option of contacting the training department of the company they are in apprenticeship with and making arrangements to change trainers should there be an incompatible relationship.

In the case of single people in training with no one to look after their residence while they are away, the residence may be broken into and personal possessions can be stolen without them even knowing. Mail can be lost, rent or mortgage not paid, car payments missed and many other basic demands of life not met. If the trainee insists on going home to check on things or quits, he loses all the time and money already invested. This should be made clear to all who decide to proceed with OVER THE ROAD truck driver training. Without these obligations on their minds, entrants have a much better chance of completing the initial training and being successful. Prior arrangements are mandatory!

## 2. CAUSES OF THE DRIVER 'SHORTAGE'

There is a lot of concern about the shortage of OVER THE ROAD truck drivers. This may or may not be so, depending on how you look at it. Since anybody in reasonably good health with a decent personal history and good driving record can enter this field maybe it comes down to, *'is it worth it'*? There certainly is no shortage of people who *think* they want to be OVER THE ROAD truck drivers. Thousands of truck driver training schools have developed in recent years to show these people how to drive a truck. But driving a truck is just the tip of the iceberg. As we have seen, *there is far more to OVER THE ROAD trucking than simply being able to drive a truck.* Because of their importance, some of the following circumstances that may have been mentioned before must be repeated in this section.

To begin with, most of the truck driver training schools fall far short when it comes to screening and introducing all these people *adequately* to the transportation industry and what it is all about. A thorough aptitude test could certainly help. These folks need to be made aware of all the conditions and limitations of life on the road as well as the responsibilities and skills required of an OVER THE ROAD truck driver. *Unpaid for waiting time is a major issue! Another is home time. I do not feel these things are always being adequately presented to newcomers at this time!*

Training is where it all begins. There is a tremendous amount of money being spent or borrowed at exorbitant interest rates for this short training period, in many cases only two weeks. *Shopping for the best school to fit your needs is very important as is shopping for the right job or company to work for.*

Because of the high failure rate of trainees to continue on after their training, it indicates that they should have been more thoroughly examined with an appropriate aptitude test *before* obligating them to this expense. Most of them are honest, hard working people looking for a better way to make a living. Most of these people are coming in cold with the blind hope or vague idea of establishing a new career that will adequately support them and their families for a long time to come.

*Driving a truck can do exactly that* but there are many different areas in trucking that should be looked at before jumping blindly into the OVER THE ROAD type of trucking that most truck driver training schools and trucking company training schools are promoting. Yes, students are promised a job after the training *but there is a reason so many jobs can be guaranteed!*

This type of trucking will take the individual *away* from his friends and family for *weeks* or even *months* at a time, in most cases. Should a young family man or woman attempt to do this, it will most likely cause extreme hardship on the rest of the family that is left without one of the major players, especially if there are children involved. This is the most difficult part of OVER THE ROAD trucking for new entrants; *being away from home and not being able to get there when you want or need to!* This is a major ongoing problem for most OVER THE ROAD truck drivers.

Being away from friends and family is bad enough but getting stuck for a day or two or more in some faraway location for a variety of reasons, with little or no compensation compounds the problem, especially if the driver could legally and safely have been dispatched. Sometimes there just are not enough loads and some drivers will have to sit out a weekend at a truck stop, *spending money instead of earning it!*

What makes it worse is that if these drivers *need* the income, *want* to work, are on the truck and available, there is rarely a company representative present and willing to talk to about it *during or after* a bad experience. Management people at these trucking companies generally have normal eight to five daytime hours and weekends off, leaving after hour dispatching or lack of it to part time, many times unqualified telephone answerers. *Usually when five o'clock comes the driver's only contact is gone for the night or worse yet, for the weekend.*

## 3. NOT ENOUGH TRUCKS

Sometimes when students finish the OVER THE ROAD segment of training and are ready to be assigned a truck and go to work, there are no trucks available for them. This means the now 'qualified' truck driver may have to go into a waiting mode, retrieve an abandoned truck somewhere or be sent home indefinitely to wait for a truck to become available. Not a happy event.

## 4. OVER-HIRING

Having no trucks available for students ready to get on the road and earn money stems from companies over-hiring to assure that there will be a constant supply of drivers for company trucks. It is very costly to have trucks sitting around with nobody to drive them. Conversely, I have seen newly qualified students right out of training get brand new trucks while I as a trainer continued on with an older high-mileage truck ready for trade-in. Personal consideration is secondary to filling the trucks with drivers as fast as they can when freight is heavy and needs to be moved.

Students are routinely herded like cattle back and forth to motels with little or no pay, far away from home. It is obviously disheartening to them but most of them are stranded and must wait it out in hopes things will work out. It is a very sad situation.

## 5. ABANDONED TRUCKS

Many new truck drivers are terrified of going into the crowded and busy streets of major metropolitan areas such as New York City with this huge equipment and also panic when it comes to being inspected at a weigh station. These things are only casually mentioned during the initial orientation period but *no amount of training and preparation can remove these emotions other than to do it and experience it!* I suppose it is similar to skydiving. The first time is the worst but the apprehension is going to be there every time you do it. Some drivers even make up excuses or simply refuse to go to New York City! This shifts the responsibility to another driver, hopefully a regional driver who lives nearby and is more familiar with the area rather than another coast to coast OVER THE ROAD driver who may now be deprived of getting under a high mileage load that would have paid him substantially more, *not to mention the added risk and responsibility of going into the Big Apple that has now been transferred to him!*

*Hundreds of company trucks are abandoned nationwide as new entrants become discouraged, frustrated and angry at the way things are done in this industry and walk away from their new occupation in disgust, even though they know this will probably permanently end their career in this field.* There are few, if any trucking companies that will hire anyone that fails to return their equipment before quitting. This is looked upon as irresponsible and unforgivable by management. Many good and potential career drivers are lost to the industry this way. What a shame that the drivers are ready, willing and capable but the *industry does not provide the basics* to make the career acceptable!

## 6. EQUIPMENT RECOVERY

As a result, new recruits and even some regular drivers are utilized as 'recovery drivers' to retrieve this expensive equipment so that another newcomer can 'give it a go'. Many times new drivers are sent by bus, train or plane to pick up one of these abandoned trucks to use as their assigned vehicle in their new career. This certainly does not create a positive image to the newcomer or anybody else for that matter. The driver who abandoned the vehicle will have the cost of retrieval deducted from his last paycheck, if he had one coming. If the vehicle has been trashed the new driver must deal with it.

# 7. POOR MANAGEMENT

We need to touch on the problem of people in top management who have no background in trucking and know nothing about the actual first hand performance of duties but are nevertheless setting company policy. Clearly, this type person cannot be knowledgeable enough of what happens in the field to be setting company policies that will dictate men's lives with no regard for the individual. Especially retired ex-military officers! This is not the military nor is it even a close proximity. Truck drivers are here of their own free will and can leave anytime they choose! When policies are laid down that are unrealistic and make no sense and management tries to militarily jam it down truck driver's throats, the result can be a mass exodus of seasoned drivers to greener pastures, taking what experience they have with them!

*Simply getting a dispatcher to talk to on the phone can sometimes be a major accomplishment!* Being slammed on hold for fifteen minutes to half an hour or more and seemingly forgotten about is not unusual with many companies. Calls are 'accidentally' dropped. Many times drivers give up in frustration. The unfortunate truth is that nothing can be done about most problems anyway and therefore nobody in management wants to talk about them.

If a load assignment has not been pre-planned in advance in preparation for when the current load is delivered, the driver may sit idly around waiting for a load for many hours or even until the next day or worse, over the weekend. Unfortunately, even a pre-planned load can disappear. If a driver is optimistic enough to think he may get dispatched after hours, he needs to stay near his truck and check his satellite-messaging unit frequently. This is seldom a happy event when no load is forthcoming! Having a TV and a laptop computer can eat up many idle hours. Reading books is a great pastime. This is a reality check in OVER THE ROAD trucking, like it or not.

When a driver is ready for time off and has made plans with his family after entering the appropriate time off message into the satellite 'communicator', many times he is left dangling as to whether or not his time off request will be accepted. This is always a really frustrating situation. I guess I am old-fashioned because I feel a lot better talking to a real person about things of this nature rather than trying to communicate via satellite, especially when it comes to getting home on a timely basis. In my experience with several trucking companies, all communication becomes slow and distant or delayed when asking about personal things such as time off or asking how much the pay is for extra-duty issues or if there even is any extra pay. It sometimes seems like you have to wring it out of dispatch a bit at a time. Answers are usually real slow in coming and sometimes you may not even get a response without asking several times. *This seems to be standard in the industry and tends to keep drivers on an emotional roller coaster.*

Additionally, many duties of the OVER THE ROAD truck driver *are expected to be performed without pay, including most local deliveries!* A man's time usually means little or nothing in this type business even though the *time and responsibility required of the job is far beyond any other profession.* The pay simply does not justify the effort in most cases. For this reason the 'shortage' will undoubtedly continue for a long time to come as those from 'normal' lifestyles get a taste of OVER THE ROAD trucking and reject it.

Following are many of the conditions that have resulted in causing such a tremendous truck driver turnover and ultimate driver shortage. Because of the great number of OVER THE ROAD trucks necessary to move the nation's goods, there is constantly a need for properly trained people to drive them. These truck drivers should be respected as top professionals and compensated accordingly. Instead they are many times treated as second class citizens by the people they haul product for and as lowlifes or deadbeats by much of the general population. Occasionally, professing to be a truck driver can bring out negative comments or looks of disdain by the so-called 'normal' members of our society. Wives of truckers are many times treated with lack of respect by new acquaintances when inquired of their husband's profession.

*There is no incentive for management to be efficient in the utilization or treatment of their drivers other than that the driver may quit.*

*Obviously a driver can quit for any reason but companies tell newcomers that they also can be fired anytime for any reason. This results in already intimidated new hires to keep their mouths shut about any blatant inequities that they experience. The end result is a continuation of <u>unfair labor practices!</u>*

## 8. SOLITUDE CAN BE A PROBLEM

Once the training is out of the way and a driver begins his solo career, the solitude and time away from home and friends can turn out to be a serious problem. The reality of exactly what it is all about hits everyone at a different time and everyone reacts a bit differently to it. Homesickness can occur. Loneliness! Uncertainty and fear! Many people quit right away. Some stick it out until the training is finished, then quit. Others hang in there for several weeks, months or even years. Most who finish the initial training and acquire adequate experience find local truck driving jobs near their homes. A few make OVER THE ROAD trucking a lifetime career.

## 9. UNSTABLE CAREER

Signs on many trucking companies' rear trailer doors asking, "How's My Driving?" or advertising for more drivers and/or owner operators, are a clear indication of the unstable aspect of OVER THE ROAD trucking as a career. Billboards along the highways all over the country seeking drivers are commonplace. Newspaper classified ads for truck drivers are plentiful. Even radio and television have truck driver commercials. Driver turnover is well over 100% in most trucking companies and may even be as high as 200% and higher. *There is no other career that does anywhere near as much continual nationwide advertising and recruiting of employees.* Most other major professions have waiting lists of people *trying to get in,* many with pensions and benefits included as part of the compensation package! Before deregulation most of trucking was that way too! OVER THE ROAD trucking is now a revolving door with newcomers constantly coming in and leaving. Benefits are scant. Compensation varies drastically. Holiday pay is non-existent.

## 10. PHYSICALLY AND MENTALLY DEMANDING

As a seasoned lifelong trucker, I sometimes forget just how physically and mentally demanding this profession really is compared to others. It requires someone being in top physical and mental condition with good common sense. I am not a millionaire and never have been. I always took it for granted that normal people generally have to work hard to make a living and I always have. Punching a clock was for others.

The fatigue factor alone in OVER THE ROAD trucking is enough to cause many people to shy away from it or give it up, once indoctrinated for a short time. Being tired and falling asleep at the wheel is one of the biggest causes of accidents and death in this profession! Many people do not know how to deal with this problem. If they would simply find a safe place to pull over and sleep a short while instead of fighting their body's craving for rest with coffee or one of the many other stay-awake techniques, it could alleviate this condition and assist them immeasurably. The driver more than compensates for any time spent sleeping with no accidents and a far more positive outlook after resting. 'Better late than never!' would best describe this scenario. Popping illegal pills is not an option and is dealt with severely.

However, becoming an OVER THE ROAD truck driver and driver trainer has exposed me to *professionals from many other fields of endeavor coming into OVER THE ROAD trucking.* This in itself has been an education for me. In the general course of conversation with new entrants from other professions coming into trucking it has become obvious to me that no other occupation *begins* to require the time and skills demanded of OVER THE ROAD truck drivers. This is a much different world! This is a world of physical activity and getting things done rather than phony stock market values determined by the paper world of the money market. *Without truck drivers the entire economy of the country would collapse in just a few days or less! The economy of our country depends on trucking more than any other industry!* Yet the truck drivers many times are not even paid *as much as a minimum wage earner for his time and expertise!*

Those in transportation management and the trucking media continually express the critical importance of truck drivers relating to the success of their companies and to the economy of the country. Yet little is mentioned about the inequitable compensation compared to all other far less demanding professions. *For the sake of change this writing will continually exhibit the vast discrepancies relating to this most important issue! INADEQUATE DRIVER PAY!*

## 11. DISHONEST SYSTEM

OVER THE ROAD truck drivers are trying to earn an honest living from a dishonest system. Why a dishonest system? Oftentimes the trucking, shipping and distribution companies' abuse of the OVER THE ROAD truck drivers' time is abominable and nothing is being done about it! If a driver does not like the way things are most companies have the attitude, 'Don't let the door hit you in the butt on the way out' or, 'Step aside and make room for the next guy.' Labor laws regarding overtime and most basic working conditions have been waived for OVER THE ROAD trucking companies. It is largely because of this abuse of a driver's time that trucks are abandoned by drivers nationwide, although there are countless other more personal reasons.

## 12. ATTITUDE

Attitude is very important! Developing and maintaining a proper attitude in OVER THE ROAD trucking can sometimes be very difficult for a driver. After the newness wears off and the job duties and career demands settle in, *there are many things that affect your attitude.* Some of those are:

1. Family relationships and adequate communication with family members.
2. Company requirements and your ability (or lack of it) to communicate with those who affect your daily activity. Poor dispatch communication results in poor attitudes.
3. Job conditions and earning capability are of utmost importance.
4. Decent equipment is necessary since this is your 'home away from home'.
5. Being able to get home regularly and on special occasions is crucial.
6. Being able to talk to a company representative that can take decisive action *after normal business hours and weekends* is very important, especially if it appears that a day or two of unproductive weekend time with little or no pay may be imminent. Buck-passing is frustrating and unacceptable but commonplace in regard to this problem.
7. Pre-assignment of another load almost always results in not only a good attitude but is usually a motivator of the first degree.
8. Knowing someone respects you and appreciates your performance as a professional driver makes a big difference.
9. Excessive waiting time without compensation can damage a driver's feeling of self-worth.
10. Anger and discourtesy are becoming more and more prevalent both on and off the highway as an unspoken form of protest.
11. Drivers of various companies many times walk by each other without so much as a glance or nod of acknowledgment that the other exists, including some who work for the same company, apparently engrossed in their own troubled thoughts. Sad!

Of course some of this may not apply to many *single, unmarried* folks with no dependents to worry about. *It is these that best fit into this type of career.* The chance of these people becoming successful with this career is much better but even they need to investigate closely before spending their time and money for training. Safe and capable handling of heavy equipment requires proper training of the many special skills demanded.

Without a doubt the pay and conditions have the greatest affect on an OVER THE ROAD driver's attitude. There are generally three prevalent attitudes in this profession.

1. Those that are satisfied with the way things are.
   A. These folks are usually the drivers who are on regular or dedicated runs that earn basically the same income every week and can get home for two or three days a week.
   B. Empty nesters that travel around the country similar to being on vacation, living in the truck and/or motels and taking in places of interest at a casual pace as they perform their duties. These folks usually have other means of income from pensions, rental property or investments and are not overly concerned about the earning capability. They are just out there to see the country and have a good time

similar to those in RVs except the truck is their RV and it not only costs them nothing as a company driver but also provides entertainment income.

C. Owner-operators in specialized hauling who are generating $1.50 per mile and up. They are usually making a reasonably good living.

D. Single folks who require little income to maintain their meager existence. The truck is their home.

2. Those that accept and tolerate the pay and conditions as they are.

A. These are long term drivers that have become accustomed to the way things are done and developed satisfactory relationships with those who control their activity. Even though they know things are not as they should be, they understand that little is going to change any time soon.

B. Women and other minorities that are escaping the responsibilities of a normal lifestyle and can realize more income as an OVER THE ROAD truck driver than they otherwise could at any other career.

C. Ex-military, ex-convicts and divorcees.

3. Those who are totally dissatisfied with the fact that they have committed their time and talents to a profession that does not fairly compensate them. They soon develop poor attitudes that are reflected by lack of courtesy in their driving habits as they become bitter about the career and take it out on anybody and everybody that they come in contact with. These folks usually change companies several times looking for something better and finally quit the profession altogether or find local trucking jobs.

## 13. CAUSES OF JOB-HOPPING AND DRIVER TURNOVER

As we have seen, due to the many different pay packages presented by the various OVER THE ROAD trucking companies needing drivers there is a tremendous amount of 'job-hopping' or 'driver turnover', if you will. In fact there is so much of this going on that it has resulted in the creation of quite a few free monthly trucker publications that are dedicated solely to the purpose of matching up people (drivers) with companies that need them. Using this as a barometer of the changes taking place at this time in truck driver careers, driver retention is *clearly* a major problem. Of course there will always be the *'grass is greener'* syndrome but it has gone far beyond that.

Many people join the ranks of OVER THE ROAD trucking with the express idea of getting enough experience to qualify for a local truck driving position near their home. These local jobs allow being home nearly every night, weekends and holidays. Usually the benefits are better and some holiday pay may be included. This type of job can provide a more 'normal' lifestyle, definitely more family oriented. This may be a good option for those with families as long as the initial time away from home during OVER THE ROAD training is fully understood and accepted by all concerned.

Most companies that need truck drivers for local work require six months to two or even up to three years of experience. Generally these local companies do not have training capabilities of their own and they hire from the OVER THE ROAD segment of the industry as beginner drivers gain experience and become proficient in handling an eighteen-wheeler and decide they have had enough of being away from home for weeks at a time.

There is plenty of time for OVER THE ROAD trucking in later years after the young family has been raised if this is what the individual is determined to do. By that time most or all the special occasions have been properly attended by those that should be there, namely *Mom* and *Dad*. Again, taking on a position as an OVER THE ROAD truck driver simply to gain experience enough to be able to acquire a local driving job is definitely an option. The problem here is that the extended time required to accomplish this can sometimes result in strained or broken family relationships.

Additionally, it is easy to become 'trapped' in the career of OVER THE ROAD trucking for different reasons. The income is many times enough to survive on and not easy to duplicate with most local jobs. Also there is the aspect of 'getting it in your blood'. After doing this for a time many people become restless and bored with regular home life and want to get 'back on the road'. Punching a time clock is not an option. It becomes difficult to apply for a local trucking job since when an interview or opening becomes available you may be a thousand miles away deeply involved with the business at hand. You are 'trapped'.

It is not a good option for a *young married person with children* to start out as an OVER THE ROAD truck driver unless they have a definite plan lined up to secure a local job ASAP. In that case I recommend calling your local community college for training, if there is one. Too many trainees start out to do this at a school far away from home. When the reality of what they have gotten themselves into hits them they are faced with the difficult decision as to whether to continue on in trucking and jeopardize their family's stability or give it up prematurely and *face the prospect of now paying off a huge loan for schooling they may never utilize!*

*All of this activity has resulted in thousands of new, inexperienced and unprofessional truck drivers on the nation's highways all the time due to the constant driver turnover. Accidents are imminent! It's scary to see how incompetent some of the new drivers fresh out of a 2-week driving school are. They do not even know the basics! Some of them cannot even drop or hook up a trailer or even get the weight distribution right. The increased danger to the public on the highways is incalculable!*

*Again, not enough is being done to retain experienced drivers in this profession as a long-term career.* In many cases the attitude of those in management seems to be that if you do not like the way things are, step aside and make room for the next guy. There is no shortage of those willing to make an attempt to do this. Basically, management's main concern is with filling the seats of their trucks. The safety aspect of retaining experienced drivers is 'out the window'. A good safety record counts for little and in fact is expected and rightly so, as is adequate compensation!

Following is an excerpt from an article in Road King magazine, written by editor Tom Berg, with his permission.

> **"Our government doesn't do much to protect truckers' wages. Indeed, long ago it exempted truckers from the Fair Labor Standards Act. That's why you drive more than 40 hours a week and are not paid overtime, and can be made to sort and restack freight in warehouses for no pay, or have to show up for an "appointment" and wait all day or night, off the clock."**

*That pretty much says it all regarding extra pay.* This sounds unconstitutional to me! If you are an owner-operator you might expect to endure this kind of time spent without pay as part of the package and conditions of 'owning your own business'. But as a company driver most folks expect to be paid for their time, regardless of the profession. In fact, *the law requires it* in nearly all other careers. Driver shortage? You bet!

## 14. STUCK ON THE EAST COAST

Since OVER THE ROAD truck drivers are paid by the mile, many of them that run 48-state dispatch prefer to get high mileage runs into the far west, away from the East Coast, especially if they live there. That assures them of a decent paycheck and the enjoyment of traveling into the most scenic part of the country as a bonus.

However, most large OVER THE ROAD trucking companies do the bulk of their business on the East Coast and east of the Mississippi River. This is because that area is highly industrialized and heavily populated. These factors cause the need for trucks to carry raw materials and finished products to factories and consumers in that area on a large scale, which in turn causes an imbalance in the overall national trucking scenario, resulting in the need for more trucks and drivers in that area of the country. Drivers that live in the West can constantly be heard complaining that they have been running loads up and down the East Coast for several weeks in spite of numerous requests to get to their homes in the West. Additionally, more and more of the longer runs are moving on the train, as mentioned before. Loads going west that could have gotten a driver home are going by rail due to cost savings!

The highways and city streets on the east coast many times leave much to be desired in the way of maneuverability for a big truck. Many of these areas were developed during the Colonial Era for horses and buggies and have been difficult or impossible to enlarge to accommodate modern-day over-sized trucks. The terrain is such that many times it is impossible to access some areas. Low bridges, narrow streets and tight turns are frequently a problem. Restrictions are prevalent! Making wrong turns or getting lost can be not only challenging but can result in accidents and exorbitant fines for inadvertently violating truck restrictions.

## 15. RAILROAD PIGGYBACKS

It does not help the plight of long haul OVER THE ROAD truck drivers when increasingly, large trucking companies are utilizing the railroad piggyback service for long runs due to driver shortage and financial advantage. Service by rail has improved somewhat from what it used to be but it still has a long way to go. I can see where sometime in the future nearly all long distance trucking might be put on the train with local drivers on each end to take care of the pickups and deliveries. Of course this will be determined by how expeditious and flexible the railroads are capable of becoming. Presently, fast and dependable rail service continues to be questionable as it always has been in the past. Train after train can sometimes be seen backed up in many areas of the country waiting for each other to clear the tracks, obviously creating a service problem. However, with government subsidies it is improving and may someday reach the point where it is as fast or faster than trucks.

Many shippers and receivers object to their loads going on the rail due to damage caused by 'humping' the rail cars. What this means is that a locomotive must hook and unhook sections of train in preparation for the long haul and due to the tremendous weight involved this can result in a tremendous shock factor that severely jolts the entire train causing damage to the product inside trailers.

Nevertheless, an increasing number of long distance loads are being put on the trains as piggybacks to save fuel and reduce driver costs to trucking companies. Thousands can be seen every day. Railroads are subsidized by the government, trucking is not! They are *supposed* to be competitors but the end result is that *they are jointly holding truck driver's pay to a minimum* with inter-modal operations, benefiting management in both. Long haul OVER THE ROAD truck drivers lose three ways:

1. The best paying high-mileage runs with ample time to deliver are gone.
2. They have to deal with the massive, time-consuming and congested railroad yards when delivering or picking up trailers.
3. They are left with making low-paying local pickups and deliveries on each end instead of running high mileage loads OVER THE ROAD as they hired on to do.

Something to keep in mind when choosing a company to work for is that very few flatbeds, tankers or moving vans are utilizing the railroad. Their operations do not seem to be conducive to do so. You may want to consider working for a trucking company that utilizes equipment such as this. On the other hand you may be interested in local delivery and pickup of these piggybacks as a local driver.

Dealing with the railroad as an OVER THE ROAD driver to pickup or deliver piggybacks can be very frustrating. To begin with, the OVER THE ROAD truck driver is deprived of high mileage. Then the OVER THE ROAD city driver who is actually waiting for a long run can lose most of a day messing with the local delivery of a piggyback at about half the pay or less than a union driver gets. Then he will be expected to pick up his own load and head out over the road in a tired condition.

Additionally, many railroad employees are very unresponsive to a trucker's frustration. Most railroad employees are union and are slow moving, non-communicative, ignorant and rude toward truck drivers. After all, we are basically competitors, right? Therefore some of them seem to relish making things just as miserable as they can for truckers.

Should the railroads ever get to the point where they are efficient enough to match or beat truck service and railroads are utilized to the maximum, there is something else to consider. Derailment or interruption of service due to earthquakes, floods or other natural disasters would have an immediate effect on all the products being transported by train, similar to putting all your apples in one basket. Not only would the trailers and product on them be delayed under these circumstances but also most likely the merchandise in the trailers would be damaged and much of it considered unusable. *This is a major advantage of shipping by trucks. Versatility and flexibility!* There is always another highway route to use and get the product there and even if a few trucks were detained or destroyed, most would reach their final destination intact, one way or another.

Yes, trucking is the only mode of transportation that cannot be completely shut down by a single event as was seen with the airlines after the 9/11 terrorist attack. In fact it was shown that service by truck was actually very competitive with air due to the long delays at airports on each end. Air freight must be picked up from the shippers by truck, then staged and loaded, then unloaded and staged again and then be taken again by truck to the final destination. All this requires a great amount of time in which trucks are meanwhile steadily traveling across the country.

## 16. NO OVER THE ROAD DRIVER REPRESENTATION

As we have seen, one of the conditions governing deregulation was that crucial labor laws were waived as part of the deal. This seems un-American, maybe even unconstitutional. It seems to restrict capitalism! I have no problem with businesses and celebrities making exorbitant amounts of money but I do have a problem with restricting the ordinary workingman from earning a fair wage for his time and efforts without negotiation or representation of any kind. If it were not for the millions of working class *there would be no country and no millionaires or billionaires!* People make it happen!

I heard that in 1937, working conditions for truck drivers were entered into the United States Federal Register to assure that their time would be adequately compensated for. Even then a driver's time away from home and on the job was an issue. Although this is hearsay it makes perfect sense. The way I understood it was that a truck driver was to be compensated for his time spent on the road from the time he reported to work at his home terminal until he returned to that same terminal and was relieved from duty. Obviously this provision is not a factor in regard to today's OVER THE ROAD truck drivers. It may be that only Teamster Union drivers were affected although that seems somewhat bazaar. What should it matter whether a truck driver is union or non-union in a case such as this? A man is still a man! Safety is still safety!

*The brutal truth is that present day OVER THE ROAD truck drivers are expected to work twice as hard and twice as long for half the pay!*

The excellent Road King article quoted earlier about truck drivers being exempted from the Fair Labor Standards Act seems to answer this question although not thoroughly or adequately enough. Why should this be so? Things have changed dramatically in the transportation industry since these archaic rulings were made. Clearly *it is time to reexamine OVER THE ROAD truck drivers' compensation!* Companies are clearly abusing truck drivers in this and many other ways.

While many OVER THE ROAD company drivers are getting barely enough miles to survive on, at the same time many company owner-operators are being run ragged with high mileage loads since the company benefits far more from utilizing owner-operators than company drivers. The truth is that owner-operators are not doing that well either due to their low rate of compensation and high rate of expenses. Owner-operators are sometimes expected to run 1200 mile runs in 24 hours with high-speed trucks without regard for safety. *And they are doing it! How safe is this?* Many times I have seen trucks sitting in the medians or tipped over in a ditch off the road when the drivers obviously fell asleep while driving. Rollovers are not uncommon.

A casual look at company owner-operator custom trucks may at first glance seem quite impressive. However if you take a closer look, evidence of neglected repairs and maintenance can sometimes be quite obvious. The income simply is not there many times to keep this expensive equipment in peak condition. Bodywork not done or performed by patching with tape and broken lights, paint falling off, missing or loose can be seen on many trucks. Tires with chunks out, cuts or poor tread depth also indicate inadequate funds to repair and replace needed and necessary items. This says nothing about the things you cannot see such as worn brake drums and shoes, bad air lines and other unexposed or hidden, worn or missing parts.

As mentioned previously it is highly unlikely that truckers will ever join together to improve their conditions and need some kind of minimum compensation legislation on their behalf. Unfortunately, for two truck drivers to agree on anything has been a continuous failing throughout the years. It seems this fact is being fully utilized by the government and trucking companies to the maximum degree. How do you represent millions of downtrodden professionals who are scattered throughout the country constantly struggling to make a decent living under archaic conditions?

The skills, talent, ambition and commitment are there but the deck is not only stacked against them but some of the cards seem to be missing. Representation is one, labor laws are another!

There is only one glaring instance where I witnessed total agreement or cooperation if you will, where 100% participation of truckers took place inadvertently. This occurred when the state of New Jersey decided to install a toll for trucks to park in the Vince Lombardy service plaza on the New Jersey Turnpike. Since this is the last service plaza before entering New York City it has always been jammed up with trucks waiting for their time to go into the city and make their delivery. Somebody got the bright idea that the continual 24-hour a day turnover of trucks in this service plaza would generate a lot of revenue if a toll was instituted for its use by installing tollgates.

I happened to be driving by immediately after the tollgates were installed and much to my surprise there was not one single truck in the entire Vince Lombardy parking lot! The huge parking lot was empty! It was the most impressive reaction by truck drivers I have ever seen and had to have been a spontaneous reaction by each individual driver as they arrived since there is no way possible that all those thousands of truckers could have been contacted for their participation beforehand.

The very next time I drove by a few days later, the tollgates had been removed and the (free) parking lot was again full to overflowing. For once the truckers won! They stuck together in their thinking! *They united, albeit inadvertently!*

The obvious reason for this unannounced and unprompted, spur-of-the-moment 100% boycott was that the parking fee would have had to be paid up front by the drivers, most without reimbursement. The point to be made is that when this situation tried to take money directly out of these truck driver's pockets up front, they unanimously rebelled! What a shame it is not this way when it comes to cooperating in regard to planning other shortcomings on a larger scale, especially when it comes to improving their long term income and working conditions. It seems that organizing this profession on behalf of truck drivers is virtually impossible at this time.

## 17. NEWCOMERS QUITTING

The ultimate result of no representation or legislation to protect truckers has been a shortage of people that are willing accept and endure this type of occupation for any prolonged length of time. Thousands are continually coming into this field having little or no idea of what is required of them. Then, as everything begins to unfold they begin to realize that this occupation will not work for them and go on to other endeavors. The stress and anxiety produced by the many different phases of this type of trucking can be extremely nerve-wracking to newcomers. It is not unusual to see them call it quits as soon as they become more aware of the ever-present risks and dangers. Meanwhile, time and money have been spent, families have been broken up, accidents have happened and people have been injured. Lives may even have been lost. This dangerous profession is simply not for just anyone. Round pegs will not go into square holes. People have different stress levels. Wives and children need to see the man of the family more than once every two or three weeks or even longer. Countless other factors need to be considered.

In all fairness, some of these trucking companies really *are* trying to be respectable employers and doing the best they can to survive the financial and operational challenges and changes of the transportation industry at this time.

Why would most companies not take advantage of the situation? Many are falling by the wayside as the events of the 'revolution' continue on. Conditions are chaotic! Competition is fierce! Rates are low! Mergers, buyouts and bankruptcies are happening constantly! The evolving of a new modern day OVER THE ROAD transportation industry is in full swing!

# 3.

# GOOD CONDITIONS, TOO

## 1. HONEST AND RESPECTABLE CAREER WITH LIVEABLE INCOME

In my experience those who are in their forties and older seem to be best suited to do this. Their families are generally raised or nearly so and they have far fewer distractions relating to personal obligations. Hopefully by now they are more responsible in their lives and safer in their driving habits, having gotten most of the reckless nature of youth out of their system. They are more stable and routine in their habits. Additionally, at this age most other professions are reluctant to hire them whether or not they want to admit it, due to age discrimination.

The fact is that driving a truck OVER THE ROAD should be and for the most part is an honest, respectable profession and a livable income can usually be obtained for those with the health, skills and endurance required. There are many gray-haired senior truck drivers out here in their fifties, sixties and even some in their seventies and eighties. Some carry their spouses with them. Many of these senior citizens thoroughly enjoy the daily activity and adventure connected with this profession. It keeps them busy and provides them with additional income for their leisure years. The on-going activity may even prolong their lives. *They have learned how to play the game!*

There are definitely positive conditions in trucking that count for a lot with new drivers, especially those coming in from other fields that were involved with high stress or monotonous routines. The excellent modern trucks and freedom of the open road can certainly offer these people a welcome change. After all money isn't everything, right? There are a great many highly educated folks out here, some with PhD's in other careers. Generally, OVER THE ROAD truck drivers can work at their own pace. No one is standing there looking over your shoulder. It is pretty much up to you to either stay ahead and keep on top of things or kick back and take it easy. Once you understand and accept the conditions then it is up to you to make the best of things the way they are. As we all found out on September 11, 2001 it is an uncertain world that we live in. Things can change in a New York minute!

## 2. MOOD SWINGS

Mood swings. A driver's emotions can go from positive to negative in the beep of the sat-com. For instance, should a driver be under a high mileage load that has the potential to generate a respectable paycheck for the week he would be in a positive mode. If this load might additionally take him by his house so he can stop there a few hours or even a day or so, now he will be enthusiastic and charged up to hit the road. If however, the sat-com should beep in a message that says he will have to give up that load to another driver for some reason, the storms of hell have hit. The elation instantly turns to anger and disappointment, gloom and doom. Many a driver has quit over just such a scenario such as this happening too often. Trying to keep the load usually fails and there is generally no one to appease the ruffled feathers of the driver that is forced to surrender his 'gravy load'. This is just one of countless scenarios that can happen to turn a driver's emotions upside down in a heartbeat.

On the bright side, this can happen in reverse. Your truck may be coming out of the repair shop after a day or so of being out of service and you may be feeling cheated because of little or no compensation for the down time and find that you are assigned to a so-called 'gravy load' such as was mentioned before. Especially if you are in winter season somewhere in the North Country and the load you are getting will take you into the deep, Sunny South. This should create a positive attitude in any normal driver, *provided he does not have this load taken from him.* It is a very erratic business.

## 3. PRIVATE CARRIERS—COMPANY TRUCKS

There are still some manufacturers and distributors that have their own company trucks so that they can maintain full control of their transportation requirements. They usually have better conditions in regard to getting drivers home for regular time off. This is because they need their trucks to return to home base for another load of their products rather than going from point to point all over the country like the truckload carriers. The pay and conditions may be better or worse, usually better. Working for one of these companies after getting a year or so experience OVER THE ROAD is certainly an option. Finding one of these companies requires diligence.

## 4. TEAMSTERS UNION COMPANY DRIVERS

There are only a handful of large union trucking companies left that survived deregulation. They are still somewhat regulated by the government and must also abide by the rules and regulations set forth by the International Brotherhood of Teamsters, Chauffeurs, Warehousemen and Helpers Union. This is a very complicated arrangement and can best be explained by a Teamster Union official at their office in any major city. There is an official book of rules that should be available to any interested parties explaining all the pay provisions and benefits, work duties and requirements as well as pension and welfare programs. This information may also be available on the Internet.

Most of the equipment union companies use is designed for versatility of operations. They have short trailers that are pulled over the road as 'doubles' or 'triples'. This allows maximum flexibility of operations in regard to servicing the type freight they specialize in which is less than truckload (LTL) shipments. These short trailers can be loaded and unloaded quickly to gain access to expedited shipments as soon as possible.

## 5. DOUBLE AND TRIPLE TRAILERS (WIGGLE-WAGONS)

The drawback to 'double' and 'triple' trailer combinations is that they are very unstable as compared to one single full-sized forty-eight or fifty-three ft. trailer. The rear trailer may go out of control because of misloading, uneven pavement or driver error and over it goes!

Exit ramps and highway construction projects are very dangerous for this type equipment, especially if the driver becomes over-confident or inattentive and drives too fast. Once that rear trailer starts whipping it is probably going to flip over.

Union operations are generally high-speed LTL (less than truckload) operations that generate more revenue that in turn provides higher pay and benefits for the union drivers and management. There is a lot of stress and pressure on everybody all the time to see that everything is done in a timely and efficient manner. There can also be labor disputes between drivers, union and management, individually or concurrently. *It definitely forces management to become efficient, as it should be! Everybody's time is worth money!*

## 6. DEDICATED ACCOUNTS

Many large industrial fleets that once employed union drivers have been taken over or replaced by the large deregulated truckload carriers. These truckload carriers can operate at considerably less cost than a fleet operating under a union contract. These are designated as 'dedicated accounts' by trucking companies and are assigned to drivers that prefer some kind of regularity, of which there are many.

There are very few large industrial or manufacturing companies with trucks of their own anymore for this reason. Looking at it from their viewpoint it is a great advantage *not* to have their own trucks. It gives them the following advantages:

1.  They no longer have to negotiate a union contract.
2.  The hassle of hiring and controlling drivers is gone.
3.  The huge driver payroll is gone.
4.  Benefits such as medical insurance and pensions for drivers are gone.
5.  Holiday and vacation pay, not a problem.
6.  Having to tie up huge sums of money buying and insuring trucks and trailers is no longer necessary.
7.  Maintenance shops and personnel to operate them have been eliminated.
8.  They now have an outside trucking company to be held responsible for any service failures.
9.  If they do not like the performance of the carrier they are using, they have many other choices.
10. Reduced overall transportation costs.
11. More $$ in the pockets of top management and/or stockholders.

In short, they have fixed transportation costs. These companies are now free to concentrate on what they do best which is to manufacture or produce goods, process food or whatever else it is they started out in business to do. They are undoubtedly enjoying much higher profits as a result of eliminating this transportation obligation.

## 7. JOB SECURITY

Also on the plus side, job security in the trucking industry has never been greater because of all the negative things. You should not have to be concerned about a layoff but if it should happen there are usually thousands of truck driving positions of all kinds available everywhere. Developing a good reputation as a safe, dependable driver can pay dividends.

Job security is almost a given since layoffs are nearly non-existent for a variety of reasons, driver shortage and turnover being the principle ones. However, since it can increase the cost of a company's unemployment insurance when official layoffs may occur it may be to a company's advantage to coerce drivers to quit rather than implement layoffs. Some companies have been known to 'starve out' any undesirable drivers by purposely depriving them of enough miles to make it worth an unproductive driver's time and effort. While this may seem to be an unfair practice it can sometimes create an incentive to the other drivers to cooperate and fall into line with the company's policies and procedures. After all, 'The tail cannot wag the dog'. This is all part of the 'evolution of trucking' process.

## 8. POSSIBLE TO EARN SIX FIGURES

A good living may still be earned in this profession if someone is willing to accept present conditions and *work the system as it is!* Pay and conditions are slowly improving as the evolution of deregulated OVER THE ROAD trucking progresses. It may get better or it could become worse!

Surprisingly, it *is* possible to *earn a wage into six figures* if you put forth the effort and develop a reputation with your company as a safe, dependable driver and *become a driver trainer!* Only a few highly experienced and thoroughly dedicated driver trainers reach this level of income at great sacrifice of personal life, with little time off on a regular basis. It also makes a big difference what company you drive for, with an attainable rate of pay and availability of students plus high-mileage runs. Husband/wife teams can earn into six figures and are in great demand with nearly all long haul companies for obvious reasons.

## 9. CAMARADERIE

There can be a lot of good humor out here between truckers from time to time. Driving at night can bring out a lot of conversation over the CB to keep each other awake and entertained. You can learn a lot about many things this way. In fact, this is a good way to gather information about changing jobs or becoming an owner-operator. As time goes by you may find yourself looking for something that will get you home more often, provide better pay or benefits and many other topics. Owner-operator 'niches' that are usually kept a closely guarded secret may be freely gained access to during these graveyard-hour driving shifts. As the nighttime hours go by, the new acquaintances can get into many topics that they normally might not discuss, just to keep the conversation going to help keep themselves awake.

## 10. RETIRED AND EX-MILITARY

Retired military personnel are good candidates for this type work since they already have a base income from their military pensions as well as medical benefits. This helps to relieve the financial pressure of waiting around without compensation that those with only one income must endure. It still does not remove the *need* for compensation regarding waiting time.

OVER THE ROAD trucking is also very popular with those who are separating from the military and seeking a new career. Most ex-military have experienced being away from home for long periods of time and have accepted it as a condition of employment. They are not particularly interested in mundane eight to five employment with somebody looking over their shoulder and seem to have a more adventurous attitude. This aspect is a big plus in being an OVER THE ROAD truck driver.

## 11. MOST LUCRATIVE PAY

The most lucrative pay packages for truck drivers at this time seem to be the driver training programs whereby the OVER THE ROAD driver trainer gets paid for all the miles the truck travels and the student receives a nominal weekly salary or lesser mileage pay. This type of pay incentive has made the truckload driver's pay somewhat comparable to what other professionals earn. Additionally, the spacious ultra modern training trucks have made a dramatic difference in overall driver comfort compared to the smaller cramped and basic trucks most union company drivers are issued. This is a definite consideration to a driver since he will be spending a great amount of time in the truck, whether union or not. The 'gypsies' of today have it much better it would seem, especially if you are a driver trainer. In fact, many older drivers are content to keep right on working past retirement age rather than lead the humdrum and inactive life of a retiree.

It is usually up to the individual to develop and pay for his own benefit package in the non-union sector. He must fund his own pension plan, pay half or all of his family medical insurance coverage, invest in IRA's and many times forfeit most or all paid holidays since they are usually not even mentioned by many companies. Individual circumstances and a positive mental attitude play a large role here.

As time goes by and the many things a truck driver must do without pay become more apparent, many entry-level drivers decide this is not for them and look around for better pay packages or more localized work that will allow more time at home. As I pointed out in my first book, under present conditions you cannot look at how much you get paid by the hour, day, week or month, in this type of work. It is the annual income and how much of it you can hang onto that really matters. As a driver trainer, the annual income is usually adequate compensation for time expended. It is mainly the solo drivers that get cut short and many of these do not have enough experience and/or do not want the hassle of becoming a driver trainer. Training is not for everyone. For this reason it is important for a solo driver to select a company offering the highest mileage pay for solos with the most benefits the first time around.

# 4.

# TRANSPORTATION, THE BACKBONE OF AMERICA

Transportation by truck is one of the largest industries in the world. While it can truly be said that trucking is the backbone of America, it goes far beyond that. The services and goods that are provided with transportation by trucks is actually the very lifeblood of the country and reach into not only every large metropolitan area but also every small town and community. Without trucks to transport goods from one place to another nothing else can happen and few other businesses could exist very long.

Everybody complains about too much government control of things and I agree that we are a nation based on freedom for the individual to do things. However, in an industry as large as transportation, there comes a time when there must be some kind of *basic regulation and control on behalf of the truck drivers* because without it, you have what you see today in OVER THE ROAD trucking; *a free for all, resulting in mass confusion, disorganization and carnage on the highways!* **Regulation of any kind is generally introduced to protect the rights of the little guy in business and/or labor, if you will. Without regulation, those with money and power can force the competition out of business and/or usurp the time and efforts of the masses at their whim and nothing can be done about it.** In OVER THE ROAD trucking it has become a case of the rich getting richer through complete control of the lives of truck drivers who have nothing to say about the pay or conditions other than quit.

All other modes of transportation already do have such regulation and control for their employees, which has resulted in a professional atmosphere for all to see. Airlines, railroads, ships and busses are all regulated to enhance safety conditions for the public and the employees. The professionals who operate them are paid well and their lives are enhanced accordingly, as it should be.

The trucking industry was headed in the right direction too, until deregulation. *Deregulation of trucking has resulted in **little or no representation** for the major players and a completely one-sided set of conditions* set down by management for drivers, with no recourse other than to leave their jobs and seek employment in another profession or accept conditions as they are, which is almost totally unprofessional. *Labor laws regarding minimum wage and hourly pay have been entirely waived by government for OVER THE ROAD truck drivers!*

But let us back up a bit and find out how all this came about.

The pay and benefits for truck drivers was coming along nicely and keeping pace with other professions such as auto and steel workers until DEREGULATION.

## 1. BEFORE REGULATION

In the early 1900's, before government regulation and the strict requirements of the commercial driver's license (CDL), anybody could buy a truck and start trucking for themselves, whether it involved a contract with some company requiring specialized services or hauling exempt commodities such as produce or unregulated products. Anybody could go anywhere. Trucking companies developed as the need arose. Many large agriculture growers developed called 'truck farms' and needed a way to get their produce quickly to market before it spoiled. Most had their own trucks for full operational control.

The only requirement to be able to drive a truck was to possess a chauffeur's license. This was acquired by a short test, a quick spin around the block in a truck with a motor vehicle examiner and attaching the driver's picture to his driver's license.

These 'gypsies', as they were called, contacted produce brokers and developed relationships with them and other customers that would provide unregulated or exempt 'back-hauls'. They were hard working men who preferred the freedom of the open road in spite of bad weather, no interstate highways and less than desirable equipment, to punching a clock in a factory or some other menial, boring nine to five job. At that time there were not too many other good choices in the private sector and the pay and time lost waiting were apparently acceptable. But that was forty or fifty years ago and longer, after the Great Depression. Since then, we have become the 'Great Society'! More education, higher pay, shorter hours, greater benefits! Work less, earn more mentality!

## 2. WHAT IS DEREGULATION?

Oftentimes in trucking you will hear the term, "Deregulation". This refers to when many decades ago the Interstate Commerce Commission (ICC) was formed and tightly regulated all trucking. In the early years of the 20th Century it was felt there was a need for trucking to be more rigidly controlled by the state and federal governments to protect the various entities affected by transportation. This included regulating freight rates for shippers, receivers, truckers and the general public. Carrier fitness was also a consideration in regard to financial stability, adequate insurance, proper maintenance and safe driving. As we have seen, during that period of history there were many trucking companies starting up and it was difficult to control the rapid growth for the benefit of all concerned.

Those trucking companies that were already established at that time were issued certificates or 'franchises' that specifically described the cities and/or states each carrier was servicing and the highway routes they were using, as well as the products they were hauling. Those certificates allowed existing trucking companies to continue operating as they were and limited others from entering the field of transportation indiscriminately, thereby undermining existing companies at that time. This limited the competition and helped to ensure a profit, strengthening the overall economy of the industry and ultimately, the country. The existing trucking companies were "grandfathered in" so to speak, and their operating franchises became very valuable. It all depended on where they were already operating. In some cases a company may have been operating only between two or three cities whereas others may have been involved in all 48 states. The only way a company could expand or another company could start up after regulation was to apply for authority from the (ICC) with shipper support showing there was a need for more service or buy out an existing company (franchise). Applying for authority was a very lengthy, difficult and expensive process and many times failed to result in new operating rights being granted. This is why the franchise certificates became valuable and could be sold for an agreed upon price to another trucking company, private enterprise or a private individual, whichever the case may be, upon ICC approval. Even then a sale could be blocked if a competing trucking company could convince the ICC that it would cause unfair competition and injure their business.

Labor was also a major consideration since driver safety and fatigue affected everybody on the narrow two-lane roads of that period, not to mention the driver's own well-being. There were no interstate highways. Trucking companies forced truck drivers and warehousemen to work beyond their capacity. Management had unlimited and complete control of truck driver's lives. As time passed, truck driver compensation and working conditions were far below acceptable standards. There was no one to represent the truck driver and warehouse labor force. People were dying due to unsafe equipment and working conditions. Benefits were inadequate or non-existent with many companies. Does this sound familiar? *Welcome back to the 1930s!*

Hence, the beginning of the Teamster's Union to represent truck drivers and protect their interests. *Over the years, truck drivers were elevated through increased pay and benefits to a somewhat honorable and respected professional status!* Labor and management came to an understanding of 'live and let live'. A fair day's pay for a fair day's labor was established and upgraded periodically as with all labor unions. If an agreement could not be reached as to what was fair, negotiations resulted in regional and nationwide work stoppages, with strikes by the union against management on behalf of the union members. Settlements took place! Driver's pay and benefits were increased as agreed upon. Freight rates were then adjusted accordingly to provide additional revenue for trucking companies to be able to provide the compensation and benefits deemed necessary for truckers to earn a fair income to support and provide benefits for their families. To get a job driving for a union company you almost had to know somebody that could pull strings to get you in. There was no driver shortage then! All jobs paid the same no matter what company you worked for if they were signatory to the union contract.

Due to crippling nationwide strikes by the Teamster's Union in the 1950's through the 1970's there came a movement in government to make drastic changes in transportation to weaken and reduce the union labor force, thereby lowering freight rates. To accomplish this, most trucking regulation was basically eliminated in the seventies and eighties. I believe it was and still is an ongoing conspiracy in the name of national security! A trucker strike could shut the country down!

## 3. AFTER DEREGULATION

Wide spread corruption and rumors of organized crime connections in the Teamster's Union helped sway public opinion that deregulation was the right thing to do. Most trucking franchises became worthless or nearly so as new companies sprang up and slashed rates of truckload (TL) and then less than truckload (LTL) freight. Driver pay and benefits diminished. Thousands of trucking companies that had operated profitably for decades in conjunction with the Teamster's Union for driver representation were forced out of business through mergers, buy-outs, liquidations and bankruptcies. The Teamster's Union shrank to a shadow of it's former self in trucking and diversified into other fields. Non-union trucking reappeared on a massive scale, mostly in the truckload segment of the industry. Representation for *most* truck drivers ceased to exist once again.

Presently, there are as many different methods of driver compensation as there are trucking companies. OVER THE ROAD truck driver pay has shrunk considerably from what it was. As a result, *drivers again work beyond their capacity just to earn a livable wage, safety is secondary and there is a continual truck driver shortage* as drivers leave OVER THE ROAD trucking for reasons previously mentioned.

Hundreds of thousands of high paying truck driving positions have been replaced by modern day 'gypsies', in the OVER THE ROAD truckload business. *What it has truly amounted to is a 'transportation revolution' that will probably continue on for many years to come! This is the truth! This is reality!*

## 4. TRANSPORTATION REVOLUTION

A lot of money changes hands constantly in trucking because it is a very high-cost industry. *Deregulation* has caused what I call the 'TRANSPORTATION REVOLUTION'. Among other things, this 'revolution' has resulted in easy access for nearly anyone to obligate themselves to paying for (or leasing) but not necessarily owning an expensive truck costing up to $100,000.00 and beyond, as long as they make a labor commitment of several years to the transportation company they choose to do this with. The truck is being used as a carrot to entice people to be sucked into one of the many *'own your own truck, be your own boss'* schemes that have been designed so that companies will have drivers to deliver their freight. It has also resulted in thousands of new-style truck driving positions that in turn provide few if any benefits and questionable pay packages. The psychology seems to be that the idea of 'owning' a Big Truck or being identified as an *owner-operator* makes up for less than acceptable income and benefits to these unsuspecting people. It certainly does not!

These new entrants into transportation are being coerced into a long-term commitment before they fully realize what has happened and then are faced with paying the consequences *up to and including bankruptcy!* This is a very serious business! It may take a year or more of continuous hard work as a so-called 'owner-operator' or 'lease-operator' before *all* the government fees, hidden expenses and responsibilities of owning a truck come to the surface and finally expose to him the reality that most times, *it just is not worth it!* The driver is now classified as 'self employed' and most of the huge expense of trucking has been immediately transferred from the 'mother' company to the individual who now thinks he is a business owner. The lease-operator programs seem to be a method for trucking companies to *profitably dispose of used vehicles while at the same time acquiring long-term drivers!* If an owner-operator is caught cheating on his logbook, the huge fines imposed are all his and the company is off the hook for any penalty. Pretty slick, huh?

Additionally, the proud new 'owner' may soon learn that even his time off does not belong to him any more. His new truck requires considerable fixing, cleaning and servicing between runs so that it will be ready to roll without worry when the time comes. The drivers who are 'fortunate' enough to sign on with a company that can provide high mileage face the dilemma of being able to continually be on the road away from home and endure the fatigue and exhaustion that goes with it. The 'jet lag' syndrome is ever-present. Speeding tickets, falling asleep at the wheel or just plain getting 'burned out' can result. It is a long-term commitment of several years rather than just a few weeks or months. This realization may not manifest itself until deep into such a program.

In the unlikely event that the driver actually acquires a truck after driving it the agreed upon period of time, many times he is stuck with the worn out behemoth because the company he is leased to will not take it in trade and nobody else wants to buy it either. Used trucks are already a glut on the market. He may wind up nearly giving it away or selling it at way under book value because he has no place to store it. Some of these pre-owned vehicles can be seen sitting in overgrown fields all over the country with faded for sale signs on them.

As far as I know all these programs relating to schooling, leasing, owning and financing are perfectly legal. However, I think the unsuspecting new drivers should be *more thoroughly informed* on a case by case basis to let them know exactly what they are getting themselves *and their families* into rather than sign everybody up without caring. Financing for schooling is a long-term commitment and in many cases it involves up to fifteen years of financial obligation that *must be repaid* whether or not the would-be truck driver continues on with this as a career. Instead, *most companies present only the positives and mask or hide the negatives.*

Company drivers do not fare much better. For a company to have a driver for six months or a year at half pay is very profitable for them. The fact that there is usually a 90-day waiting period before most companies even provide medical insurance saves the company even more money while leaving the driver and his dependents at risk during that period. This is exactly what has happened and is continuing on a massive scale.

Many trucking companies are now not only profiting from transportation services but also from driver training school financing, truck financing and truck leasing programs as well as selling service and products to their contractors and drivers. *Many thousands of new drivers have become a major source of income to the trucking companies they work for, as well as to law enforcement, truck sales, truck repair services and many other businesses as they travel about the country!*

Again, the danger to life and limb is far greater in this profession than almost any other. Even if the new entrants may be informed of this *the reality may not sink in until they are actually out on the road and deep into training and witness people lying dead on the road!* The brutal truth is that hundreds of OVER THE ROAD truck drivers are killed every year for a variety of reasons. Upon this realization many trainees pack it in regardless of the huge new debt they may have obligated themselves for. It is not worth risking their life or the stability of their family! Bankruptcy becomes acceptable.

Deregulation of the trucking industry has resulted in unlimited access of the transportation business to anyone who has the financial backing and ambition to go after any and all types of trucking. Since truckload business is the simplest type of trucking with the largest volume of products, most if not all of this business has been diverted from the Teamster Union based companies to 'truckload' carriers such as Schneider, J. B. Hunt, Swift and many others. Of course this affected the rates of hauling by lowering them, which in turn resulted in lower pay to the drivers.

Everything changed! Rates got lower, trucks got bigger and runs got longer. Instead of a driver going from terminal to terminal as before, it became from shipper to consignee with a single driver taking the load all the way from start to finish. This, while simplifying the overall movement of freight, produced other problems to the drivers such as long periods of time on the road away from friends and family. And with no intermediary to speak for them the drivers began to inadvertently donate a lot of extra work without pay as 'part of the job', not to mention many hours of sitting idle without pay waiting to load, unload or get dispatched on a load.

## 5. NO UNION REPRESENTATION ALLOWED

Let me again make one thing perfectly clear at this time. I am not in any way trying to promote membership in a union. As pointed out earlier that causes more problems.

However, present day deregulated OVER THE ROAD trucking is the only major profession in this country that has no representation for skilled labor. As mentioned before, the Teamster's Union in the past negotiated pay and conditions for truck drivers that assured *a fair day's pay for a person's time and skills*. Since this put too much control in the hands of labor and union officials in an industry that could *totally shut the country down*, the bureaucrats initiated deregulation with a *provision that there could be no unionization of the deregulated OVER THE ROAD segment of transportation!*

The result is what we presently see which is free-for-all trucking bordering on chaos, with *nowhere for truck drivers to go to deal with their problems and complaints*. The scenario is, 'Like it or leave it'. This is exactly what is happening! They are arriving and leaving in droves! Thousands of newcomers are being trained constantly and *after they fully understand for themselves through experience what is involved,* most of them quit within 90 days! By then they have seen several meager paychecks and what is involved in earning them. This realization alone causes mass exodus! It simply is not worthwhile!

Because of this there has been an *ongoing two to three hundred percent turnover rate in OVER THE ROAD truck drivers throughout the trucking industry ever since deregulation took place over two decades ago!* What this means is that a large company with several hundred drivers may plan on hiring more hundreds of beginner drivers every year because drivers are coming and going so fast! It also means that *there is a constant flow of inexperienced, harried, unqualified and unprofessional truck drivers in control (hopefully) of heavy, awkward, high-speed equipment sharing the highways with the general population, who themselves are mostly unprofessional drivers!* Improving this scenario would seem to be a priority for safety's sake if for no other reason. An industry with this much constant turnover in skilled labor indicates a *serious lack of proper screening and aptitude testing as well as a lack of basic human needs and professionalism.* This situation has gone far *beyond acceptability* and too many lives are being affected in a negative way because of it. *Accidents are imminent!*

There are simply too many people flooding into this field if only for a short time. The highways are constantly full of beginners who know nothing about handling heavy equipment simply because they are willing to work and/or donate their time for less than a professional wage. As the word gets out and more people become aware of the shortcomings of this profession, fewer people are willing to attempt it. However, much of this negative aspect is overshadowed by the intrigue, adventure, hopes and dreams.

*Death and carnage on the nation's highways should ultimately force positive changes to prevail on behalf of OVER THE ROAD truck drivers.* The questions are, "How long will it take?" and "How many more lives will be lost and/or affected in a negative way"?

## 6. PRESENT OVER THE ROAD TRUCKING IS IN ITS INFANCY

OVER THE ROAD truck driving as a profession is still in its infancy. If you consider that motorized transportation in it's entirety is only about one hundred years along and the present OVER THE ROAD trucking portion was singled out through deregulation only about twenty years ago, it puts things more in perspective. With this in mind, trucking of *all* types still has a long way to go, as do all other modes of transportation. I wish I could see how trucking will be one hundred years into the future.

Those who read and comprehend this book can consider themselves properly informed as to the reality of how trucking really is. If they are still interested in becoming an OVER THE ROAD truck driver in spite of being made aware of the way things are done, *they just might make it!*

# 5.

# WHY ALL THE TRUCKS?

To the average citizen of the United States that utilizes the nation's highways on a regular basis, this question has probably entered his or her mind at one time or another.

Why all the trucks?

The simple answer is, "To move the nation's goods."

A favorite old trucker expression is, "If you've got it, a truck brought it!"

Another is, "Without trucks, the nation stops".

While these answers are all basically true, it is much more complicated than that. It has been estimated that there are close to 20 million commercial truck drivers of various types of equipment in this country. Trucks are everywhere!

The general population of this country has no idea of what takes place in the life of an OVER THE ROAD truck driver every day (and night) so that when they go to the department store, super market, shopping malls and strip malls, the shelves are full. Additionally, even their place of work has undoubtedly been supplied by trucks or is waiting for the arrival of the necessary product or merchandise to allow them to earn a living at whatever their trade may be. Without these dedicated men and women truck drivers to keep this constant flow of goods moving across the nation's highways nobody would have food for their tables or clothes for their backs. Most would not even be able to earn a living because there would be nothing for them to work with. *Everybody needs trucks whether they realize and want to admit it or **not**!*

A simple visit to any local supermarket will show that garden-fresh fruits and vegetables, fresh-caught fish and seafood as well as meat and dairy products are taken for granted. Most of these extremely perishable products are trucked in from many hundreds or even thousands of miles away. *Freshness of product is not only expected, the public demands it!*

## 1. INTERSTATE HIGHWAYS DEVELOPED

Back in the fifties when I learned to drive a truck, everything was different. Some things were better than now, most were worse. There were few interstate highways then. The interstate highway system was promoted in 1956 by President Dwight D. Eisenhower as a necessary way to expedite transportation of goods in peacetime and the movement of troops and equipment in the event of another war.

It is common knowledge that way back in 1919, then Lieutenant-Colonel Dwight D. Eisenhower led a military convoy across the United States to determine the feasibility of trucks carrying men and equipment long distances. It was obvious that better highways were badly needed. Motorized transportation was in its infancy. When Eisenhower became President, having been an ex-general in the military who saw a lot of action in Europe during the Second World War, he had the vision and power to make it happen. The German autobahn network impressed him during WWII. Our interstate highway system has been a major factor in our trucking and transportation being able to develop this great country into what it is today. Of course this involved years and years of highway construction at great expense. Traffic congestion and construction detours were prevalent throughout the country. They still are. *Trucking played a major role in this dramatic success then and continues to do so now.* The end result has been dramatic for our great country and the interstate highway system was instrumental in helping us develop into the greatest nation on the face of the earth. It also allowed us to develop bigger but not necessarily better trailers for the trucking industry.

## 2. PROBLEMS WITH OVERSIZE EQUIPMENT

Why do I say not necessarily better? Well, it *was* better up to a point because it eventually allowed shippers to move their products on pallets instead of having to hand unload everything onto the floor and then hand reload the same product back onto pallets at the consignee's dock on the other end. This kind of double handling was not unusual. In fact, it was the norm. In addition, it was the driver who was expected to do all this handling or pay a laborer out of his own pocket, referred to as 'lumpers'.

Lumpers are self-employed, independent laborers that load and unload trucks by hand should manual labor be required. Usually, they deal directly with the truck driver in making a verbal agreement as to how much they will charge to load or unload a truck. Then the driver gets a receipt from the lumper after the work is completed and gets his money back from the company he drives for. This method of loading and unloading trucks came about to relieve warehouses and manufacturers of the hassle of labor disputes. It also provided an incentive to get the work done faster and more efficiently, since the more trucks a lumper unloads, the more he earns. They earn by the load rather than by the hour, like the warehouse employees. This also allows the truck driver to relax and get rested up in preparation for his next dispatch rather than to load or unload his own truck, if he chooses not to.

When I started trucking in the fifties, a thirty-two ft. long trailer was considered large and they were only 12 ft. six inches high by 96 inches wide. Before that, trailers were only twenty-eight and thirty-ft. long, 12 ft. high, and smaller. As they increased to forty-five ft. in length it made the movement of goods and products of full truckloads much simpler in most cases. Since standard pallet size has generally been considered to be 40 x 48 inches, a truckload usually consisted of twenty-two pallets because of weight restrictions. Twenty-two pallets at 48 inches (four ft.) long loaded side by side (eleven pallets on each side) figures out to a little over forty-four ft. by the time you consider that you lose a bit of length due to product overhang off the pallets and imprecise measurements of pallets and equipment. The previous smaller trailers could not accommodate a twenty two-pallet load without hand-stacking some of or the entire product on the floor. Forty-five ft. long trailers were perfect for such a palletized load. A forty-five ft. long trailer allowed a shipper to load eleven pallets side by side and end to end, totaling twenty-two pallets on a trailer without handling the product thereby saving a lot of time and money for everybody involved. Material handling is costly and time consuming. Everybody loses except the lumpers, of course.

But forty-five ft. long trailers were not big enough for those industries that had lighter, bulkier products such as paper towels, toys, Styrofoam and many other items. It was to their advantage cost-wise, to have larger trailers that would accommodate more freight for a slightly higher freight charge. Hence the increase in size to where now in my opinion, the present over-sized 53' trailers have created a safety hazard and greater risk to a driver *with no additional pay.*

Presently, standard size trailers are fifty-three ft. long. Some are even fifty-seven ft. and longer, built to accommodate those shippers of light, bulky products. This is where the problems come in. These trailers are now so immense that they have become counter-productive for the truck drivers. They have caused it to be much more difficult for new drivers to learn how to handle such a large unit combined with the much longer power tractors of today, since length laws have been relaxed dramatically. It is truly amazing what the power of money can do to change laws in favor of those willing to make political contributions among other questionable tactics. Public safety has taken a back seat when it comes to equipment size. Additionally, truck drivers have had to accept the responsibility for the safe maneuvering of these over-sized monsters for the same or less pay. They are more difficult to maneuver and more difficult for other traffic to deal with on the open road.

Most trailers are now built to the present most popular size which is fifty-three (53) ft. long, thirteen ft., six inches (13' 6") high and one hundred and two (102) inches wide. Why one hundred and two inches wide? Because that allows a shipper to load the 40 X 48 inch pallets in side by side the short way (sideways), and now they are able to ship up to thirty pallets of lightweight merchandise. However, these 53' trailers have caused several problems for drivers.

1.  If these trailers are loaded too heavy on the rear, they cannot meet the bridge law requirements of many states, especially California.
2.  If a driver tries to pull out of a tight spot in a parking lot from between two other trucks to the right or left too soon with the trailer tandem axle slid all the way forward (toward the tractor) to comply with the weight distribution laws, the rear of the trailer may over-swing into the vehicle next to it and cause damage. This never happened with a forty-five or even a forty-eight ft. trailer. Additionally, these drivers are responsible for this damage and an accident of *any* kind may cost them financially and will affect their safety record. Because of this, many times a driver will drive off and not even acknowledge a mishap to protect his safety record, pocketbook and future employment. I have actually seen this happen and before I could acquire the identity of the truck, it had gone back onto the asphalt jungle and was lost in the confusion that seems to prevail in heavily congested areas. In one instance, a driver caught into an unoccupied tractor parked in a crowded truck stop. He nearly tore the entire fenders and hood off the parked truck and then tried to get away before somebody saw what had happened. Fortunately for the missing driver of the damaged tractor, another trucker backing into a parking spot was blocking the driveway so that the culprit could not escape and ultimately justice was done. Surprisingly, this happens frequently. Never park on the end of a row where your vehicle is vulnerable for this to happen. Take an inside spot or park along a curb.
3.  Taking these trailers into downtown New York City, Chicago, Los Angeles and many other major cities in the country can be a serious challenge for an *experienced* driver, never mind about new drivers. It was difficult to maneuver the smaller trailers in

these tight circumstances but now it is nearly impossible in some cases. Accidents are imminent!

4. In the far western states such as Washington, Wyoming, Utah, Nevada and many others, the wind can sometimes blow at speeds up to eighty and ninety miles per hour. These high volume van trailers are so tall and long that they are not unlike the sail on a sailboat when it comes to catching the wind. If a driver gets caught out there during this high wind his truck may easily be blown off the road or over on it's side, even with a load on. It happens all the while. There is little that a driver can do to prevent this from happening because even if he stops, the wind may blow his trailer over before he can get it headed into the wind. Shorter trailers with less height are not affected as much. The more surface, the more likely to be blown over! Flatbeds and tankers have a definite advantage because of their low profile.

5. Most of the time there are up to seven or eight feet of unused space in the 53' trailer depending on what the product is. Only a small percentage of shippers can load these huge trailers to full capacity and still meet the legal weight requirements. This extra space is wasted much of the time while the risk and responsibility to the driver has been greatly increased permanently, without additional compensation.

6. Maneuvering these 53' monsters in cities and towns around corners or other tight spots can be a genuine challenge. All over the country there are crushed guardrails, broken fences and considerable other evidence of where these trailers proved to be more than some harried driver had been able to handle properly. When attempting to go around the corner on a city street, a driver must be on maximum alert. In making a right turn he must be concerned that an auto driver may try to dive inside his trailer when he swings wide so as not to run over the curb, traffic light pole, a pedestrian waiting to cross, or an auto parked too close to the corner while at the same time being careful not to get hit by traffic coming the other way in the lane he had to swing into to have enough room for his maneuver and again at the same time being careful not to collide with the traffic coming from his right in the street he is turning into. In the middle of all this if the traffic on his right, waiting for the red light, is too far ahead so that he cannot complete his turn without someone backing up or somehow proceeding through the red light, the driver must stop and wait for space to be made for him. When this happens the situation continually changes as other traffic and pedestrians proceed into other locations as they go about their business. The world does not stop just so a truck driver can keep from having an accident. In fact, many times the impatient drivers of smaller vehicles let a trucker know he is #1 by raising their middle finger high in the air. If this seems like a lot of information all at once, try the actual maneuver. All of these factors must be simultaneously on the mind of the truck driver trying to do this or he may have an accident and cause serious damage to his equipment and/or the property or pedestrian he is trying to maneuver around. The entire procedure usually takes place in a matter of seconds, much faster than it took you to read and comprehend this paragraph. Quite a responsibility, not for the faint of heart! This is no game for sissies!

7. When approaching a left turn with two turn lanes, it is necessary for the truck driver to stay in the rightmost lane to avoid collision with traffic on his blind (right) side. A wide swing toward oncoming traffic is usually necessary so that the smaller traffic in

the left lane next to him will have no problem or interference from his following 53' trailer as he is rounding the corner.

8. The height of these huge trailers as stated before, contributes to the possibility of being blown over in a high wind. It also presents a problem in going under many bridges that were built decades ago with the much shorter 12' trailers in mind. Tree limbs that stretch over the right lanes on many city streets must also be avoided as well as poles that lean over the gutter lane in some streets and many building overhangs that are too low at various places of business.

9. New entrants (truck drivers) coming into the field of transportation are definitely intimidated by the size of these trailers. It is one thing to decide to want to be a truck driver but quite another when they are faced with the unforeseen difficulties of doing so. Many would-be truck drivers simply give it up on the first trip or two when training in the field simply out of fear. Oversize trailers have definitely contributed to increasing the on-going driver shortage.

10. A good share of the truck stops and rest areas were designed for the much smaller (shorter and narrower) equipment of years ago and have difficulty accommodating the larger trucks of today. Many accidents (incidents) occur in these cramped and crowded truck stops and parking areas as drivers struggle to squeeze into a place to park for the night in a spot designed for the smaller trucks of yesteryear. This has presented another problem, hit and run. As explained before, many of these minor and some major accidents happen when no one is around to see them and the culprits quickly drive away to avoid having it go on their record and possibly deducted from their pay. Many truck stops and rest areas have had to be closed for this reason, contributing to the parking shortage.

11. Some states restrict over-size trailers from using highways other than interstates since they feel they are unsafe and require too much room to maneuver. I tend to agree with them and do not understand why this was not checked into before all these major changes were gone ahead with. Winding mountain roads with 'switchbacks' restrict these trailers. Somebody surely did not do their homework but it is the truck driver who must pay if caught on one of these restricted roads.

Another little known fact is that there are and have been for at least twenty years even larger trailers, fifty-seven ft. long. I noticed them over twenty years ago when I lived in the south and was informed that they are generally used only on interstate highways in the south and haul light, bulky commodities. At the time however, I was nowhere near an interstate highway and parked at a convenience store next to one of the behemoths. Once again no additional pay to the driver, just added risk and responsibility.

## 3. BIGGER TRAILERS WOULD BE MORE DANGEROUS

Standard size trailers are presently 53' long by 102" wide and there is talk of increasing the length by several more feet. In my opinion, length increases should have stopped with 48-ft. long trailers. They were far safer, more maneuverable and if simply widened from the previous 96 inches to 102 inches (present width of 53' trailers) would probably have been able to accommodate 99% of current available loads. Relatively few of these 53' trailers are loaded to full capacity.

Standardizing larger trailers than the present 53' trailers will undoubtedly result in more accidents and tougher parking conditions than currently exist which is already a major problem. 53' trailers have also caused problems for drivers in regard to proper weight distribution because of the longer rear overhang. State bridge formulas require specific distances between axles for proper weight distribution that cause the vehicle to be in violation if they are not complied with. This situation did not exist as much until trailer length exceeded 48'. It is the driver's responsibility to see that weight distribution is correct. *If he is unaware or complacent about it, it will cost him money!* While weight laws enacted long ago were originally intended to prevent or lessen highway deterioration they also seem to be another method for state governments to generate revenue from truck drivers.

# 6.

# A STORY THAT NEEDS TO BE TOLD

Those who think it is all fun and games out here are in for a rude awakening!

It is time for OVER THE ROAD truck drivers to stand up and be heard! Everybody in trucking knows there are problems and they know what the problems are. *The root of the problem is not enough money!* Truck drivers are all complaining and bellyaching to each other about things but little or nothing is getting done to fix it! Even increasing the rate of mileage pay would do nothing to compensate for the massive amount of time spent and many duties performed without pay.

This is a story that needs to be told! There are too many lives being affected in a negative way simply out of ignorance! Safety! Career change! Unprofessional conduct! Unprofessional conditions! Fatalities! All these and more need to be explored and the information made available to not only those thinking of participating in OVER THE ROAD trucking but to *those who are concerned about making it safer and more acceptable with better drivers and to those who regulate trucking!*

The average person simply would not believe some of the conditions expected to be endured by OVER THE ROAD truck drivers at the shipping and receiving departments of many multi-million and multi-billion dollar industries. This would fill another book. Truly incredible! Most of the executives running these industries are completely out of touch with reality and with the fact that OVER THE ROAD truck drivers are people too and should be accommodated as such! It is these same truck drivers that bring in supplies to operate the plants and carry the finished product from the plants to the users or consumers on a timely basis so that the shipper may exist. Providing sub-standard facilities such as porta-toilets without running water in the parking lot for outside truck drivers to use in sub-zero or triple digit temperatures is stark evidence of this uncaring attitude.

There are maintenance and janitorial services available to maintain a more acceptable environment on-premises at most companies. This is where a hard-working trucker should also be able to relieve himself and freshen up a bit after driving hundreds or even thousands of miles to deliver their product. If this service would reduce some CEO's million-dollar bonus by a few dollars, it would be money well spent.

## 1. NOMADS OF AMERICA

Millions of eighteen-wheelers can be seen on the nation's highways every day, transporting product from farms and manufacturing centers to distribution centers and factories to be processed or consumed. It can be a very frightening experience for drivers of smaller vehicles who must share the highways with them. Each of these trucks require a safe, responsible driver, sometimes two drivers as a team for expediting. A good share of these truck drivers are of the long haul, OVER THE ROAD variety that this writing is about.

If you have ever gone by a truck stop at night and seen all the trucks parked there, you may have wondered about the people who drive them. Most of these drivers are simple ordinary people like yourself, trying to earn a living. Some trucks have become a temporary home to many single folks and couples that may not have any other place to live. I have seen entire families living in trucks semi-permanently, including children and pets.

An interesting thing to realize is that most or all of the trucks in every truck stop will be gone within twenty-four hours and parked in a different truck stop or location for the next night as they progress toward their destination. These are the modern day Nomads of America. This is why years ago we used to call them 'Gypsies'. This constant shuffle from truck stop to truck stop is kind of like musical trucks instead of musical chairs because of the shortage of parking spaces in many of them. If you do not get there early you may not find a parking space.

The trucks circle around and around, looking for a parking space and waiting for each other to back into the spots designed for the much smaller trucks of the past. At times it can become quite a frustration for experienced drivers when a novice tries to put his rig into a difficult spot and completely ties up the traffic flow for twenty minutes or half an hour. Since a certain kind of camaraderie exists among drivers, most try to assist each other in these circumstances without being asked. Most of them had to go through this too and understand the new driver's plight.

With this large OVER THE ROAD equipment, in limited conditions you need all the help you can get. There are multitudes of new truck drivers out here that are trying to gain enough experience to make a new career for themselves in trucking without having an accident or mishap. More than once I have had to back another driver's rig into a parking space or loading dock to help him out. If you have ever visited a truck stop at night you know what I am talking about.

When doing city deliveries, assistance of any kind is appreciated rather than a middle finger stuck high in the air from an automobile driver that does not understand the truck driver is having difficulty backing or may have taken a wrong turn and is trying to get his rig turned around in a too small or restricted area. *Incredibly, the bureaucracy is presently trying to get even bigger trucks allowed on the highway!* What in the world are they thinking?

## 2. BIG DEMAND FOR TRUCK DRIVERS

Transportation by truck is unlike any other field of endeavor because of the wide variety of choices. There are local and short haul trucking and there is OVER THE ROAD. There are dry vans, refrigerated vans, household moving vans, doubles and triples, flatbeds, drop-decks, oversize trailers, boat trailers, auto transports, inter-modal containers, piggybacks, curtain vans, tankers, haz-mat loads, dumps and belly dumps and undoubtedly others not mentioned. They all need drivers! Company owner-operators and lease-operators have become more prevalent in recent years and are heavily promoted because of the many advantages to trucking companies by utilizing them.

*Great caution* is advised *before* obligating yourself to lease or purchase a vehicle through the seemingly unlimited plans available to unwary individuals hoping to improve their station in life with honest efforts, through hard work. Most of these plans are designed by the companies to *benefit the company at the effort and risk of the drivers*. Because of unrealistically low freight rates, many present day OVER THE ROAD trucking companies can operate far more profitably by paying the drivers *less than professional pay*, with reduced or no benefits. The majority of the owning and leasing programs are based solely on cents per mile income, which can be less now than it was *thirty years ago* when the price of fuel was a fraction of what it is now and equipment cost and maintenance were also much less. *Beware!* Some of these trucks are 'sold' or 'leased' several different times to various individuals who attempt the programs without success and give it up! Most of the trucks end up being returned to the companies running the programs, then re-leased or sold again. It seems to be a plan for a perpetual revolving door, with drivers constantly coming in full of hope and excitement and going out in despair.

## 3. COMPANY DRIVER VS. OWNER-OPERATOR

We will be looking at information and opinions about leasing and owning programs as well as independent owner-operators.

Remember this; driving a company truck is one thing while 'owning' your own is *quite another*. As a company driver your liability is limited and there are usually some benefits, albeit limited. Usually there are provisions for paid time off for vacations and you do not have to be concerned about your truck when you are gone as long as you have secured it at a company approved facility.

As an owner-operator, the immense overall cost of only *one truck* combined with maintenance, insurance and licensing *can cost more than many houses*. There are ongoing and hidden operating expenses that must be satisfied periodically by the owner-operator every week, month or annually as the case may be. *A potential owner-operator must take this aspect of trucking fully into consideration!* He is now *self-employed* and subject to all the rules and regulations that go with it. *Variables beyond your control dictate your success or failure!* If you take time off, all the payments must still be met! You are now 100% responsible for everything! Good luck!

## 4. OWNER-OPERATOR SCAM

It seems to me that the countless lease and owner-operator programs set forth throughout the industry are nothing but a *giant smoke screen* that is blinding the truth that *OVER THE ROAD truck driver pay is far less than what it should be!* These programs seem to have diverted attention from the *real* problem of *inadequate driver compensation* to 'Which is the best lease or owner-operator program?' when in reality *few of those programs are worthwhile* since the low rate of income causes the drivers to *support their trucks 'out of pocket', further eroding their net income!*

I am all for the entrepreneurial spirit and 'own your own business' scenario but what we have here borders on scam and once again, seems to be supported by the government. *People with no prior experience of any kind in transportation are being coerced to 'Own your own truck, be your own boss!'* after only a few months behind the wheel. Owner-operator companies have nearly perfected getting people to work for less than a fair and equitable amount *and like it because it appeals to their ego!* The many that fail and fall by the wayside are apparently at an acceptable level since they are nevertheless transporting the nations goods as they struggle to survive. Clearly, it is 'If you can't make it, step aside and make room for the next guy.' Sad, but true! *If this is not a plan for a perpetual revolving door I do not know what else to call it.*

## 5. COMPANY OWNER-OPERATORS

In my opinion, owner-operators signing on with large trucking companies that offer less than realistic compensation are not truly owner-operators. They have merely *taken on the obligation of paying for (not necessarily owning) and maintaining an expensive piece of equipment and have given up what few company-paid benefits company drivers do enjoy.* These so-called 'owner-operators' are coerced to run to the limit of and beyond their endurance for many thousands of miles per week in order to financially survive at less than a realistic rate of pay. Many of them claim to consistently run between *six and eight thousand miles a week* with the help of a co-driver. *I have overheard them say that with less than 6,000 miles a week they cannot make it.* Setting a pace such as this is destined to result in safety shortcomings from fatigue as well as premature equipment failure. Additionally, *these drivers are depriving the regular company drivers of enough miles to survive on* by skimming off the easiest and longest runs, assisted by the companies because of the *increased profitability to the company by using an owner-operator as opposed to using a company driver.* Safety and logbook demands have been relaxed for them since they are not on the company payroll.

## 6. PAYING THE BILLS

The truck or lease payment becomes the first consideration of a new owner or lease-operator and is deducted from your settlement up front, leaving you with the balance to pay your personal bills. Many of these owner-operator individuals are usually not concerned with how much they earn per mile as long as they can simply pay their bills and meet their other personal obligations. Some of these people never imagined that they would be able to acquire such an expensive item as an OVER THE ROAD tractor due to prior inadequate income and poor credit history in their past.

This kind of thinking may be okay or it could be disastrous, depending on each individual circumstance. If they are not cautious and selective in which plan they choose to go with *they can wind up owning a huge package of heartache and failure.* On the other hand some companies have designed programs that are more realistic than others provided a driver is willing and able to hang in there for the duration of the contract and work hard for the entire length of it, more or less becoming a slave to the company. Working smart is important, too. Keeping a lid on expenses by buying cheaper fuel and finding deals on truck maintenance can help.

## 7. GENUINE OWNER-OPERATORS

*Genuine* owner-operators own a tractor and trailer and deal directly with brokers, shippers and receivers at a *realistic income* of $1.50 or even far more per mile. These are *real* businessmen and at that rate can generate much more income with far fewer miles, thereby causing less wear and tear on their equipment and themselves. *Many of these owner-operators are very successful!* It usually takes many years working as a company driver to gain enough experience and business contacts to accomplish this. These are the real pros but even then *it is still a challenge to be successful,* as with any business.

These businessmen are usually better and safer drivers since they try to protect their 'large cars' from being involved in any event that may result in damage to their 'money-maker'. Probably if more trucks were operated by responsible drivers with this mindset combined with realistic income the highways would be a much safer place.

## 8. CONSPIRACY?

At the risk of sounding paranoid it almost seems as if the owner-operator scenario might be the result of an ongoing conspiracy if you will, by the federal government in conjunction with those in control of the transportation and manufacturing industries to keep a handle on the overall effect of trucking costs in relation to the economy as a whole, since *there are no provisions for even minimum wage, much less overtime!* Lobbyists and politicians have made and continue to make a lot of money getting and keeping transportation deregulated for the benefit of the bureaucracy and the federal government. Lack of driver representation eliminates concern about a nationwide trucker shutdown that *would bring the country to a standstill!* Would our government instigate such a thing? What do *you* think?

Consider the following:

1. Truck drivers have been classified by the government as 'unskilled labor'.
2. Truck drivers have been exempted from the Fair Labor Standards Act'.
3. Deregulation laws included restriction of union participation by OVER THE ROAD truckers.
4. Representation of OVER THE ROAD truck drivers barely exists.
5. Government regulation of truck drivers with an hourly logbook while paying them by the mile driven does not make sense.
6. There is no provision for a minimum wage of any kind.

Clearly all of these things have been well thought out by the bureaucracy and *any change to improve the plight of the OVER THE ROAD truck driver is highly unlikely to ever take place.*

## 9. OVER THE ROAD TRUCKING HAS BEEN SINGLED OUT

Premium pay for those in other professions increases the cost of everything from automobiles to airline tickets *without a whimper.* In addition, they all enjoy *regular cost of living increases. This is the capitalistic American way!* OVER THE ROAD trucking is the *only* major profession that has been singled out by the federal government and industry to *waive labor laws that were specifically designed to enhance safety and fair compensation.* The result is an erratic, confused transportation system *struggling for survival* that *unfairly exploits its multi-talented labor force; the truck drivers.* The demise of tens of thousands of union trucking companies after deregulation and resulting loss of high-paying truck driver jobs is stark evidence of this! Unrealistic logbook rules and uncertainty of income while at the same time increasing the possibility of fines from citations has contributed to this loss. Countless dependable, responsible and highly experienced truck drivers have been lost to the highways due to the revolving door that has been created in trucking. Many abandoned single-purpose truck terminals can be witnessed today throughout the country. Ghost terminals, if you will. They are a grim reminder of how significantly things have changed.

## 10. INCREASE IN FREIGHT RATES IS NEEDED

Since there is no longer a rigid regulatory agency in regard to freight rates, the carriers themselves will have to take on the task of adjusting rates to where they can afford to increase truck driver pay and benefits to an acceptable level.

If truck drivers were paid comparably to all other professionals, freight rates would undoubtedly have to be increased somewhat which could raise the price of consumer products because of the millions of truck drivers involved. If so, *the increase would be so slight that it would have little or no effect on the overall economy and could greatly enhance the safety aspect of big trucks on the nations highways! It would result in higher quality drivers with professional attitudes, pushing most of the present undesirables aside.* Lazy, unproductive and uncaring truck drivers could be weeded out through attrition. Standards could be set and expected to be adhered to or the drivers terminated. Additionally, **with this many drivers earning substantially more income, it would *stimulate the entire economy* with the increased purchasing power of OVER THE ROAD truck drivers as they traveled throughout the country. Motels, restaurants and department stores would certainly benefit. Houses and cars would be bought!** *Working people spend money! The more they make, the more they spend!*

And even if it did result in a noticeable increase in freight rates to provide fair and comparable compensation for a major profession such as this, *it is long overdue!* If paying truck drivers fairly would reduce bonuses for top executives, sorry about that! Surely, they will always somehow receive enough to justify their efforts. Chalk it up to the cost of doing business as in all other professions. Expecting people (truck drivers) to work for nothing is an atrocity! *We need to get back to reality!*

## 11. FAST TRUCKS, AN ENTICEMENT TO WORK FOR LESS

As mentioned before, many small trucking companies entice drivers to drive for them by offering the finest and most up to date equipment available *with no restriction on speed!* They openly encourage their trucks to be driven at excessive rates of speed while carrying loads that could not possibly be time-sensitive. Some even offer to pay the speeding tickets. In some cases an experienced driver is paired up as a team with an inexperienced greenhorn and they are told to accomplish high-mileage runs in unrealistically short periods of time which would require driving sometimes into triple-digits (100 MPH and up)! *There are many solo drivers running the mileage of two drivers, getting by on little or no sleep!* Is this what we want roaring across the nation's highways? *The momentum of that much weight (80,000 #) at those speeds is virtually uncontrollable! What if a steering tire should blow? What about reaction time to stop in the event of an emergency?* But quick turn-around of equipment assures maximum earnings for their investment, without regard for life or limb of the drivers or those they may come in contact with. Reduced rates of pay to the drivers are compensated for with high mileage, *if they survive.* No benefits are provided and driver burnout is commonplace. *Safety is seldom an issue; money is the prime objective!*

## 12. 'KNIGHTS OF THE ROAD' ARE TREATED LIKE 'PAWNS OF THE ROAD'

In the old days truck drivers were often referred to as 'knights of the road' and treated accordingly with courtesy and respect. Times were tough and people worked hard. There seemed to be a better understanding by everyone as to the importance and responsibility of truck drivers.

Now most people, including those in management of large trucking companies, shippers and receivers, either do not fully realize the demands expected of OVER THE ROAD truck drivers and the skills and endurance required to meet them or *they do not care! Cost of living on the road for an OVER THE ROAD trucker is rarely mentioned!*

The main thing management is concerned about is that they want a load taken from one location to another at the appointed time without any problems. The irony is that they leave this responsibility almost entirely up to the underpaid OVER THE ROAD truck driver to accomplish this. The fact that many of these truck drivers are barely getting by and not earning enough money to pay their bills *is generally of no concern to anyone but the truck drivers and their families,* in spite of all the lip service to the contrary.

They are paid the same for hauling a load of high value, time-sensitive or hazardous products as they would be paid for a load of scrap paper or some other mundane item of far less concern. It matters not that OVER THE ROAD truck drivers are being exposed to hijackers with high risk to life and limb, traffic citations, hazardous weather and financial disaster from exorbitant fines with no consideration for these things in their compensation package. This lack of concern can continue on with back-to-back trips continuously as long as the driver can endure the pace. Truck drivers have become 'pawns of the road' with little respect in today's world. They are dispensable.

## 13. WITHOUT TRUCK DRIVERS, NOTHING MUCH ELSE CAN HAPPEN

The fact is that while each segment of the trucking industry looks at things from their viewpoint only, it remains that *if there is nobody to drive the truck, little else can happen!* Some of the people in trucking management are prior truck drivers who themselves could not withstand the conditions of being on the road but do understand many of the ongoing problems because of having 'been there'. Many of them develop short memories. Others of those in transportation management have not driven truck at all and are making decisions that adversely affect the daily lives of long-time experienced truck drivers in a negative way. *It is too bad that so many people are ruining a great profession!* I apologize if this sounds a bit cynical, but I feel *the truth must be told! If conditions are to improve the problems must be brought out in the open,* not swept under the rug and ignored. *Again, dialog is badly needed if improvement is to take place.*

## 14. CHANGE MAY TAKE DECADES

As time passes and the evolution of OVER THE ROAD trucking takes place, a more professional atmosphere and compensation package for OVER THE ROAD truck drivers *should* hopefully develop. This will probably take several decades or more. Most of those that control such things are satisfied with the way things are now in regard to driver pay. They are the people that are profiting most from present conditions. Until the driver turnover and/or shortage reaches an unacceptable level to those controlling such things, nothing much will happen in the area of improvement unless laws are passed.

*It is those that are most concerned about the carnage on the highways that must help to influence changes to happen sooner!* There are many groups, committees and organizations that already exist and are studying the problems of fatigue, safety and accidents! It is these that must be made aware of where the answers are that they are looking for. *Most of those answers are in this book!*

# 7.

# COST AND QUALITY OF TRAINING SCHOOLS

## 1. GETTING THE OVER-RATED CDL

This is where it all begins nowadays in almost all cases. Becoming a non-union company driver. Getting trained and acquiring the much over-rated commercial driver's license (CDL). Why over-rated? Because the federal government would have the public believe that the CDL is the answer to the public outcry about truck accidents and unprofessional truck drivers careening down the nations highways at breakneck speeds, endangering the lives of all others on the highway. While the CDL actually did result in reducing the number of drivers involved with drugs and alcohol, *it did nothing to help with the problem of tired and fatigued drivers.*

This book is intended to provide an in-depth look at the cost and quality of training schools. There are many thousands of truck driving schools to choose from and it can be difficult to determine if they are only in it for the money or are genuinely concerned about what happens to the students after they 'graduate'. The base cost of this 'training' can be anywhere from $1500 to $10,000, depending on the school and what they offer. *Higher cost does not always insure better training!*

It is important to investigate as many schools as possible before making a decision of which one to go with. I suggest talking with someone who has already completed their training at a school if at all possible and getting their opinion about the quality of instructors and cost involved. I recommend a bona-fide community college with several years experience in this field.

## 2. TRUCK DRIVER TRAINING IS A MULTI-BILLION DOLLAR INDUSTRY

Please understand that many 'trainees' in truck company training programs may be highly experienced drivers simply changing jobs and their training mostly involves learning company procedures in the new company with a trainer. *It is with these experienced students that a trainer may be able to maximize their miles and therefore their income by running as a fully qualified team on high mileage runs.* Much of the following does not pertain to them.

Driver training! As a trainee, you only get out of it what you put into it.

While this is true to a large degree, many of the truck driver training schools and driver trainers are themselves inadequate.

The better 'primary' schools last as long as eight weeks and the training is much more thorough. Then, the 'on the job' training with an OVER THE ROAD driver trainer may take another six to eight weeks. By the time a trainee completes three or four months of intensive training he should be adequately prepared to take on a position as a solo OVER THE ROAD truck driver if his OVER THE ROAD trainer was thorough in his training. Eight weeks in paper school and eight weeks on the road. Now we have a good start in producing a *qualified* OVER THE ROAD truck driver. This is rarely if ever the case!

Instead, it seems as if many or most of these schools that specialize exclusively in truck driver training are actually in competition with each other to get their 'share' of people willing to commit to paying for training. Remember, shorter training periods (two weeks) allow more enrollment capability (money). The schools know that most of these students will not make it anyway and most of those that do will probably not stick it out!

Many schools have become 'head hunters' simply to get people to sign the loan agreements! From what I have heard community colleges appear to be the most affordable and most professional in their training. Since they are professional in teaching for other careers they can be expected to present their course in a thorough and professional manner with highly qualified instructors.

A little known fact by the public is that most states have 'job-training' programs, sponsored by the federal government in the form of grants of up to $5,000 that do not have to be repaid. This was told to me by several students I had. In reporting to their local unemployment offices these students were informed of this program as a way of securing a CDL and becoming an OVER THE ROAD truck driver.

It should be noted that students were *not* informed of these grants by lending institutions even though they were aware of them because there is more money to be made by obligating the unemployed student to a long-term *private* loan at high interest rates. *It is all about money!*

Let's look into this "truck driver training" and do a little math.

## 3. TRUCK DRIVER TRAINING SCHOOLS

Keep in mind that most of the private truck driver schools are only two or three weeks long and then the 'graduates' are sent to an OVER THE ROAD trucking company to finish the OVER THE ROAD segment of the training with an on the job driver trainer for several weeks before being assigned to their own truck.

Consider the following. There are many thousands of truck driver schools. If only one thousand (1,000) schools in the entire United States sign up an average of only ten (10) students a week at one thousand (1,000.00) dollars per student, that comes to **TEN MILLION DOLLARS ($10,000,000.00) A WEEK.** In a year that would be **TEN MILLION** times fifty-two (52) or **FIVE HUNDRED AND TWENTY MILLION DOLLARS ($520,000,000.00)!** That's a lot of money in anybody's book. In addition, these figures are a gross under-statement because in reality there are *many* thousands of truck driver training schools and the cost of training is from fifteen hundred ($1,500.00) to ten thousand ($10,000.00) dollars per trainee rather than the one thousand dollars cited. Figure it out! We are talking about **BILLIONS OF DOLLARS** a year! In addition, the interest from these school loans can many times double, triple and even quadruple the original amount.

Some students have shown me their financial documents where with interest, the original loan of $7,500.00 came to $28,000.00 financed over a fifteen-year period, for a *two-week* training session that was poor and incomplete. This borders on being a scam or worse! In addition there is talk that more of these schools are going to raise their prices to $10,000.00 for what is presently a *two* or *three week* training period! The training in these schools is supposed to meet minimum federal standards but from what I have heard from some students, *some schools are not teaching even basic shifting and backing procedures!* They leave this most important part of the training up to the OVER THE ROAD driver trainer who expects (rightly so) the student to already have acquired these skills during his 'basic training'.

This is unfair to the OVER THE ROAD driver trainers who are paid no extra for this additional unexpected and time-consuming training! It can be very frustrating to the trainers who themselves may have little patience or experience in dealing with this part of the training. Poor attitudes can develop as tempers flare as the unsuspecting trainers attempt to teach the novice skills that he should already have learned. Because of this many trainers stop training. If the students were adequately trained at the schools instead of being quickly herded through to make room for the next group coming in, it might be worth the many thousands of dollars as an investment in their future. Two or three weeks are not enough for that kind of money. Some kind of investigation could be in order here. This is getting out of hand!

Instead, the federal government many times provides grants of up to $5,000.00 per student to some or all of the training schools that participate in these 'job training' programs, providing windfall profits to the schools. While this may be a good thing for those who cannot afford schooling and need a job, it almost makes it *too* easy for an individual to jump in, uninformed as to the hazards involved in this profession. It seems some trucking companies with schools are profiting as much or more from training as they are from trucking and therefore encourage all interested and qualified people to 'sign on the dotted line' with little consideration for their personal lives. The schools make money off the financing no matter what happens to the student so they are not overly concerned about whether or not the student is successful!

The fact is that it is the individuals involved in trying to improve their lives and willing to work hard to do it, the 'working man' if you will, that are not only left out of all this money but bearing the burden, along with the taxpayers. It appears that *some* of these training schools and maybe some trucking companies are becoming very wealthy at the little guys' expense. Yes, this *is* the American way but I think it is going too far in this case.

I fear this has caused these private schools to be more concerned with first getting a *financial commitment* from the individual and then letting the student worry about whether or not this type of career will work for him or her and their family instead of the other way around, as it should be. It has become a 'Let the buyer beware' scenario, *all at the expense of those that can least afford it.* This is impulse buying of a career, fueled by the hopeful excitement of the moment, since most of these folks need a better job to support their family. Many of these students drop out of training before it is finished and many others only stick it out long enough to fulfill their financial obligation. Of these a small percentage may continue to try out various OVER THE ROAD truck driving jobs with several of the many thousands of long haul trucking companies advertising for OVER THE ROAD truck drivers. The long-term retention rate in OVER THE ROAD trucking is very low. I do not know of any official statistics on this but I have heard several times that only about one out of every one hundred and fifty applicants continue on with OVER THE ROAD TRUCKING as a career. Many applicants cannot even qualify for reasons of a poor driving record, poor health, drug usage or a criminal background. It is not quite as easy to come on board as people may think!

There are minimal federal requirements on length of training time in schools but none with an OVER THE ROAD driver trainer. That's right! It is up to the individual trucking companies as to how much risk they are willing to take. A trainee can actually go directly from any truck driving school onto the open road if a trucking company allows them. God help us!

If anyone is anxious enough to try this and willing to 'give it a shot, what have I got to lose?' they had better think again! They have a lot to lose, including time, money and family stability as well as their credit rating if they do not repay the loan. However, I feel that most of the *trucking* company schools are more interested in a successful conclusion of training for the simple reason that *they need drivers*. I would like to think these trucking companies are a bit more conscientious about obligating folks without having only the money in mind.

Some of these so-called 'Truck Driver Training Schools' appear to be nothing more than a backyard mud lot scam. Others that appear to be more legitimate are simply in it for the money with no regard for the well being of the individual. Still others that are genuinely interested in training and supplying truck drivers for the over 650,000 trucking companies that need to fill their empty seats, appear to be operating on the theory that if you throw enough mud against the wall some of it will stick. They are obviously playing the numbers game!

For what it is worth, a common complaint many trainees have about the schools is that when orange traffic cones are used in backing exercises rather than using real trailers to back in between, it causes the student to be somewhat out of touch with the reality of the event. Some schools also use smaller trailers to train with instead of the now commonly used fifty-three ft. trailers. When the students complete their training and achieve solo status they are then faced with maneuvering and backing around the real thing and they have to start from square one. They are now in the high-pressure area of the real world, dealing with real truck drivers and real conditions. It is a whole new ball game! This is not a good situation nor is it conducive to retaining these new intimidated drivers.

Information about the actual work and conditions of pay or lack of it, is not included in any training program I have heard of other than the rate of pay per mile. The new entrants are led to believe that it is a somewhat normal job with adventure and travel as a bonus. They are told they can earn $30,000 and up the first year and more each year thereafter as their rate of pay per mile increases if they hang in there. Not many do!

Nothing is usually mentioned about the many hours of waiting around without pay that is expected of drivers, little or no layover pay and no provision for overtime of any kind! Neither is it mentioned that there are few if any paid holidays and the benefits are many times poor or non-existent. The on-going problem of being away from home for long periods of time may be mentioned but minimized.

For those that *do* qualify and decide to make the huge transition of becoming an OVER THE ROAD trucker, the training needs to be intensified at the *beginning* of this transition *in the school, before* the students are turned over to the OVER THE ROAD driver trainers. *Two weeks is not enough!* There *are* truck driver training schools with eight week programs that are very thorough in all aspects of the job including backing, shifting and on the road experience in realistic conditions. These schools are hard to find but they do exist and include room and board for the same price as the 2-week schools that are inadequate and incomplete. You had better shop around!

## 4.  GETTING YOUR MONEY'S WORTH

Truck driving schools! There are thousands of them all over the country! The prices they charge for the short duration of the training period they provide can sometimes be exorbitant. Another of my recent trainees said he paid $8700.00 for a two-week session. This included a motel room, two meals a day and a bus ride to get to the school from where he lived. The school said he could have ten years to pay it off at 21% interest, which brought the final cost to over $17,000.00! *For two weeks!* As you can see, it is very important to investigate thoroughly before doing this. Again, I recommend a training school at a trucking company that can provide a job when you are done. Keeping everything under one roof can be a definite advantage. The trucking companies will also provide transportation from home if you need it, with food and lodging and I never heard of them charging near that much. They have a lot to gain from treating students fairly since they need drivers for their trucks. Many of these companies advertise for trainees in the free monthly trucker publications found in truck stops. They can also be found on the internet.

Many trucking companies that do not have a school depend on private truck driver training schools to get the preliminary training out of the way and then recruit the graduates to finish their OVER THE ROAD training with them and eventually become a driver for their company. Some of them even make arrangements to pay off part or all of the debt the student incurred with the school they attended, provided the student agrees to drive for them for a year or two at a reduced rate of pay. Everybody wins *if* the student is able to fulfill his obligation without jeopardizing his family life.

Some of these trucking companies have *also* developed finance plans for schooling that can obligate you for payments for many months at high (20% and up) interest rates. They have found another way to make money it seems. They have become a finance company! Be sure to check them all out and do a fair comparison to select the company that best suits your needs. After compiling all your information, *take it to a lawyer!* You need an outside opinion by a professional before you sign anything! Do not be in too big a hurry! Very few people will follow this advice but I feel it is very important! A lawyer will make you think! Many recruiters are similar to a car salesman. They coerce people to 'Sign now before it is too late'! They get paid so much a student. Do not forget this!

I have developed a starter kit for would-be truckers that includes a list of many of these trucking companies with schools and their toll-free numbers. The starter kit also includes information pertaining to income taxes, driver training notes and forms for data accumulation for each trip. You will find a list of the details at the end of this book. The income tax expense report alone is well worth acquiring the kit not only for new entrants, but also for those already driving truck as well as owner-operators.

## 5.  NOT ENOUGH TRAINERS

A major problem on entry into OVER THE ROAD trucking is that when students finish their initial training and are ready to go into the 'on the job' training with an OVER

THE ROAD driver trainer, many times there are not enough driver trainers to accommodate all the trainees. This causes the company to have to either hold the students somewhere until a trainer becomes available or send the students home to avoid the cost of motels and waiting pay, if any. It is very important to have an understanding about this potential problem up front, before it happens. Since recruiters get paid so much a head, many times they will say whatever it takes to get someone to sign onto their company's program even if they have to 'stretch the truth'.

*The fact is that OVER THE ROAD truck driver trainers are in such short supply that some major companies are actually putting two inexperienced drivers straight out of training school with no OVER THE ROAD experience at all, directly into a truck together and turning them loose on the highway!* **This is for real, folks!** This information comes from a student who experienced it. Also, some companies are so short of OVER THE ROAD truck driver trainers that they are even allowing new solo drivers that have only a few months experience themselves to be driver trainers! These are desperate, 'blind leading the blind' scenarios that are putting everybody on the highways at greater risk! No company names, please.

*In the case of a trainee with no prior experience the trainer should always be present to observe and advise him in advance of happening events and never retire into the sleeper berth to sleep!*

## 6. NEED FOR GOOD DRIVER TRAINERS

The need for qualified OVER THE ROAD truck *driver trainers* has greatly increased as a result of this 'driver turnover' situation. *Being one of these truck driver trainers has now become one of the most lucrative professions in modern day trucking.* To be a conscientious and effective trainer is not easy and requires tremendous patience, endurance and skills not to mention experience and training capabilities. People skills are definitely a big plus. A training position usually results in better utilization of time through better, longer runs with more miles and therefore more income. However, there is no guarantee of that either. You can sometimes find yourself feeling like a combined baby-sitter for a student and security guard for equipment if you have to wait a day or two or more for a load. It can be very frustrating to both the trainer and the trainee!

As for being a trainer, the student is expected to do most of the driving and backing into customer facilities. Sometimes it is necessary for a trainer to do difficult things as the student looks on, to avoid a backing accident. Since shippers and receivers are usually on a tight schedule, trainers sometimes must take on the most difficult backing tasks to save time, prevent an accident and accommodate the customer who is probably impatiently waiting for the truck to be backed into his dock. This can result in the trainee getting less badly needed first-hand backing experience in the actual backing of a rig into tight places and therefore may be improperly prepared to accept solo status when the training period is finished. A good trainer will try to see that his student gets enough experience of all kinds whenever possible and take special measures to do so.

On the up side for a trainer there are many trainees with prior experience who are simply changing jobs for some reason. Most companies require that job changers go with a trainer for a short while to simply learn company procedures and operations. It is with these a trainer may be able to generate some very good mileage running as a team.

## 7. WHY A SHORTAGE OF DRIVER TRAINERS

Why is there a shortage of driver trainers? There are many reasons.

1. Most OVER THE ROAD truck drivers value their privacy. These drivers would not train at any price.
2. Driver trainers should not trust the driving of a novice enough to sleep while the trainee is driving. This reduces the aspect of a trainer earning more money with more miles.
2. There can be personality conflicts between trainers and trainees.
3. Sharing space in the tight quarters of an OVER THE ROAD truck can be very trying, especially during non-productive waiting periods.
5. Lack of or inadequate training to prepare trainers.
6. Inadequate training by schools to prepare trainees.
7. Failure of the trainer to have personal notes explaining to his trainees how things are done.
8. Failure of the company to *adequately* explain to the trainee that he is going to be a *guest* in the trainer's *home* and should respect his position and authority. This stems from the fact that the *company* has to understand this before it can be passed on to the trainee. Only those who have done this can *fully* understand this problem. Some students can test a trainer's patience to the limit and the trainer must work things out on his own the best way he knows how. This is not a ride around the block to try out a used car.
9. Company demands on trainers without compensation. It takes a lot of time and patience to *properly* train a novice simply to back these huge units up. There are straight backs, forty-five to ninety degree backs and tight backs between two other trucks that can result in crunched fenders or broken mirrors if a trainee is too lazy, over-confident or in too much of a hurry to *get out and look*. Many trainers simply refuse to let the student even try to back into tight spots and do it themselves. Backing can be very frustrating to trainer and trainee. Since many of these trainees do not last long anyway, trainers can feel their time and efforts are being wasted on them. Unfortunately there is no way to differentiate between a trainee that will stick it out and one that will quit after a short time.
10. Not enough more miles to make it worthwhile even though the trainer gets paid for all the miles he and the trainee drive together. Many good trainers have given up training for this reason. An experienced OVER THE ROAD driver does not like to feel like a baby sitter. This feeling can develop if a company does not provide loads enough to keep the truck moving. Under present conditions, miles are usually the only pay incentive. If a trainer with a trainee only gets the mileage of a solo driver, why inconvenience himself?
11. Shifting skills. Most new entrants have never driven a standard shift vehicle of any size and it is very difficult for a trainer to try to show and explain to these trainees how and when to change gears without jamming and crunching them. The short training period at driving schools is where this *should* be accomplished. This is why automatic transmissions in trucks make a trainer's job immeasurably easier.

## 8. LACK OF *QUALITY* DRIVER TRAINERS

There are many reasons why a new entrant may pack it in early, seemingly without giving trucking an adequate chance. One of these reasons could be that the trainer he was assigned may have had an abrasive or overpowering attitude that simply scared the trainee off. Many of these trainers are not themselves qualified to be in a position of showing new entrants the many necessary things needed to be successful with trucking as a career. They can become over-tired, impatient, irritated and rude to their students due to constant sleep interruptions and jostling about by the trainee as the trainee fumbles about in unfamiliar territory, struggling to do the right thing that may be obvious to the trainer. It requires a tremendous amount of patience and self-control on the part of the trainer. In addition to these possible shortcomings the trainer may not have provided adequate preparatory notes for the students to read. It can become very disconcerting living in these tight quarters with a total stranger for several weeks of training, especially if there is no meeting of the minds through proper preparation and communication.

I remember an incident where my trainee and I were dining with another trainer who worked for the same company as us. In conversation, the other trainer stated that he lets his students know right up front that for the next five weeks they will be riding with 'god', meaning himself! Both my student's and my jaws dropped and we stared at each other in disbelief! It was obvious to us why this trainer did not have a trainee with him.

I wish I could say that there is no room in truck driver training for a trainer with this kind of mentality but unfortunately because of the trainer shortage, many trainers do have this attitude and little or nothing is usually done about it.

On the other side of the coin some *trainees* can have a 'know it all' attitude, finishing the trainer's sentences and taking over the conversation before the trainer has a chance to make his points about various conditions. *Students that purposely fail to fall in line with a trainer's way of doing things can present a real challenge!* Little events can become big problems over the several weeks of travel with each other. Because of the massive influx of trainees from all walks of life, a trainer must maintain this realization and be willing to adjust or be flexible in many of his training and living habits.

Therefore trainers need to be schooled in how to communicate tactfully, taking into account the many personality conflicts that can arise and how to handle them. Ex-drill instructors from the military tend to be poor trainers for obvious reasons. A trainee is already very nervous and on edge about changing jobs, starting a career in a new field and facing huge equipment that he knows little or nothing about. Then the aspect of traveling all over the country and trying to find locations he has never been to before while maneuvering a huge, ungainly piece of equipment can be a deciding factor to quit upon the realization that he will soon be alone and expected to do it all by himself.

In my opinion, a trainer should have at least two winter seasons under his belt in which he would be exposed to complete winter driving conditions himself. Otherwise how in the world can he show someone else how to prepare for those conditions? As the saying goes, 'Talk's cheap, seein's believin'". Realistically however, this simply is not possible due to the driver shortage which also includes a shortage of driver trainers. Presently a 'blind leading the blind' scenario definitely exists. If the compensation more adequately justified the effort there would be more qualified, experienced drivers willing to train and less inclined to quit and go somewhere else as a solo driver. Being an OVER THE ROAD truck driver trainer is not easy!

## 9. DRIVER TRAINERS CAN MAKE GOOD MONEY

If you become a driver trainer, you must realize that new trainees are many times trying harder than normal to do everything safely and according to proper procedure. Entering a new field of any kind can be very trying on the applicant and they are in a 'prove yourself' mode. Accept their efforts accordingly and try to be confidant in their abilities, within reason. Usually if given half a chance, their common sense will prevail. You must learn to be patient and 'bite your tongue'. Being a driver trainer is probably the toughest of all truck driving careers. A driver trainer must be gentle, understanding, patient, flexible and ready to take control of the truck in an instant in strenuous circumstances that may cause a trainee to fall apart. Being a trainer can also be a most rewarding career when a student is successful. A good trainer is helping someone improve their life.

A driver trainer can make more income at a lower rate of pay with the assistance of a responsible trainee with prior experience to help with the driving. It is possible for an experienced driver trainer to travel anywhere from five to six thousand miles a week if he has his training methods properly developed, an experienced trainee changing jobs from a different company and the company he drives for has the available freight. Two drivers on a truck can easily travel over 1000 miles a day under normal circumstances. Safety is a definite consideration here, of course. It is extremely important to have a handle on your 'fatigue factor'. This requires operating and rest routines with professional attitudes by both drivers. Time zone changes can cause 'jet lag' traveling east to west and back. Several days off between trainees are sometimes needed to restore your energy.

For example at only 30 CPM, five thousand miles will generate a $1500 paycheck to a trainer. And at 40 CPM a trainer traveling six thousand miles in seven days will see earnings of $2400 in a week. That is a mighty impressive piece of change. This is being done regularly with some companies. It is not likely those driver trainers are going anywhere! But remember, *all the money in the world is useless to you if you or your trainee should fall asleep from fatigue and kill yourselves.* Know your limitations and live by them. It is no shame to park the truck and sleep when fatigue is trying to overtake your body. A short nap can do wonders!

Remember this. It seldom makes a difference where you as a driver want to go or what *you* want to do with most companies. It will be whatever comes across the screen of the sat-com that will dictate those events completely. As an OVER THE ROAD driver you must learn to accept the assignment and work with it by using your knowledge and experience to juggle things to try to deliver early, re-power the load or drop it at a company facility and get reassigned to another load. Any of those things should result in more paid miles. As long as you get decent weekly mileage, where you go usually does not much matter.

## 10. PREPARING TO BECOME A DRIVER TRAINER

Becoming a driver trainer has both advantages and disadvantages. The biggest benefit to the trainer is hopefully, increased income from more miles. A driver trainer generally gets better, longer runs since obviously two drivers can put more ground behind them much faster than a solo driver and with greater ease. Logbook demands are more easily met. However, there are several things a person must accomplish to be a successful driver trainer.

1. Having a set of personal notes to present to new trainees is important to develop a 'meeting of the minds'. These notes should present your way of doing things to the newcomer and try to answer as many questions as possible about the way things are done to succeed in this kind of work. The first several days should be spent instructively with open communication between trainer and trainee. The trainee drives and the trainer observes and advises. However, it might be better if the trainer drives the first few hours to give the student a chance to relax and observe how the trainer handles the truck in regard to traffic and following distance.

2. A trainer must develop a mental attitude that is patient and understanding of the student's nervousness. This is a very difficult time for trainees and many will give it up right away if the trainer is too demanding or impersonal. Forcing a trainee to drive a truck too fast can produce fear and anxiety in a new driver as well as be unsafe. A trainee needs to drive so that he feels somewhat 'comfortable'. It does not matter if it takes longer to get somewhere as long as you get there without any problems. Better to be a little late than to have an accident. Personally, I do not want to be traveling across the country in a truck at breakneck speeds with an entry-level driver at the wheel. Alternatively, driving too slow can cause a hazard to other traffic.

3. When a trainee makes mistakes and they all do, a trainer must be understanding and organized in instructing the student in how to correct those mistakes. Unless there is a possible imminent safety failure, being a silent observer and leaving the trainee alone can many times be the best thing to do. Then at an opportune time ask if he would like some helpful advice. Present him with his mistake during a quiet time and explain what he did wrong, why it was wrong and how to correct or prevent it from happening again.

4. Most students can be expected to drive from eight to ten hours a day as the trainer observes. Then the trainer may drive several more hours as the student observes before stopping to get some sleep with the truck sitting still. The two can usually easily travel from six to eight hundred miles a day like this, even more in good conditions.

5. Remember, it is with the trainee's presence that a trainer will be able to accomplish service to the better runs and maintain a fully legal profile in your logbook, thereby increasing the trainer's income. Both parties should come out winners.

## 11. TRAINEE REPRESENTATION

Representation for trainees should also be looked at. Because of the shortage of driver trainers many trainees are expected to wait around sometimes for several days or more for a trainer to become available to train them after they have completed all other orientation and are ready for their OVER THE ROAD training. Trainees that have been sent home to wait for a trainer usually have no income during that period. If the trainee has no alternate income or employment during this waiting period, it does not take long to become financially troubled, to say the least. The student understanding this possibility and making preparation *before signing on* seems to be the only cure for this. Adequate financial preparation by the trainee in advance would seem to be mandatory and a basic requirement before accepting the trainee into the school. Obviously most of these folks have quit their previous jobs and if their spouse does not work there is no income to meet their basic expenses. Some companies do provide nominal compensation during this unproductive waiting period but not many.

## 12. STUDENTS QUITTING DURING TRAINING

As stated before, many times students may not finish entry into this field because of family considerations. At the beginning, hopeful young mothers may go along with their husband's desire to do this. However when the actual training begins and the absence of the husband and father of her children becomes a realization to her, it can become an overwhelming obstacle for her to be without her man. This can happen at any age for that matter. Especially, should the training take the new student near his home and he stops by to 'see the family'. Some companies allow this; most do not. It is almost like the trainee has been temporarily abducted. The reason is, many times should a trainer stop and allow a trainee to visit his family en-route to a delivery, that will end the training session right there. I had it happen several times!

*Physical contact with their family combined with homesickness or the fatigue of training can be a terminating influence!* Even though they will express confidence and assurance it will not make a difference, once the family reunites during training many times it results in the trainee ending his training, then and there. Preventing this physical contact with family during training can result in the student concentrating on the training session and successful completion of it. Yes, it is difficult but once the commitment has been made you might as well finish it. As confidence in your ability of the profession is gained, family considerations can usually be overcome long enough to get adequate experience to find a local job, if that is your goal. The end justifies the means.

As explained before, conflicts with a trainer can also result in a student packing it in before he finishes training. This happens frequently. There is no intermediary. Trainer and student are paired up indiscriminately and the chips fall where they may. *It is entirely up to them to work out their differences as they go along!*

## 13. TRAINEE BONUS NEEDED

Trainee incentive might also be considered by trucking companies. If the student knew he would be eligible for a sizeable bonus of several hundred dollars upon successful completion of five or six weeks initial training OVER THE ROAD, it could make a tremendous difference in his attitude about not getting home even if he had to remain six months or so with the company as a condition to collect. Getting over this hurdle might result in a good many new drivers that would have quit to stay on longer, maybe for a long-term career. *Money is a motivator*!

## 14. TOO MANY NEWCOMERS

Of course it is doubtful if anything such as this will take place since there are too many unsuspecting people available to try a new career. Many of these new entrants may have worked at low-paying or stressful careers and they are willing to initially overlook the unpleasant and unpaid parts of this profession. As time goes by and the job becomes more mundane, they begin to realize that things in this line of work are very much one-sided, *all in favor of the employer!* The demands of and responsibility of drivers are *tremendous! There is little or no incentive for management to be efficient in the use of their drivers* since there is little provision regarding compensation for unproductive waiting time. Welcome to OVER THE ROAD trucking!

## 15. DRIVERS FOR SALE

Recently I learned that drivers are actually being provided, or 'sold' to investors who need drivers for their trucks. This is happening because investors sometimes buy trucks as a tax hedge and need someone to drive them. This has gone on for years and seems to work out as a tax advantage for people in high-income categories that need tax deductions. Heavy trucks can be depreciated off very quickly, providing huge tax advantages for those willing to take the risk of putting a $100,000.00 truck on the open road in all kinds of weather in the hands of a total stranger. Because of the current driver shortage, qualified, experienced drivers for these trucks can be difficult to find.

What has taken place is that some large trucking companies that need drivers to haul their loads are now willing to be flexible to the point of signing on these investor's trucks and *provide the investors* with drivers from their driver training schools *for a charge of up to $7500.00 per truck!* This is another method of generating revenue in the modern day trucking scenario while at the same time attaching more trucks and drivers to the company. Astounding! Capitalism truly is wonderful for the paper pushers.

But what does this make the driver? A commodity to be bought and sold? Something like a slave, huh? I would think the industry needs to work things out so that any *money produced by a driver should go to the driver, not an entrepreneur.* Maybe the driver turnover problem could be reduced if good drivers could realize a greater return on their time and skills instead of dragging everybody else along on their coattails (at the truck driver's expense). Additionally, it does appear that even the new trucks of investors that can barrel down the highway at speeds approaching 100 miles an hour are attracting enough drivers to fill the seats. Special arrangements with the 'mother companies' are sometimes made to assure these drivers of high mileage and loads going where they want to go. Company drivers get what is left, usually the shorter, tougher runs involving delays, therefore producing less income.

I also heard that even some truck driving schools are getting up to $750.00 from companies for each driver they send to specific companies.

## 16. MEXICANS WORK HARDER FOR LESS

Another developing situation is a result of the North American Free Trade Agreement regarding Mexico. This agreement provides for Mexican truck drivers to now come into the United States and deliver loads that previously have provided jobs for Americans. It is a well-known fact that Mexicans earn far less than Americans which could eventually have a negative effect on the American OVER THE ROAD truck driver pay. An excerpt relating to this potential problem from the same Road King article as previously mentioned is; **"Spencer (Todd Spencer of the Owner-Operator Independent Drivers Association) says Mexican drivers, and those from other impoverished societies, will 'work like dogs' and not complain because they don't know the language and don't know they have some**

**human rights. Some pay is better than no pay, which is all that many of them have in their home countries".**

I have seen some of these Mexican drivers on the road and heard them over the CB radio and from my experience I see not only a safety problem but also a social problem developing. Mexican drivers are many times over-aggressive in their driving habits and can be somewhat abusive to their American counter-parts who do not speak Spanish. American drivers take offense at these foreigners coming into the country with such an attitude that cannot or will not speak English. It creates a feeling of, 'Go back to your own country if you do not want to fit in here'.

If this is our government's answer to the OVER THE ROAD truck driver shortage the American OVER THE ROAD truck driver may be in for a big disappointment for a long time when it comes to an increased pay and benefits package. The conspiracy goes on.

I have seen Mexican trucks when I have been near the Mexican border crossings and some of them leave much to be desired in regard to condition, which affects safety on the highways of the United States. Clearly the safety requirements of heavy trucks in Mexico are not near as demanding as here in the U.S. or Canada.

# 8.

# UNDERSTANDING LOGBOOKS

Logbooks are one of the most misunderstood facets of trucking and with good reason. The main reason new entrants have so much difficulty understanding logbooks is because *logbook rules do not make sense and nobody can adequately explain how they function in relation to fair driver compensation! As long as drivers are paid by the mile driven and regulated by the hour, logging legally will unlikely ever result in fair pay; only considerably less pay. Safety will always take a back seat because of it and the driver's neck will always be in the noose!* While there is *no provision for minimum pay* for the OVER THE ROAD truck driver there is now a *minimum fine of $500* for any logbook violation under the new rules.

Due to the possibility of being fined for procrastinating, forgetfulness or just plain cheating, logbooks actually have become a major time-consuming distraction from what is genuinely important in a truck driver's daily activity such as equipment checks to prevent breakdowns and directions to keep from getting lost, among other things.

In irregular operations of OVER THE ROAD trucking, because of erratic scheduling and countless unscheduled interruptions throughout the day, it seems like logbooks have principally been designed to generate revenue for regulatory agencies and place responsibility on the truck driver in the event of an accident. Anybody who thinks differently has never experienced OVER THE ROAD trucking as an irregular route truck driver for any prolonged length of time. Lawyers love logbooks!

Most trainees have difficulty trying to understand logbooks in which they must record many hours per day to perform various duties and waiting periods that they are not compensated for, sometimes resulting in little or no pay for an entire day's effort and time spent. The fact is that this activity is *nevertheless required by law to be logged and can be enforced by the DOT.* The result is *the driver may use up many of his available hours by logging 'on-duty, not driving' and then will have fewer hours to drive, which is his only method of earning a paycheck!* Ideally a solo driver should realistically be able to drive between six and seven hundred miles a day, depending on how fast his truck will go and what the speed limits are where he is traveling. That many miles every day would generate an acceptable income. As you have seen however, there are many times this will not be so.

**The truth is if OVER THE ROAD truck drivers entered everything into their logbooks every day exactly as they utilized their time, many days there would be very little time left available to actually drive the truck. Most experienced OVER THE ROAD truck drivers fail to log as much as 30 to 40 hours per week of this unproductive but required and mandatory activity as described in this writing. This amounts to as much time lost to a driver as most people's entire workweek, all without compensation. Regulating truck drivers by the hour effectively reduces their mileage pay significantly,**

**coercing them to 'juggle' their hours accordingly so that they can generate a somewhat reasonable paycheck each week. It is this fact that has resulted in regulatory officials trying to 'catch' truck drivers in the act of 'cheating' on their logs and then charging exorbitant fines.**

This is why experienced drivers soon learn to *log by the mile rather than by the hour*, to prevent using up all their available driving time performing non-paying activities. Since unproductive time was not logged or was minimized, the driver now may have *worked and/or waited many hours without pay* and juggled his logbook to allow him time to drive as long as he can to produce a paycheck. *This is a major cause of many OVER THE ROAD mileage-paid truckers to be going down the road in an exhausted or fatigued condition.* **This is exactly what logbooks are supposed to prevent!** Additionally, should a driver have spent this waiting time to pick up a 'high value load', most trucking companies instruct the driver *not to stop for any reason for several hundred miles* for fear of getting hijacked. **This compounds his fatigue! He is now a prime candidate for a 'falling asleep' accident!**

Consider this. Even though a driver is expected to perform numerous tasks for which he is not compensated, if he should have an 'incident' or accident while doing these things he *will* be held accountable. He is also expected to enter these activities on line 4 of his logbook as 'on duty, not driving' using up his 14-hour day. Is something wrong with this picture? Who can blame these drivers for trying to earn a decent paycheck? Lawyers and officials, that's who. The same people who designed them.

For example, in mountain country it may take considerably longer to accomplish traveling only a few hundred miles due to slow travel climbing mountains and then slowly descending down the other side in a safe manner. Highway shutdowns due to construction, accidents and weather can also cause major delays as can slow travel on winding, narrow roads and countless small towns with 25 and 35 MPH speed limits on back roads. All this and more will result in a drastic reduction of paid mileage if you log it like that and you will have a greatly reduced paycheck at the end of the week.

In this example if a driver goes 500 miles and it takes 12 or 14 hours to do it due to the various conditions mentioned previously, the driver will simply divide 60 or 65 MPH into the miles driven to comply with the speed limit and use that result for his log hours. This is probably the most common method of logging by drivers that is prevalent throughout the transportation industry today. This is routine logging by most experienced OVER THE ROAD truckers so that they can realize a livable income.

Maintaining logbooks creates a tremendous amount of lost productive time for truck drivers *and* management when checking them. The time required of truckers to make logbook entries and the money the companies spend checking them could be better utilized to *enhance truck driver's pay* where the *real* problem is!

Those that are qualified, experienced team drivers know only too well that logbooks for teams should not be required for them. Logbooks for them are an unnecessary diversion and a complete waste of time that could be better spent doing other things. The stress and anxiety caused by having to maintain logbooks is very counter-productive. Instead of being able to concentrate on their productivity, truck drivers are constantly fiddling with meaningless logbooks that are useful only to lawyers trying to place blame should there be a lawsuit.

What the lawmakers *seem* not to understand is that, one day a truck driver may drive an hour or two, feel tired, stop and take a nap. Then he may again drive a couple more hours, get tired and stop to nap again and again until safely reaching his destination. Another day, that same driver may feel well rested and drive ten hours straight to his destination and still feel like driving some more. *This is how the human body functions rather than like a machine that can be set to perform the same every day. The logbook does not allow for such individuality or realism!*

As I wrote this book and read excerpts to other drivers I occasionally got feedback from them. One such feedback was from a driver who had been brought into an Oregon weigh station because of a flat tire on his truck that he was unaware of. This driver logs everything exactly as he functions and the scalemaster was impressed with his honesty. To make a long story short, while awaiting the tire repair truck the scalemaster admitted to this driver that most weigh stations are 'vultures' that prey on truck drivers to produce revenue for the state, just as suggested in this writing. *Suspicions confirmed!*

It is commonly known by experienced truck drivers that 'the top two lines on the logbook are your friend and the bottom two lines are your enemy.' This refers to the graph on a logbook, which consists of four lines. Line one is 'off duty', line two is 'sleeper berth', line three is 'driving', and line four is 'on duty, not driving'. The first two lines indicate rest periods and the last two lines use up time available to drive, thereby eating into your paycheck.

## 1. IS FALSIFYING LOGS BEING ACCEPTED?

While all this 'logbook juggling' is considered falsifying logs and is illegal, *it is commonplace and it is unspoken by everyone that this is expected and maybe even accepted within reason, by everybody as necessary for drivers to not only fulfill their trip assignment requirements but to acquire a paycheck for themselves!* Nearly everyone 'looks the other way' until something unforeseen happens, *such as an accident!*

Should this occur, the logbook is viewed as a legal document that will be *scrutinized in great detail* to determine accountability. If a fatality is involved, the truck driver will be dealt with unmercifully. *Suddenly, safety and compliance become important issues and driver pay irrelevant! Logbooks are the first thing law enforcement and lawyers ask for even though they know logbooks are unrealistic in regards to pay and rest for the driver!*

The 'sleeper berth' requirements would seem to be proof that lawmakers are aware that there is need for flexibility regarding a driver's sleep requirements. This is evidenced by the fact that even if a team driver is in the sleeper and reading a book or working on a laptop, it counts as 'sleeper time' during which the driver is supposed to be resting up for his turn to drive. But if this driver should make the mistake of venturing out into the cab for some reason such as preparing to use the rest room upon entering a weigh station or rest area, and be sitting in the passenger or 'jump' seat, as it is called, he can be cited by the DOT for not being logged as 'on duty, not driving'! The fine is over $200! Very expensive just to perform a basic bodily function! Ridiculous! Simply another way to relieve the truck driver of more money.

There is little provision in the logbook for the driver to make his own decision to *drive when he feels rested and rest when he feels tired! In fact he could be penalized for doing so!* In other words, if a driver feels *alert and rested* and wants to drive but his logbook shows no 'hours available', he cannot drive or he will be in violation. On the other hand, the driver may *feel too tired to continue on* but is informed by dispatch that the load must be delivered on time. Then, when the hands of the clock reach midnight and another 24 hour day begins, hours available are picked up from the *previous week*, allowing the driver to now drive legally again! At midnight! Is this bazaar or what? How many of the lawmakers or officials could perform according to the rules they are making for truckers to comply with? My guess is, none! *You simply cannot put being tired on a schedule as a logbook tries to do.*

The bottom line is that there are definite laws relating to logbook entries by truck drivers. Failure of the driver to comply with these laws, whether through ignorance or by design, can result in huge fines and even *termination and incarceration of the driver!* Prison!

The end result of those drivers that do comply with the logbook rules is that they are constantly 'running out of hours' and have to be re-powered (swap loads) by another driver to meet the appointments on time. This is another earnings reduction that contributes to the 'driver shortage'.

Hazardous materials (Haz-Mat) and routine daily activities, as well as hours spent driving the vehicle, have specific logging requirements. Again, each of these functions demands the driver to make entries in his logbook showing time expended, thereby leaving him less time to accumulate income by the mile, *his only method of earning!* Many hours a week can be eaten up this way, *all without compensation!* This will cut deeply into a driver's paycheck that can *never be made up!* This is of little or no concern to those in management or those making the laws. *It is very easy for the bureaucracy to make unrealistic laws for others, knowing that they, themselves, will never have to live by them.*

New Jersey is in the process of passing a law that will charge someone who causes a fatality by falling asleep at the wheel with vehicular homicide, punishable by up to *10 years in jail and a $100,000 fine.* Other states are looking at similar laws that are specifically directed at truck drivers. *If truck drivers were fairly paid, pushing themselves beyond the limits of their endurance would no longer be necessary and this problem would be all but eliminated.* Who can argue with this? There would be no good reason to go 24 hours without sleep and continue to drive in such a tired condition as many OVER THE ROAD truck drivers do now.

**With fair and adequate compensation, a truck driver would never have to be concerned about a DOT inspection because he would be able to log truthfully!**

## 2. THE CONTROVERSIAL 'BLACK BOX'

This is a device that can now record all truck driver activity throughout the course of the day and would ultimately result in the much coveted 'fair days pay for a fair days time and effort'.

Under the present haphazard conditions, initially this recorder would immediately cause most drivers to run out of the necessary driving time needed to generate enough income to make it worthwhile to drive a truck because it would eliminate all cheating, altering and creative logging that now takes place. The many time-consuming duties and activities previously mentioned in this book that are now performed without compensation and therefore not logged by most truck drivers would now eat a big hole in the 14-hour daily allowance of logbook time. This would force a great many truck drivers to seek employment elsewhere either with a company that does not yet utilize the 'black box' or even a different profession. It would also result in many loads not getting delivered on time and cause companies to lose business.

The end result could be such a significant driver shortage and loss of business that trucking companies would finally be coerced to compete with each other to acquire truck drivers by offering the long-coveted guarantee to truckers of income for time committed, recorded and regulated by the 'black box'. *The dreaded 'black box' just might be the ultimate answer to truck drivers finally being fairly paid!* It won't happen overnight. It will initially cause a lot of driver anguish and exodus from trucking! **Obviously the trucking companies do not want them or they would already have them. They are very aware of what the end result would be!**

## 3. LAWMAKERS LACK UNDERSTANDING

To elaborate further, federal regulators have been studying logbooks for several years, supposedly trying to improve on them to provide for better safety through more rest provisions and time off requirements. But how can they legislate what they do not understand? *Understanding can only come from actually performing the many functions and duties constantly demanded of OVER THE ROAD truck drivers.* What lawmakers also fail to acknowledge is that when most normal human beings have time off, they do not necessarily spend all this time resting. Instead, if after a short rest they cannot return to work, they will busy themselves with things people do such as shopping, reading, watching TV or countless other things. Demanding that truck drivers shut their truck down when they feel fine and could safely continue on does nothing to enhance safety and in fact *is counter-productive in that regard* and is frustrating to truckers.

Regardless of how logbook regulations may be changed, experienced OVER THE ROAD truckers will soon figure out how to work things out to their advantage so they can earn a 'decent living'. The fact remains that *paying these drivers strictly by the miles driven with no provision for time or talent, will not work when it comes down to safety versus income. To put it simply, people have bills to pay and earning money is how they do it!*

Understand that it is not the demands of the logbook instigated with safety in mind that are so objectionable. Clearly the logbook is intended to create conditions that will result in fewer accidents caused by tired drivers. *What is objectionable is the lack of any provision for drivers to be fairly paid to comply with those demands!*

## 4. LOGBOOK REVISION

Trying to regulate a human being's rest times in OVER THE ROAD trucking is an exercise in futility. It is like trying to regulate other bodily functions such as bowel movements. If a person were constipated it would be of no use to have a document demanding that it take place. It just is not going to happen. The next day the same person may have the same problem again or could reverse and have two or three movements. The point is the human body cannot be controlled by a piece of paper called a logbook in regard to rest or anything else, for that matter. Things simply must happen spontaneously in due course and should be logged that way and the driver paid accordingly.

Logbooks were originally designed to coordinate union activity of city delivery drivers who usually had to work on a freight dock in the morning loading trucks, then make deliveries and pickups throughout the day, then return to their terminal and unload trucks and work on the dock at night. Ten hours driving, five hours on the dock and eight hours off duty to rest up for the next day or tour of duty. Provisions were also made for line-haul drivers. All this was intended to assure safe conditions in the various areas of daily activity in the transportation of goods. Basically, it worked! *Unfortunately, deregulation of trucking has almost completely reversed all of these safety provisions,* one way or another! Only the remaining union-regulated operations have continued on as before. *It still works for them!* **It requires that management be efficient!** *Paying OVER THE ROAD truckers by the mile has clearly resulted in management becoming lazy, complacent, thoughtless, uncaring, unresponsive and grossly inefficient in dealing with the needs of truck drivers.*

A driver may log many hours in the sleeper when he was actually wide-awake, performing unpaid for work duties. Then his logbook will show more hours available to drive and allow the driver to generate badly needed income after being delayed. Of course this is fine with the company since they need that truck to be moving toward destination ASAP.

It appears that the unrealistic logbook rules are not really meant to be complied with in present day OVER THE ROAD trucking by mileage paid drivers. Why say such a thing? Well, they started out with good intentions when trucking was in its' infancy. The Teamster's Union and management were at odds as to what constituted a fair day's pay for a fair day's work. In those days things were considerably different from what they are today and everybody tried their best to make the work effort coincide with the logbook requirements. City drivers did city work and were paid hourly and OVER THE ROAD truck drivers ran the long miles for mileage pay. Even in those days it was obvious that these two segments of trucking needed separate and distinct rules governing the various activities of each.

Seeming proof that logbook compliance is not realistic or is ignored in today's OVER THE ROAD trucking is:

1. Thousands of OVER THE ROAD trucks are all over the country every day without sleeper berths whereby the drivers can be seen sleeping over the steering wheel or propped up against the door window, taking a nap while sitting up. Are these drivers logging 'on duty, not driving' or 'off duty'? It undoubtedly depends on their method of compensation. Hourly paid drivers are probably logging 'on duty, not driving' while mileage paid drivers are most likely logging 'off duty'. The rule is that you cannot log in the sleeper if there is none.
2. Traffic delays due to accidents, construction detours, weather and such are logged as 'on duty' by hourly drivers and 'off duty' or 'sleeper' by mileage drivers.
3. Waiting time of any kind is logged by the hourly driver as 'on duty, not driving' and by the mileage driver as 'off duty' or 'sleeper'.
4. Mileage drivers also log getting directions and getting lost as 'off duty', those paid by the hour, 'on duty'.
5. A mileage paid driver riding in the jump seat does not usually log 'on duty, not driving' as required. Occasionally, a hotshot DOT scale master may catch a violator in the 'jump seat' and collect a couple hundred dollars from him.
6. Breakdowns, drop and hooks, fueling, maintenance and random drug screens, all of which may take considerable time are usually logged as 15 minutes 'on duty, not driving' if at all, even if they take an hour or more.
7. Loose-leaf ringbinders for logbooks are not only legal, but also encouraged by some companies, for increased time flexibility. Stapled logbooks require that no pages be missing whereas with loose-leaf pages there is no such requirement.

Following is an example of time lost without pay in a typical, normal day's activity. Keep in mind that the mileage for these unpaid for activities is not usually calculated into a driver's pay either.

| | |
|---|---|
| Deliver a drop trailer at 0700. | 0700 ½ hour |
| Find an empty trailer to pick up a load on, bobtail 40 miles. | 0730 1 hour |
| Construction traffic backup. | 0830 ½ hour |
| Find the shipper location. | 0900 1 hour |
| Drop the empty and find the loaded trailer. | 1000 ½ hour |
| Get checked out, do logbook. | 1030 1 hour |
| Go to scale at truck stop, adjust weight distribution. | 1130 1 hour |
| Fuel the truck and perform a daily pre-trip inspection. | 1230 1 hour |
| Wait for flat tire repair. | 1330 2 hours |
| | to 1530 |

Total time spent without pay that should be logged as required by law is 8 ½ hours, count them. *Now the driver is ready to get on the road and start his trip toward his destination.* He already has more time in his workday than many 8 to 5 people and has not yet earned a dime! No paid-for mileage has accumulated, thus far. Get my drift?

*Like it or not, the truth is that the previous scenario takes place every day in the lives of millions of OVER THE ROAD truck drivers.*

In truth, logbooks have probably caused as many drivers to be driving tired and have accidents as they have prevented. Maybe more! Since there is no way to monitor this aspect there are obviously no statistics on that.

Logbooks have hamstrung trucking companies from making a profit and drivers from making an adequate living in the guise of safety for decades. Many trucking companies have paid huge fines into the tens of thousands of dollars and their CEOs even sent to jail, simply for trying to get the job done! Logbook requirements and the resulting fines from noncompliance and violations have unnecessarily bankrupt more than one trucking company. Logbooks have certainly been a great method for the government agencies to generate revenue!

While those in other fields of endeavor are concerned about getting their annual three to five percent cost of living allowance and/or pay increase, *this aspect is not even mentioned in OVER THE ROAD trucking!* Neither are holiday or sick time pay.

One thing about logbooks for sure is that you had best have it current before crossing any state scales because you never know when the official may decide to walk out of his 'chicken coop' over to your truck and inspect it. Also, if you should get pulled over by the highway patrol for any reason, your logbook is usually the first thing they ask to look at. If it is not current, they can either fine you or shut you down for ten hours or both. It happens all the time. Be prepared! They want your money!

Occasionally, logbook violations can run into the thousands of dollars in fines, especially if you are an owner-operator. They can be fined $25,000.00 to start with for falsification and the company they are leased to may have to pay an equal amount plus other charges. This does not help the driver shortage problem at all but the object seems to be for law enforcement to get as much money as possible before the owner-operator and the companies they are leased to go broke or bankrupt. No mercy!

## 5. ACCIDENTS AND LOGBOOKS

As explained previously, the most important thing in trucking is not getting to your pickup or delivery on time. Yes, this is important! But far more important than anything else is, *do not have an accident!* Especially a moving accident that involves another vehicle. Additionally if there is a fatality, everything changes.

First of all, minor accidents such as backing into another truck at a truck stop and breaking a mirror or denting a fender will merely put a blemish on your record and possibly result in a safety talk, maybe cost you a few dollars.

However if either vehicle is damaged badly enough so as to need towing from the scene, this makes it DOT reportable. What that means is that any or all drivers may be temporarily suspended *without pay* until there can be an audit of the logs and the company they drive for performs a safety investigation to determine liability. *This can take several weeks or even months, depending on the severity of the occurrence! Without pay!*

Should there be a fatality, *regardless of who was at fault,* the truck driver's logs most probably will be audited for the entire previous year and any discrepancies taken into account. If the driver logged a fuel stop at one location and documentation shows he was at another location at that time, it constitutes a fraud. Even if this driver did not cause the accident involving the fatality and this can be proven without a shadow of doubt, because of falsifying his logbook he may be subject to criminal fines and even jail time. Other discrepancies will also be taken into account. The driver may not only go to jail and pay some fines but this could end his career as a commercial truck driver. It could cause him financial disaster and/or destroy his family. It does not matter if his record is impeccable!

Another interesting and important thing for you to remember is that if your actions cause others to have an accident, even though you were not involved in it, you can and probably will be held responsible, as it should be.

The honest truth is that for the risk involved regarding safety and the exorbitant fines for failing to comply with the many rules set forth by all the governmental agencies, law enforcement and the trucking companies themselves, *it is a wonder there is anybody willing to get involved with this profession!* Telling it like it is!

## 6. DOUBLE STANDARDS

It is significant to realize that the very Federal Government that is instigating all the laws and regulations that must be adhered to by private enterprise (and truck drivers), *exempts themselves from having to follow those very same laws!* This includes not only logbooks not being required by military or government personnel but expensive and complicated emission requirements demanded of industry are also exempted by military and government-operated vehicles.

It is obvious to them that these cumbersome and unrealistic logbook and emission requirements are so stupid and difficult to comply with that they relieve themselves (U.S. Government) from having to do so! However, failure of private individuals and businesses to comply can result in fines beyond comprehension (ability to pay) and even incarceration (jail)!

Enforcing these laws continually generates millions of dollars in compliance activity and fines to the private sector for both truck drivers and the companies they work for. It places an unfair and heavy burden on all parties involved in trying to operate according to the law while releasing those who make these laws from having to comply with them at all!

Additionally, I just learned that the new 2011 logbook rules proposal also exempts all drivers involved with oil companies. How can this be? Money yields power!

It seems clear to me that logbooks merely appease those safety-minded organizations and pressure groups that demand government action in regard to highway safety. In my opinion, they have failed miserably and are highly unrealistic in regard to today's OVER THE ROAD trucking profession.

## 7. CHANGE IS NEEDED

A question I have is, "Why should OVER THE ROAD truck drivers have to cheat on their logbooks just to have enough time available to earn what still amounts usually to sub-standard pay"? The obvious answer is, "They shouldn't"! Nobody else does and it is unsafe. *The system is wrong and needs to be changed!* Deregulation accomplished exactly what it was intended to; lower freight rates through lower driver pay. However, this resulted in a direct negative effect on safety to human lives and injuries caused by multitudes of inexperienced and less than desirable drivers coming into the field on a continuing basis!

**Answer: Get rid of logbooks! Bring on the 'black box'!**

# 9.

# BETTER PAY AND BENEFITS OVERDUE

Since I have the greatest respect for those genuine professionals with OVER THE ROAD truck driving skills and commitment, it is mandatory that in this writing I continue to opt for better compensation on their behalf. The money is there. It simply is not getting to the right people. Too much money is going into the hands of a few.

## 1. THE KEY TO IMPROVEMENT

*Seemingly, the only key to improvement would be to increase freight rates!* As a now retired consumer, I am not anxious to pay more for things any more than anyone else. However, it goes much deeper than that. Not only is it the principle of things, all this has a direct influence on safety! Safety could be tremendously enhanced because OVER THE ROAD truck drivers might act and operate more like the professionals they are instead of all the 'hurry up and wait' that presently exists, scratching like chickens in a feed lot over every available dollar. Many of these drivers defiantly crowd in ahead of each other without mutual consideration or respect. Present circumstances have bred an attitude of 'every man for himself'.

Let us back away for a minute and take a short view of the bigger picture.

There are the elite few of our society that receive (not necessarily earn) salaries and bonuses totaling millions, no, tens and hundreds of millions of dollars a year.

## 2. HOW MUCH MONEY IS ENOUGH?

Talk show hosts that rake in 40 million dollars a year for five three-hour shows per week to bash politicians and advocate that the poor should pay more taxes!

Movie stars that demand from three to thirty million dollars per movie!

Television stars, getting more in a week than the average individual can earn in a year, maybe in a lifetime.

Millions of dollars in daily giveaways to contestants on television shows.

Soap opera and sit-com actors, game show hosts and many others are getting millions of dollars a year!

Rock Stars bringing in millions!

Sports stars that demand and get several million dollars a year!

CEOs that are rewarded each year with staggering millions (through questionable means) even after bankrupting their companies.

Politicians that vote themselves exorbitant raises in middle of the night sessions, even after the public previously rejected those same pay raises!

These people and more are wallowing in wealth beyond anyone's wildest dreams. Some have more money than they and all their family members combined can possibly spend in several lifetimes.

These are the very people that complain about unions, promote more taxing of the poor and think that if someone is willing to work for $1.00 an hour, that's okay. They have no compassion for those that work hard just to survive paycheck to paycheck, barely getting by week after week. It is real easy for them to sit on their pedestal and brag about how people should work smarter instead of harder. However, a good share of these 'favored' rich inherited wealth, were celebrities children or came from wealthy families and cannot or do not want to relate to those of the 'working class'. Of course, there may be a few exceptions.

## 3. WHERE DOES THIS MONEY COME FROM?

Money is generated from manufacturing, labor and services rendered. Food, clothing and housing are basic needs. Distribution by trucks is mandatory.

*Millions of ordinary workingmen and women through their productivity and their purchasing of commodities generate money.*

Manufacturers and other large businesses need people to work in their facilities. This means people earn a paycheck and spend it on living expenses. Robots have not taken over yet.

The multi-billion dollar corporations of this great country provide ridiculous amounts to the following entities either directly or indirectly, through advertising or various other means. Of course marketing of products is necessary but $3,000,000 for 30 seconds advertising on the Super Bowl? Come on!

One hundred million dollars to a rock star from a soft drink company.

Time is bought of the talk show host because the people that listen to him supposedly buy things from the companies that support his show.

An oil company easily paid over two hundred million dollars to satisfy an oil spill in Alaska. Then another major oil spill in the Gulf of Mexico cost more millions.

Hundreds of millions lost to the taxpayers in the Silverado Savings and Loan scandal years ago, swept under the rug.

More billions in stock market fraud, wiping out the life savings and pensions of untold numbers.

Ponzi schemes! And on and on.

How much is enough? Especially when much of the lowly 'working class' can barely meet their monthly bills, many of who are losing their homes. *These are the people that are generating the money!*

I have no problem with this unbalanced wealth *as long as the workingman also receives a fair days wage for a fair days work!* **This is all I ask for those in my profession!**

Instead, OVER THE ROAD truck drivers have been systematically *excluded* from adequate compensation for time, talents and effort expended!

With adequate income to the OVER THE ROAD trucker, the money saved from fewer accidents, injuries and lawsuits would be impossible to determine but should nevertheless be significant. Everyone would benefit from it in the form of lower insurance rates. Hospitals, doctors and lawyers are getting much of this money now. Maybe this would also allow the public to be able to better afford the slightly higher prices generated by slightly higher freight rates to adequately support the highly professional OVER THE ROAD truck drivers constantly trying to earn an adequate income by the elusive mile. Racing down the highway at speeds approaching triple digits to make up for lost time might be reduced or eliminated. Career truck drivers could be fairly and adequately compensated for their efforts, just like everybody else. OVER THE ROAD truck drivers should be treated by others with respect and appreciated for their profession instead of looked upon as second-class citizens because they are willing to take on a task that stops most people in their tracks for many reasons, mostly lack of income. *Money is a motivator! Just ask any CEO!*

There I go, getting carried away again.

## 4. FAIR DAY'S PAY IS NEEDED

OVER THE ROAD truckers can be heard on the CB radio regularly, *pushing themselves to the limit of their endurance and beyond* at a lower rate of pay so they can increase their earnings to an acceptable level by acquiring more miles. Why should this be? *Can this be safe?* Sitting idle all day and attending the truck while waiting to get loaded, unloaded or dispatched pays them nothing! *Can anybody think that is right?*

OVER THE ROAD truck drivers are entrusted with expensive equipment and product many times worth well into six figures. Is it not worth something for the drivers to safeguard these things? Should something happen to this equipment or the product they carry, *the driver will be held responsible! Yet, the pay is zero! How can this be so?*

**This is exactly why I have a problem with great numbers of millionaires and billionaires that never seem to have enough, some of whom have rocked our nation's economic stability to the core with their corrupt, scandalous greed. These 'educated idiots' have no conscience when it comes to the plight of the honest, hard-working citizen that this country depends on to get the 'nuts and bolts' work done at the grass-roots level. In fact they take advantage of the working class any time it will put more money in their own pockets! To them it is a game. They are all wrapped up in their own self-importance! Movies such as 'Other People's Money' and 'Wall Street' explain it very well. If this sounds like sour grapes, so be it. I have no problem with someone becoming wealthy but not if it causes grief and suffering for countless others when depriving them of their income by cheating them out of their just pay. There will always be rich and always be poor but everybody deserves a fair day's pay for an honest day's time and work effort, especially in the trucking industry. Expecting truck drivers to commit their time without compensation is nothing short of corporate theft! It is unconscionable! It is wrong and should be stopped!**

## 5. MILEAGE DISCREPANCY

One of the biggest problems with trucker's pay is mileage discrepancy.

To begin with, any miles accumulated as a result of making wrong turns or getting lost are definitely not compensated for, even though the law requires that the time lost is to be recorded in the driver's logbook, thereby eroding logbook time available to earn a paycheck. Miles are usually determined by computer, point to point.

A significant thing that reduces truck drivers' earnings is the discrepancy between the miles driven and the miles paid. This has always been a problem, even in union operations.

Most OVER THE ROAD truck drivers are paid by the predetermined mile. The mileage of a trip is determined by different methods, depending on the company you work for. These methods include:

1. Hubometer readings. A device is attached to the hub of a drive wheel that accurately measures actual miles driven. This method would seem to be the most fair and accurate, since many times a driver may become lost or make wrong turns trying to find a customer. It also automatically compensates for any detours due to foul weather, construction, accidents and the like. Very few companies use this method due to being too open-ended.
2. Odometer readings. This method was used in the past but was unreliable because of the possibility of a mechanical failure of the odometer cable. However, modern trucks have electronic odometer readings so possibly this is not a factor anymore.
3. Household Mover's Guide. These are the distances that moving companies use to determine their rates for moving a customer from one location to another. However these distances are said to be less than actual mileage by from ten to sixteen percent.
4. Rand-McNally, post office to post office. These distances are also said to reduce a driver's actual mileage by up to sixteen percent. This is a relatively obsolete method since the advent of computers.
5. Computer designated. Zip code to zip code! This is probably one of the most commonly used methods in these times and probably the most accurate, other than hubometer readings. However this method does not compensate for route changes due to various conditions unless a driver specifically gets with his dispatcher to include the extra mileage. Even then, there is no way to always be certain the changes have been made by the dispatcher. There is no provision for any extra miles either.

What most of this translates to is that sometimes the truck driver may actually drive six hundred miles in a day and get paid for only five hundred but is expected by law to log six hundred.

Additionally, an OVER THE ROAD truck driver is in actuality a *city driver* also and performs this segment *almost entirely without compensation or may be paid a token amount, at the whim of his fleet manager if he is lucky*. It is incredible how this has become an expected and even acceptable condition of this occupation! By that I mean, *expected* by management and *accepted* by the drivers! In truth, it has *not* been accepted by many truck drivers and the result has been for them to change jobs or quit driving truck altogether! The risk is too great and the pay too little. Again, any time spent hunting up customers, tied up in traffic or waiting to load or unload is expected to be logged as 'on duty, not driving', for which the driver is paid nothing!

I expect that eventually, several things will happen to make it more attractive to become an OVER THE ROAD truck driver. I predict the following:

1. All large fleets will have trucks with automatic transmissions.
2. All large fleets will utilize electronic or paperless logs or logs will be eliminated with the 'black box'.
3. All large fleets will utilize the E-Z-Pass method of toll payment and/or toll charge cards.

4. All large fleets will utilize the Pre-Pass method for weigh stations with an Automatic Vehicle Identifier (AVI).
5. Global Positioning Systems (GPS) will be utilized in all trucks for directions.
6. Freight rates will increase.
7. OVER THE ROAD truck driver pay will increase.
8. Benefits will improve.
9. The OVER THE ROAD truck driver image will improve.
10. Computer dispatching will assure more time off at home.
11. Management will become more efficient, resulting in improvements in the previous items.
12. The public will be better educated to properly share the highways with big trucks.
13. As a result of these things, trucks will become safer on the highways.

Hopefully, my predictions will happen sooner rather than later, if at all.

On the downside for nationwide drivers, most long runs will probably be put on the train and deprive long haul truck drivers from acquiring the high mileage of those runs. Traveling coast to coast will mostly involve several short runs rather than one long one except for teams.

## 6. HOW ARE THESE THINGS IMPORTANT TO A TRUCK DRIVER?

The main reason these things are important to a truck driver is that a company that will introduce these items is showing that they genuinely care about their drivers and are taking steps to make life easier for them. In doing this, companies will also be helping to increase their own overall profit picture through improved safety methods and driver retention. The end result should be more experienced drivers and fewer accidents. Let us take a look at these items, one at a time.

1. Automatic transmissions. When automatic transmissions for trucks first came out several decades ago, they were scoffed at and scorned. No self-respecting truck driver would consider such a thing! Real truck drivers used manual shift transmissions, the more gears the better. Duplexes, triplexes, eighteen speeds, it was a talent and pride of driving. It took a real master to do it right!

   However, because of the many thousands of new entrants coming into this field, as a driver trainer I welcomed the time when I was able to have an automatic transmission to train with. Especially since the driver training schools leave much to be desired in this area of training. After years and years of listening to gear jamming, grinding and crunching, it was a pleasure to have all that eliminated. Teaching new drivers to shift gears manually is one of the most time consuming and frustrating parts of being a driver trainer! Then, after all this training, most of the new drivers quit anyway and all the effort was wasted! Having an automatic transmission allows more time to concentrate on the more important aspect of maneuvering the truck in a safe and controlled manner. It definitely makes a trainer's job much easier. Of course, it could cause a problem for those learning to drive on trucks with automatic transmissions if they decide later to hire on with a company that only has manual transmissions.

No more missing gears when climbing or descending mountain grades resulting in trucks stalled going uphill or out of gear runaway trucks going downhill.

4.  Paperless logs. There are pros and cons to this. No more cheating, puzzling and trying to figure out how to juggle everything so that the time expended fits into the way the bureaucracy wants it to look. I hate to think how much time and aggravation have been lost on these 'comic books'. From what I have been told, everybody likes paperless; the driver, the company and the DOT. Paperless logs appear to make everyone's job easier and definitely save everyone a lot of time. Unfortunately, in today's world of trucking, drivers lose a lot of time doing unpaid-for activities that are automatically logged as 'on duty' by the paperless log system.

    Because of satellite tracking and control I can see where logs could be discontinued altogether. It is realistic rest periods that are of prime concern. The other activities are relatively mundane and not of primary interest. Electronic 'black boxes' are also being considered. However, mileage pay will need to be supplemented with hourly pay or changed somehow to compensate for time lost due to the many various duties presently done without pay that eat up the driving time.

3.  E-Z-Pass payments of tolls at the tollgates allow trucks to smoothly continue on their way through the tollgates or bypass them completely. Those without them must come to a complete stop at the tollbooth, dig out their cash, wait for change and a receipt, file the receipt in a secure place and then squeeze back into mainline traffic. If they should lose or misplace the receipts they may not be able to recover the money from their company. This means they will be out that money.

    Many of these tollgates have up to a dozen or so lanes that traffic goes through which means that after paying the toll, all these lanes must merge back into the two or three main line lanes of traffic. This can sometimes be a bit of a challenge, with all this traffic racing and squeezing together. Accidents are commonplace! Not a good situation. Meanwhile the traffic with Pre-Pass is able to keep moving and avoid most of this danger and hassle of using cash and receipts.

4.  Pre-Pass Automatic Vehicle Identifier (AVI) at weigh stations works similar to the toll E-Z Pass. Trucks equipped with Pre-Pass can be monitored as they are moving at road speed by a scale strip imbedded in the highway and/or overhead detectors that pick up readings when approaching the weigh station from a sending unit attached inside the truck cab. If everything is as it should be, these trucks usually do not even have to slow down, while those without them must go into the weight station and wait their turn to be checked. Worst case scenario here without an AVI is that upon going into a weight station, the scale-master may notice something else he wants to inspect such as a headlight not working, connector hoses dragging on the walk-plate or any number of other things. It is their job to be observant regarding equipment violations. A logbook inspection may also occur. This could once again cost the driver money out of pocket!

5.  GPS (global positioning system) units that can show exact location of a vehicle in relation to where the destination is are unbelievable in performance. A driver can see

where he is on a computer screen that shows the city streets he is driving on and his location on the streets as he progresses toward his customer until he arrives. There are also mobile phone services and laptop programs that provide GPS directions.

6. A key factor that would provide adequate funds to put a compromise plan into effect would be a slight increase in freight rates that could be passed on to the consumers who would scarcely notice it. An increase in freight rates seems to be the only answer to provide the OVER THE ROAD truck driver with adequate income. This is what happens when any other professional in any other field requires compensation that matches his time and effort.

7. Income *should* eventually self-correct as time goes on. This will not happen overnight. The conditions of OVER THE ROAD trucking are such that this *must* be looked at if a company expects to *retain* top quality drivers. As in other professions, when the money gets right there will no longer be a shortage of OVER THE ROAD truck drivers.

8. More benefits should also become a part of the pay package. The entire medical, pension, holiday and vacation pay as well as sick time, *must* eventually be considered.

9. Computer dispatching should help to lessen or eliminate confusion and cross dispatching.

10. Mixing company drivers and lease or owner-operators is part of the problem, since in most companies the owner-operators demand and usually get the better loads. This may be a tough problem to solve and may also be one of the last, possibly never fully resolved as long as the different factions exist in the same company.

11. Management needs to recognize that drivers require better representation, resulting in better pay, dignity and respect for the drivers and ultimately, better drivers for their company.

12. Educating the public about how to safely drive around big trucks is going to take a long time. Maybe a television show about truckers similar to 'Cops' about law enforcement would help. Showing actual 'on the scene' activity to the viewing public might make an impression as to just how deadly this heavy equipment really is. If disastrous events could be shown daily and then an explanation of how it could have been prevented, it would go a long way toward opening the eyes of those that think cutting in front of an 80,000# monster is a joke or a thrill. Showing dead bodies and severed limbs would not be a pretty picture but if it would save lives, it would be worth it!

13. *When OVER THE ROAD truck drivers no longer have to go roaring down the road to make up for lost time to produce an acceptable paycheck, danger on the highways should subside considerably.*

Changes surely will not happen all at once. Some have already happened. Without driver representation it will take many years, probably decades to sort things out before the bureaucracy will fully understand and make the necessary adjustments.

# 10.

# THE UNPROFESSIONAL PROFESSION

Why, 'The unprofessional profession'?

Professionalism is not truly professionalism unless you are paid professionally. Today's OVER THE ROAD truck drivers are *not* paid as such and as a result many do not *act* professionally nor do they even *look* professional for the most part. That is why you see people looking like hippies, bums and social rejects getting out of $120,000.00 Peterbilts and Kenworths.

The fact remains that they *are* professionals, *even though the federal government has **officially downgraded** them to the status of unskilled labor to prevent them from organizing.* That's right! *Truck drivers are officially classified by the federal government as **unskilled labor!***

Under present conditions, why would someone from a so-called 'normal lifestyle' want to do this? As a comparison, the U.S. military used to be the same way until pay improved, with somewhat regular hours for them. We now have the finest volunteer military in the world!

If you want to get a sample of the reality of OVER THE ROAD trucking, go to any busy, crowded truck stop and watch all the ongoing activity. Walking around the fuel islands can sometimes seem like putting your life at risk. Drivers pulling into the island to fuel up are usually in a big hurry for one reason or another and those done fueling can sometimes nearly run you over in their haste! A stroll across the truck stop parking lot can also be life challenging with the many trucks that are hurriedly arriving and leaving as they go about their business. Pedestrians are difficult to see from inside the high cabs of large trucks. This heavy, awkward equipment presents a constant challenge that is more than most people can accept in more ways than one. Even when they do see you, some of these maniacs threaten to run you down in their haste! Additionally, after parking in some of these congested truck stops it is with apprehension when I return to my truck for fear that someone may have backed into it and fled!

## 1. DISRESPECTED PROFESSIONALS

*Present day non-union OVER THE ROAD company truck drivers are the most over-worked, under-paid, unappreciated and disrespected professionals of any occupation!* They are expected to be polite and many times only speak when spoken to, never complain, be available constantly, meet all appointments on time and *comply with an unrealistic set of rules laid down by the government, regulated by a logbook.* These OVER THE ROAD truck drivers are under the constant scrutiny of various state weigh stations, federal DOT, state police, county police, city police and company paid-for outside agencies.

## 2. OVER THE ROAD TRUCK DRIVER PAY—WHAT HAPPENED?

Yes, driving an eighteen-wheeler OVER THE ROAD is adventurous and can be very enjoyable at times but frankly, most are not out there for the fun and games. *They are there primarily to earn a paycheck to pay bills and support families, just like everybody else!* A fair day's pay for a fair day's work does not sound like too much to ask. We have all heard the cliché, 'Time is money.' Unless you are an OVER THE ROAD truck driver, that is. Why should this be so?

Transportation, because of its very nature, requires that anybody involved in the demands of operating the necessary heavy equipment, should be of at least average intelligence and common sense to function safely and be compensated accordingly.

What determines the worth of a man?

What determines the worth of a job?

These two questions need to be looked at in depth to discover why there is such a huge turnover and resultant shortage of OVER THE ROAD truck drivers. It is difficult to separate these two questions in OVER THE ROAD trucking, so we will examine them together.

Generally, the answers to these two questions are based on the following criteria:

1.  Education (training and/or experience) Although the initial training is usually inadequate and incomplete, after someone becomes an OVER THE ROAD truck driver he will be in a continual learning mode. The knowledge he gains through experience is invaluable. The ongoing requirements and demands go far beyond any other position in any other transportation profession. The learning never ends.
2.  Time at work (hours working and/or on the job).
    Few other professions require being on duty and away from home twenty-four hours a day, seven days a week, sometimes for months at a time. This condition alone is in excess of what most people can accept as a condition of employment.
3.  Conditions at work (quality of life).
    Living in a truck as you continually travel thousands of miles through fog, rain, snow, ice, blizzards, floods, high wind and sandstorms would not seem to be overly desirable for anyone to endure, not to mention congested and high-speed traffic.
4.  Responsibility (security and safety for others).
    Being knowledgeable in legal requirements of two countries (U.S. and Canada) for safe handling of heavy equipment and product hauled, securing the loads and hazardous material demands that if not properly adhered to can result in thousands of dollars in fines, is absolutely mandatory! Additionally, drivers usually have no choice in whether or not they must haul a particular product. Nor can they refuse to go to Canada or anywhere else, for that matter! 'Forced dispatch' means exactly that! It should also be noted that a driver is not only responsible for the security of his rig at all times but also the load he is carrying.
5.  Commitment (time away from home on the road).
    The commitment in OVER THE ROAD trucking is far beyond any other profession!
6.  Skills (talent).
    Turning corners and backing these huge rigs into spaces many times designed for the much smaller equipment of the past can be a serious challenge. Staying safely in

a traffic lane only a couple of feet wider than the truck continually for thousands of miles a week regardless of all other traffic and conditions is no small feat.

7. Safety risk (to self and others).

Being able to safely maneuver monster-sized equipment on the highway day after day, week after week, month after month, year after year in such a manner as to be safe to themselves and the general public is not only necessary but mandatory!

8. Appearance (clothing or uniforms).

Admittedly, many OVER THE ROAD truck drivers could stand some improvement in this department.

9. Common sense (instant decision making).

Millions of lives every day depend on OVER THE ROAD truckers to safely handle their rigs under all conditions as they travel in heavy traffic as well as on the open road at highway speeds. Constantly making the correct split-second decision as circumstances demand requires uncommon, common sense.

All these things and more are necessary to become a safe and successful OVER THE ROAD truck driver! Additionally, the high mileage required of this profession to generate a decent income exposes holders of CDL licenses to the possibility of having their licenses suspended or revoked due to stringent laws regarding traffic violations and other driver activities in the name of safety. I am not saying these requirements are not necessary; only that the drivers have this also to be concerned about on top of all the other seemingly endless demands.

Huge fines going into the tens of thousands of dollars are ever-present should a driver not comply with all of the above-mentioned items!

Additionally, every large trucking company has taken considerable time, effort and expense to produce what is called a 'Driver's Manual" that includes all the duties and responsibilities demanded of their drivers, most without pay. Reading and absorbing these huge manuals can take quite a while and there is no doubt as to how important it is to a company that their drivers comply with the contents. These books spell out truck driving safety and there are many helpful things included. There are also many difficult and demanding functions required with no mention of compensation and the threat of termination prevalent throughout.

## 3. PAY AND CONDITIONS

*Yes, a truck driver is expected to always be rested, meet all pickup and delivery appointments on time and comply with all laws and company requirements. He is also expected to find any location to make a pickup or delivery on time, many times with poor or no directions, accomplish city delivery and pickup work in strange cities, put on chains in the winter without compensation, be a safe driver, wait around for free, be courteous, communicate properly and only get paid by the predetermined mile. Other than that, it's a great career!*

Truck drivers *being paid solely by the mile has resulted in over-hiring* and the combination of these has resulted in:

1. Not enough miles, therefore not enough pay.
2. Not enough miles, which produces bad attitudes.
3. No incentive for management to be efficient.

4. Excessive sitting without pay.
5. Depression.
6. Family problems and breakups.
7. Excessive driver turnover.
8. Poor quality of life.
9. Phenomenal pay loss.
10. Fatigue.
11. Unprofessionalism.
12. Unsafe driving trying to make up for lost time.
13. Over-aggressive driving.
14. Discourtesy.
15. Dangerous and impatient driving habits.
16. Poor highway sharing.
17. Speeding tickets.
18. Driver pushing beyond his capacity/endurance.
19. Driving in bad weather when should be parked.
20. Every man for himself, 'don't get in my way' attitude.
21. ACCIDENTS.

Admittedly, pay per mile provides incentive to the truck drivers. The problem is, presently there is *too much incentive to the point of being dangerous to everybody on the highway, including themselves!*

Conversely, being salaried or paid hourly may not provide enough incentive to some drivers and could actually be counter-productive in some cases. *I believe American management with ingenuity, like those in other countries of the world, could work out a combination of the two so that everyone would come out winners!* The tools are there; all they have to do is use them! This is the American way!

The sat-com would definitely play a key role in this solution. Any truck so equipped can be tracked and it's productivity monitored by satellite anywhere in the country. Daily activity is recorded by computer and archived for future reference, if needed.

If after watching the many OVER THE ROAD truckers back into tight dock locations or worse yet, between closely parked big rigs in a truck stop, anybody doubts the skills, talents and abilities demanded of this profession, they need to give it a try themselves! *The fact is, most lay people would be challenged to even start the engine of one of these big trucks, never mind move the truck around a parking lot and certainly not backing one up!*

Additionally, many times it is the 'wet behind the ears' college graduates that are misdirecting and cross-dispatching OVER THE ROAD truck drivers and making the job miserable for them. Cross-dispatching refers to the many times drivers are trying to get home and they are given loads each other should have gotten so that they will have to stay out longer, delivering more freight instead of going home. They simply do not understand or care about the conditions these professional truckers must endure. They are too busy being 'managers' and many are in 'on the job' training!

Consider this! Since newcomers are initially paid at a greatly reduced rate of pay for the first few months and sometimes do not reach peak pay for several years, it appears that whenever feasible, many of the longer runs are being dispatched to them as a cost savings to the company. For instance, most trucking companies have a starting mileage pay in the neighborhood of .25/mile while the most senior drivers may have a rate of .40/mile and up. This means that using a new driver will save the company about .15/mile, which figures out to $150.00 for every 1000 miles driven. Since the average mileage for a driver is about 3000 miles a week, the company can save $450.00 a week simply by using a newcomer. Multiply that by 52 weeks in a year and you have a savings of $23,400 per driver! Multiply that by 1000 drivers and it comes to a whopping $23,400,000.00! Quite a piece of change and that is only based on 1000 drivers! There are millions of truck drivers! No insurance for the first 90 days of employment results in further significant savings to the company. Other things that can be figured in are lower Social Security and 401K matching, Medicare, workman's compensation and undoubtedly other things I have not thought of.

Additionally, the more senior drivers will be assigned to the shorter, more difficult, time-consuming runs resulting in much fewer miles and less overall income to them.

*Yes, many companies prefer to deal with the massive driver turnover instead of increasing overall driver pay because they are profiting from it in a big way! Even if there are major accidents with injuries and/or loss of life, it is affordable! They are willing to sacrifice safety and experience for profit by utilizing the lower cost of newer drivers. It has become a proven way of doing business for most companies at the expense of their drivers and loss of safety on the highways to the public due to inexperienced drivers. We are talking about not millions but **billions** of dollars every year in savings to trucking companies, all at the expense of the truck drivers!*

## 4. GETTING PAID AS A PROFESSIONAL

Of course, 'anybody can drive a truck'. So can anybody fly an airplane, be a railroad engineer, captain a ship and all other careers requiring people skills. There are training programs for all of them.

It does not make sense that truck stops are full of billions of dollars worth of trucks carrying billions of dollars worth of merchandise and the people in control of and responsible for all these billions of dollars worth of equipment and product many times do not earn enough income to make a decent living.

Should an accident happen, *it seems that it is always the truck driver* that is looked at as being at fault; *guilty until proven innocent.* This is a standard risk in this profession! The liability and responsibility placed on *OVER THE ROAD* truck drivers is disproportionate and inappropriate in most cases. Sleeper berths are provided with the trucks but there is usually little or no provision for motel stays or adequate layover pay. Movies and television advertisements many times portray truck drivers as rough and unshaven in a less than desirable environment. Unfortunately, when the public views a truck driver in a negative scenario it seems to fuel the idea that all truck drivers are less than professional. Could it be that this portrayal of truck drivers results in inconsiderate and unsafe driving by the public? Could all this unpleasant imaging contribute to the 'driver shortage'?

If these truck drivers were wearing uniforms and had the image of professionals, it might go a long way toward negotiating for better pay. But most trucking companies do not want to spend the money for uniforms due to the high driver turnover and many drivers would not wear them anyway. Providing company paid-for, button up the front uniform-style shirts would certainly be a good start. Requiring drivers to wear them would also be necessary since many drivers object to being 'cloned'. Traditionally, truck drivers are a very independent group. Long hours and hard work in a nationwide, all-weather environment at marginal pay are not conducive to sheep-like mentality. Lots of luck getting them to wear uniforms! Only if the pay was higher and uniforms were mandatory would this happen, similar to United Parcel Service (UPS) and other high-paid company drivers. Owner-operators will probably never wear uniforms. What it actually boils down to is a 'cart before the horse' scenario. When the compensation package is enough, people will comply with the necessary requirements to get and keep their jobs. This is a necessary major hurdle that must eventually be crossed sooner or later, one way or another if OVER THE ROAD truck driver pay and image are to improve.

Training in accident prevention and operating procedures are certainly important but it is impossible to cover the many countless spontaneous events that can happen daily without a moments notice. People's lives are at stake and *everybody* depends on the truck driver to make the right decision whenever a novice or less than professional driver screws up and causes a dangerous situation. Over eight hundred people a week die out here on the highways, *many of them truck drivers!* The OVER THE ROAD truck driver must be concerned not only about his own safety, *but that of the thousands of people he passes by on the road every day*. It is his responsibility to see that he does not cause harm to any of them, regardless of *their* ignorance. *Not one! Ever!*

An interesting fact to consider is that when the entire airline transportation system was shut down for a week due to the terrorist attack on our nation, trucks stepped in and handled the airfreight portion of their operations quite adequately for the most part. However, should the trucking industry ever experience such a complete shutdown *for even a few days*, the country would also have to completely shut down for lack of goods and services. *This fact alone should be enough to emphasize the importance of truck drivers to our nation* regardless of all other concerns.

Using the previous criteria as a guideline, it seems to me that an OVER THE ROAD truck driver who dedicates 100% of his time to his company for weeks at a time, accepting responsibility for equipment and merchandise which together can sometimes be worth in excess of several hundred thousand dollars, should be worth at *least* as much as their counterparts in other professions with the possible exception of commercial airline pilots. None of the before mentioned occupations other than airline pilots, require advanced education. None of the before mentioned occupations require time away from home for weeks at a time or on weekends and holidays. None of the before mentioned occupations require comparable skills, talents and responsibility of the OVER THE ROAD truck driver. But *all* of the before mentioned occupations provide higher pay, better benefits and better working conditions!

UPS (United Parcel Service) is the largest trucking company in the world. They are also members of the Teamster's Union. *Efficient management* has allowed this company to become very profitable and provide everyone with premium pay and benefits! This is the way it is supposed to be, not necessarily with a union!

Firemen may sit at their company station for weeks or even months at a time and never get called to action. But their presence is mandatory in the event of an emergency occurring that they are trained to deal with. Suppose these firemen were only paid if they went to a fire or other such emergency of their calling. *Simply being available and on duty, away from home and at their station justifies their pay, even if they do nothing but remain in readiness to act if needed.* They generate no revenue and in fact cost the taxpayers a considerable amount of money, to which no one objects because they are very necessary for the protection of life and property should the need arise. This is as it should be and I have no problem with it. *But where is ours?*

What has been shown here is that in all *other* major professions, the 'professional' is compensated according to the value placed on him by the public and the company he works for. Then the funds to provide payment for his income are included in the cost of the service provided and everybody is happy. Why should compensation for OVER THE ROAD truck drivers be any different? *Especially since safety on the highways or lack of it, is a direct result of inadequate compensation!*

Is it any wonder that most OVER THE ROAD truck drivers feel underpaid, angry and are many times looking for another job?

**In the final analysis the problem facing truckers comes down to the method of pay. Being paid by the mile simply is not working.**

## 5. EARNINGS FOR OTHER TRANSPORTATION RELATED CAREERS

In other transportation professions, just compensation for the skilled employees is generally considered first rather than as an after thought as it seems to be with OVER THE ROAD truck drivers. Government, industrial management and labor organizations in those careers closely regulate the professionals' hours with safety and home time being major factors that must be dealt with up front and the conditions adhered to, to the letter.

Compensation for a commercial airline pilot to fly a large jetliner is well over $200,000.00 a year, not including pension and medical benefits, holiday and vacation pay. Pilots generally are allowed to fly something like eighty hours a month and are provided with up-scale hotel accommodations whenever an overnight stay is required. Most of them are home a week or two every month. Once the plane is in the air, the automatic pilot takes over and the pilot and co-pilot can take turns monitoring the gauges, radio and relaxing. My former neighbor, who was then a pilot for a major airline, said it was the most boring job in the world. In spite of all this, it seems some airline union or other is always threatening to go on strike for more of everything and get it. The public pays for the increase in the form of higher airfares. *This is the American way!*

A railroad engineer earns a respectable income and the train is on tracks, monitored by computers constantly for safety and service control. They also enjoy full medical benefits, pensions, holiday and vacation pay, with regular time at home. Watching light signals, monitoring gauges and sounding the horn at crossings seems to be the toughest part of that profession. Extra duties and overtime are compensated for. Trains can be seen waiting for each other to pass constantly, sometimes for long periods of time. Waiting is part of the job, just as it is for a trucker. The big differences are that when the railroad crew's time runs out due to unscheduled delays, a fresh crew is brought out to run the train and the old crew relieved, wherever it may happen to be. Time-and-a-half is paid to the railroader for over 40 hours and double-time for working on holidays. Six-figure incomes are commonplace! *In stark contrast, the trucker gets nothing for his time!*

*Airline baggage handlers are listed in the top ten highest paid laborers!*

Assembly-line employees at auto and truck manufacturing plants with boring, repetitive jobs are guaranteed premium hourly wages and the entire medical and pension benefits packages are included. These people are also home every night with their families. Their pay and benefits have significant periodic upgrades also, paid for by the consumer. Once again, time-and-a half over 40, double-time holiday pay!

Teamster union truck drivers under contract with the National Master Freight Agreement earn over twenty dollars per hour for city delivery and up to fifty-three CPM for driving OVER THE ROAD with motels provided whenever necessary. They too, receive a full pension and benefit package that assures them of a respectable income, paid time off for vacations, medical care, retirement, and regular time off at home. *There is a provision for compensation for every duty and function the driver performs, as there should be!* Time-and-a-half over 40, double and triple time, depending on circumstances. The consumer pays!

At this time I feel it is necessary to elaborate a bit on the union aspect of trucking since OVER THE ROAD truck driver compensation already passed this phase of the evolution process once and has now reverted back to the previous 'sweatshop' position of being overworked and underpaid.

The way it was decided was that the average *safe and realistic* speed of a truck driver is 50 miles an hour. This meant that for a 500-mile day, a driver would take 10 hours (500 divided by 50). All runs were figured using that criteria and a driver knew up front what each run would pay. If a driver got tired and stopped to take a short nap or wanted to stop for personal reasons, it did not matter because the pay was already set in advance and everybody knew what it would be. It remains this way today for all union and many of the competing non-union freight companies because *it works!*

Bus drivers are tightly scheduled to comply with safety requirements. Although busses travel coast to coast, the drivers are usually scheduled to meet each other at halfway points throughout the entire country and then change buses with one another, each returning to the place they started from. Guaranteed pay and full benefits are included!

Longshoremen at seaports are earning from $80,000 to $150,000 a year to move shipping containers onto ships for overseas voyages and off ships so they can be loaded onto trucks for delivery to final destination. Manual labor is minimal due to using cranes and forklift equipment. These people work in a protected environment away from the rigors of public activity and responsibility. Duties and responsibilities are spelled out in detail in their contract and the benefits are all inclusive. They are home every night, weekends and all holidays with provisions for time and a half, double or triple time if required to work extra time during the week, weekends or holidays. Yes, they must be able to handle heavy equipment and rigging safely which is certainly very important. But what heavy equipment can be more difficult to operate than a free-wheeling OVER THE ROAD eighteen-wheeler in all kinds of weather, traffic, parking and docking facilities, many times designed for the much smaller trucks of twenty or thirty years ago?

It is significant to note that all of the before mentioned transportation related professions have representation to negotiate their pay and benefits! As a result they earn a respectable income with good benefits and are home regularly, some of them every day. If necessary, motels are provided to assure proper rest and creature comforts.

It is also significant to note that the big difference between trucks and trains, cranes and planes is that a truck driver must be in continual, unrelenting control of his vehicle at all times. *He must constantly and unceasingly be fully awake, alert and prepared to safely do everything without assistance,* while engineers, pilots and longshoremen *operate machines that do most of the work. In some cases they simply monitor them in a relaxed atmosphere, generally with the assistance of others!*

In my opinion, *just being able to qualify to be an OVER THE ROAD truck driver and acquiring a CDL should warrant equivalent compensation to a longshoreman!* Then the aspect of being taken from a protected environment (truck terminal) and thrown into the superslab asphalt jungle to spar with millions of other vehicles driven by every conceivable mentality on the planet and perform the countless duties of the trucking profession *should justify an additional amount, including health and pension benefits, paid for by the employer!*

If the *mileage* pay were *higher* than union pay to compensate for the many unpaid-for activities of an OVER THE ROAD trucker, it *might* be more acceptable. But the fact is, mileage pay is not only lower but *much* lower and *none* of the time-consuming extra duties are compensated for nor do they get comparable benefits, vacation or holiday pay, if any at all.

In addition, most of the businesses the OVER THE ROAD truck driver picks up from and delivers to have employees with normal hours of employment and compensation that these truck drivers must constantly deal with. Many of these people develop attitudes toward the OVER THE ROAD truck drivers that obviously reflect their feelings of disrespect toward these drivers because many times *these people also are aware of the limited pay and poor conditions of the OVER THE ROAD truck drivers and look down on truckers for accepting such conditions!* Some even make derogatory comments about it. I have heard them.

Even the California Highway Patrol pays their officers $35 per hour and as state employees receive full pension, welfare and retirement benefits, including several weeks paid vacation and all the major holidays, also at full pay. This pay is fully justified by the fact that law enforcement is a high-risk profession and one of the most dangerous due to the criminal aspect. However, it ranks *behind* OVER THE ROAD trucking in the number of annual fatalities.

Los Angeles Police Dept (LAPD) officers starting pay is around $4000.00 per month with full benefits and a month vacation *from the very first year*. Training pay is around $2200.00 per month for 6 months. They have a 36-hour, 3-day workweek with 4 days off every week. Additional time worked is paid for. They are fully vested for partial retirement after only five years should they decide to pursue other careers. Full retirement requires only 20 years. Then after a few years off, they can return to duty with full pay and benefits while still collecting their first pension.

Interestingly in Europe, OVER THE ROAD trucking *is* highly regulated. *Truck drivers are treated as professionals and paid accordingly!* From what I understand in talking with one, they are salaried and receive up to *six weeks paid vacation with fifteen paid holidays a year*. European trucks are not allowed on the highways on the weekends from Friday midnight to Sunday midnight. *European OVER THE ROAD truckers are highly respected as professionals and there is no truck driver shortage in Europe!*

## 6. RECRUITING FOREIGNERS, MISFITS AND ODDBALLS

For those who consider truck drivers uneducated or lacking intelligence, they should have to experience some of the shippers and receivers truckers must deal with, as well as truck stop personnel and even some of those on our own management team in companies we work for. Yes, there may be some ignorant truck drivers but the fact is that there are *also many highly educated OVER THE ROAD truck drivers that have come in from all other professions.*

It is also significant to realize that many OVER THE ROAD trucking companies are actively recruiting *foreigners, ex-convicts and illiterates* as a routine because *they will more readily accept the pay and conditions* of an OVER THE ROAD truck driver. Some of these recruits barely speak

English and have extreme difficulty meeting even the minimum licensing requirements. However they somehow acquire a CDL, many times illegally, and are out here fumbling around on the highways with a big truck, *creating a very dangerous scenario.* Obviously these minorities, misfits of society, ex-convicts, derelicts, uneducated illiterates and imported non-English-speaking foreigners are actively being recruited to keep the pay and conditions less than what they should be rather than retaining present drivers! Non-English speaking truckers sometimes rudely tie up the CB trucker channel for long periods of time with each other, making it difficult for anybody else to communicate. Obviously they are unfamiliar with our customs, highways and cities, creating this dangerous scenario. The highways are full of them!

Although the majority of OVER THE ROAD truck drivers are honest and respectable and are average or above average in intelligence and skills, there is definitely an open door for many who are not. These things will never change until, other than to legitimate minorities that door is closed, resulting in not enough *suitable* drivers to fill the seats. *Most people in our society have no idea of the growing number of low caliber OVER THE ROAD truck drivers they and their families are exposed to daily on the open road!* I did not realize it myself until I witnessed it. Even though this may be only a small percentage of millions of truck drivers, how can it be acceptable if it results in accidents, injuries and loss of lives because of it? In addition, the numbers are increasing. *Long-term retention of experienced, safe drivers would seem to be a desirable alternative.* But how can this retention happen? Read on.

## 7. RECRUITERS

Truck driver recruiters are commonplace. Large OVER THE ROAD trucking companies, to coerce experienced drivers from other companies to go to work for their company, generally pay recruiters a set amount or fee for each driver they recruit. Some companies have full time recruiters in the field with large company-owned RV campers that travel around the country and visit truck stops in areas where they need drivers the most. Many driver recruiters were OVER THE ROAD truck driver themselves at one time or another. They are familiar with the problems and circumstances that concern truckers and use this to their advantage when trying to convince a driver to leave his company to work for theirs. *Clearly, the constant need for 'on the road' driver recruiters reinforces the notion that things are not as they should be in this industry.* Most honest recruiters will freely admit to that and even state that they stopped driving OVER THE ROAD themselves because of the many shortcomings still facing the very drivers they are trying to recruit. Newspaper ads for driver seminars in hotels are commonplace. The cost of recruiting truck drivers is very high! *This is more money that could and should go toward better pay to retain experienced drivers!*

Truck drivers themselves are being offered large sums as driver recruiters to coerce their comrades from other companies to change jobs. This is promoted by trucking companies as a way for their drivers to earn more money instead of increasing regular pay. This obviously seems like a great idea for those in management because it utilizes their drivers in a positive way while coercing their drivers to accentuate the positive aspects of the company, more or less brain-washing themselves whether or not they succeed in recruiting anyone else. The end result hoped for would seem to be more drivers for the company and more income to the driver without an across the board pay increase to all drivers.

While this may be possible on a sporadic basis, generally most experienced truck drivers have the attitude that when it comes to changing jobs, 'If you've seen one, you've seen them all.' and stay where they are because they have probably already done some job-hopping. They know that other truck drivers get bonuses for recruiting them and that the recruiting driver may paint an unrealistically rosy picture just to earn a bonus.

Even if a company driver is successful in recruiting other drivers, it is very difficult to follow up on any such recruitment to collect such a bonus because most companies that have such a recruitment bonus program are so large that the recruiting driver has little way to check on such things. It is not a case of everything being entered into the computer so that the recruiting driver automatically gets the bonus, as it should be. The recruiter must personally follow up on each person he was in contact with to see if they came on board with his company. The recruited driver must also put the recruiting driver's name on his application. Then, the company must honor it! Good luck!

It can result in a recruiting driver becoming more involved in trying to recruit than doing his own job as a truck driver, spreading himself too thin, if you will. Besides, it takes a special type of person to be a successful recruiter and although a few may be successful, most will fail. Even a successful driver-recruiter would have quite a chore earning any kind of a regular income from bonuses. I say leave the recruiting to recruiters and give me a fair days pay for a fair days work as a truck driver. Then they might not need so many recruiters. I think most other OVER THE ROAD truck drivers will agree with me.

## 8. SIGN-ON BONUSES

Some companies have offered experienced drivers what is called a sign-on bonus of up to $5000 to change jobs. If experienced drivers were adequately compensated, this expensive effort would not be necessary. Jumping from company to company is costly to everyone and has become almost commonplace. Again, *it makes more sense to put the money where the work is!* Frankly, I am tired of all the freeloaders sucking off the system at the truck driver's expense and effort, including recruiters. *Ultimately, the money to pay for all these recruiting efforts must come from working truck drivers generating revenue by hauling freight!*

## 9. PROFESSIONAL APPEARANCE IS LACKING

Being an OVER THE ROAD truck driver *should* be looked upon as a highly respected and honorable profession. Instead many people in our society view all truck drivers somewhat with disdain, maybe with good reason. Certainly they are not paid as professionals!

Appearance has a lot to do with it and a visit to almost any truck stop can sometimes be a startling experience. Many of the 'professional' drivers look like homeless refugees or vagrants. The pay and conditions are certainly a big factor. A person should be *proud* to be introduced as an OVER THE ROAD professional instead of *embarrassed* when people who are informed of your career begin to make derogatory remarks. I want to emphasize that the *vast majority of OVER THE ROAD truck drivers are decent, hardworking and honest.* Most of them do not like to be associated or affiliated with those of questionable character or slovenly appearance in this profession *either*. It seems like it is always the *few* that affect the *many* in such matters.

Most OVER THE ROAD truck drivers are very friendly, compassionate, understanding and even religious God-fearing people! Possibly the challenging overall job conditions have been an influence in this and it is difficult to explain unless you have 'been there'. Enjoying the work while accepting the conditions probably has something to do with this 'bonding'.

# 11.

# OVER THE ROAD DRIVER PAY, THE _REAL_ SAFETY ISSUE!

_We have seen that a major factor that must be considered in regard to highway safety is driver pay!_

_It is the driver pay and conditions that need to be upgraded to an acceptable level!_ Getting home every weekend or at least more frequently would certainly count for something. Being paid a fair wage if the company cannot get you home regularly is only fair and just.

Unlike those in other professions, an OVER THE ROAD truck driver many times has to try on his own to make things happen to improve his income by:

1. Calling customers.
2. Being early for pickups and deliveries.
3. Asking questions.
4. Send inquiries to his dispatcher about delivering early or utilizing a drop yard.
5. Trying to get a pre-planned load.
6. Many other common sense things as they happen.

Unfortunately those in dispatch and operations in many trucking companies have voice mail and sat-com systems that _seem to be purposely designed to keep drivers from direct communication._ This apparently allows them time to do things at their convenience and have time to think things out to their advantage. By the time an answer comes back to a driver trying to get a phone number, pickup number, directions or whatever else is needed, the driver can get lost or lose his place in line to load or unload. _Response time has become another major complaint among truck drivers!_

Communication is always one-sided when the driver needs to get information that may require a bit of effort on the part of his dispatcher or when it comes to questionable pay issues that may come up. The necessary authorization numbers that are required to put additional money in the pocket of the driver can sometimes be very elusive.

One of the few advantages to being a company lease-operator over a company driver is that the lease driver can sometimes pick where he wants to go, more or less. They are not forced to go to New York City, Canada or any other place they do not want to go. Keep in mind that the truck driver orientation classes are full of former lease and owner-operators that did not make a success of it.

Drivers put forth great effort to meet pickup and delivery schedules only to be greeted with, "Park in the lot and put your CB radio on channel so and so. We'll call you when we're ready." Then it is the unpaid-for waiting game. An hour or two of free waiting time might be acceptable. But excessive unproductive time affects drivers' pay as well as their attitude and burns up their logbook time. Additionally, it is common knowledge that in regard to waiting time, logbooks are fraudulently juggled to a driver's advantage so much that they are called 'comic books'. But even this 'juggling' simply does not compensate drivers enough for the lost time they had counted on to earn a livable paycheck to maintain their families and pay their bills. There are other unsafe 'games' that are played that I dare not get into, for fear of inadvertently promoting them.

The way it is now, if an OVER THE ROAD truck driver gets a good long run that will compensate him for time he has lost sitting around without pay, even though that driver may be too tired to *safely* complete the run, most drivers will push themselves so they will not lose such a high-mileage load to another driver. *This is the real safety issue. Driver compensation! Not logbooks!* Any experienced driver can easily juggle his logbook to show what officials want to see! Everybody knows that; it is common knowledge. Even paperless logs do not give an honest appraisal of downtime. Since they are produced by satellite, there is no way to know for sure whether a stopped truck has a sleeping driver in it or a hungry driver has gone in to eat, shower and make a few phone calls or watch TV. The paperless log automatically shows the driver in the sleeper berth after two hours even though he may be getting in eighteen holes of golf or jogging.

## 1. PAY AND CONDITIONS ARE RELATED TO SAFETY.

The *pay and conditions for the key players of a trade determine the level of professionalism it can reach.* In regard to this, it is obvious that some areas of trucking have advanced far beyond others. For OVER THE ROAD truck drivers with a casual attitude who are unconcerned about earning capability and just want something to do, this can be very good. It is probably the large numbers of this type that have been instrumental in reducing and/or holding the pay scale down. But if the primary purpose of the individual is to maximize their earnings to support their family, the income can many times be very disappointing and frustrating, especially if they are the only breadwinner. *It is the latter that are more prevalent!*

***Long-term retention of experienced, qualified OVER THE ROAD professional truck drivers is needed to maximize safety on the highways. How to accomplish this is largely what this writing is all about!***

Entry-level screening requirements are sometimes very lax, allowing simply anyone willing to 'give it a shot' to join the ranks of handling enormous equipment in ever-present dangerous conditions. 'Steering wheel holders' if you will. Warm bodies! Believe it or not, I have heard dispatchers refer to new drivers as *'pieces of meat'!* Unprofessional driving of eighteen-wheelers can be witnessed constantly, as can poor driving of vehicles from the private sector. *This combination is a formula for disaster!*

Psychological considerations, education and questionable background information on applicants are many times *completely overlooked* due to the 'driver shortage'. Temperament is an important consideration when dealing with other traffic on the highway. *The general motoring public, lacking the knowledge of sharing space with big trucks, constantly causes many dangerous situations.* Irate emotions and a 'get-even' mentality when someone drives unprofessionally can result in accidents, injuries and death. It happens every day, everywhere. *Discourtesy and road rage are constantly present!*

OVER THE ROAD trucks on the nation's highways are obvious to the most casual observer. Sooner or later trucks travel on every local city street, county road, state and interstate highway. Many drivers of private vehicles view them as nuisances that block their view or slow them when they want to get somewhere in a hurry. It seems that whenever someone has a tight schedule to meet, one of these big trucks is always in the way to cause him or her to be late. Others are intimidated by their size and being in close proximity to trucks can be frightening to many drivers, *including me!*

Trying to pass big trucks or getting passed by them on the open highway can sometimes be a very dangerous occurrence. Wind, dust and road spray can cause smaller vehicles to have a difficult time when attempting to pass a truck or when being passed by one. Trucks create a powerful *invisible wake* behind them, similar to a boat creating a wake in the water, which is *highly* visible. In both cases other traffic is affected by this wake and must be prepared for it in advance to maintain control of their vehicle. Being aware of this 'invisible' wake is important to following and passing traffic for accident prevention. *Both hands on the wheel please, not two fingers or one wrist as you text or talk on the phone or put on your makeup!*

Watching the weather channel on TV becomes a priority in an OVER THE ROAD truck driver's life, especially in the winter. *48-state travel in bad weather is a major concern* and many times there is no avoiding approaching storms. A truck driver is exposed to all kinds of weather and natural disasters such as *floods, hurricanes, blizzards and tornadoes.* This is one of the most challenging aspects of trucking. *Fog, smoke, blinding snow and dust storms are treacherous. Mountain travel and dangerous highway conditions can be disastrous!* Becoming stranded as a result of weather conditions or an unexpected breakdown can be very uncomfortable and even fatal. *Being aware of and prepared for this possibility is very necessary!*

Rush hour traffic is another big concern. Traffic is fast and very heavy in highly populated areas. Again, *the general population has little or no concept of the reality of sharing the highways with big trucks.*

Low bridges and overpasses are a constant threat to truckers that are continually going into areas they have never been to before. Many times by the time you see the clearance or truck restriction signs you have already made the turn and must now find a way to either turn around and go back or worse, *back out,* with impatient traffic trying to go around you! Here comes that middle finger again!

Security is an important aspect of the transportation industry. There are many hijacked loads occurring constantly, nationwide. High value loads are always at risk and the drivers hauling them are in danger of being mugged or worse by the hijackers. People working for the very companies that ship them many times target these high value loads to be stolen.

Small companies make no secret of the fact that they provide drivers with the finest looking, ego-enhancing trucks that are capable of triple digit speeds, *to make up for being paid less.*

Trucking is a serious business! *The general population needs to realize that highways are a place of work for the professional truck driver as opposed to a place of commuting, travel and good times for the public.* The truck driver has to share his workspace with anybody and everybody that decides to enter the highway regardless of their driving ability or condition of their equipment. If the average person had as many interruptions and intrusions into their jobs as a truck driver does his, *it would be very difficult for them to accomplish anything!* What may be fun and games for one can be deadly serious for the other!

Many drivers of cars *and* trucks develop an attitude of 'Us against them!' Cars against trucks! Trucks against cars! Emotions flare! The result is many times disastrous! There are some mighty stubborn and ignorant drivers out here! Cars end up looking like accordions and truck drivers lose their jobs! *People die unnecessarily!*

Traffic is getting heavier every year as the population increases and vehicles are traveling faster. Most super-highways are virtually obsolete! Danger is ever present! Imminent disaster lurks constantly! *After* an accident happens is the wrong time to think about how it could have been prevented. *It is too late then!*

**While it is convenient for the media and those making laws regarding safety to point the finger of blame at tired truckers, the truth is that truck drivers would not be nearly as tired and fatigued if they were fairly compensated for their time and talents and a far more professional atmosphere could prevail!**

*Driver fatigue* is definitely a major consideration in OVER THE ROAD trucking! Irregular hours concerning driving, sleeping, waiting, crossing time zones and many other things contribute to a 'jet lag' condition. Broken and interrupted sleep sessions occur constantly. There is no regularity of any kind regarding these matters. Logbooks are a bad joke! *Safety is certainly affected by all these things!*

# 12.

# MANY THINGS TO DEAL WITH

## 1. GOOD HEALTH IS IMPORTANT

One of the most important things trucking made me aware of and thankful for is my good health. Without that, I never could have gone where I have gone, done what I have done or seen what I have seen and gotten paid for it, to boot. My world has been adventurous, interesting and very much on the go for the most part. It has also been somewhat financially rewarding and allowed me to enjoy my time off in larger blocks of quality time. Some kind of irregular physical exercise can be a big help. I like to walk as much as I can whenever I am in a 'waiting mode'. This is said to be one of the best exercises and is free. Some truckers carry bicycles with them and others use weights or springs in the cab. Anything is better than nothing. Avoid buffets. Some of these are excellent but very damaging. I love them! Once a week is enough for me. Less is better, but the truck stops price buffets cheaper than dinner meals to reduce waitress demand.

One of the best ways to stay in shape is to unload your own loads rather than hire a lumper. Even though many times this is not feasible due to circumstances, there are going to be times when it may be possible to do this, especially if you are driving solo. An interesting thing to note here is that most trucking companies will pay an outside lumper whatever he asks but if their own driver offers to unload the same load, he will be paid at a standard, usually much lower rate. For instance, a company may have an $80.00 rate limit for it's own drivers but a lumper may demand and get $200.00 and more for the same task. This does not make sense to me! Learn to live with it!

If you are pulling a flatbed, the effort of installing tie-down chains and binders, straps and tarping provides a considerable amount of exercise that burns up a lot of calories. Sideboards and canvass bows also require considerable effort. You may need to wear coveralls for this.

Eat properly and stay away from deep fried food. Chef salads are great as are fruits, nuts and vegetables.

Truck drivers are required by law to have a complete physical examination every two years to comply with federal DOT health requirements. Your company should pay for this.

On the other hand, due to the endless nationwide travel, truck drivers can be in a state of 'jet lag'; tired and fatigued and not too interested in taking a walk in a strange place where getting mugged is a possibility. Ever-present hot dogs, fast foods and buffets do not help. Being available for dispatch requires nearness to your sat-com should a load suddenly become available. When waiting to load or unload, you must be always ready to back into the dock. The OVER THE ROAD truck driver must always be available at somebody's whim if he wants to maximize his productivity. This can definitely put a crimp in any exercise routine. You will definitely have to work at it!

Since OVER THE ROAD truckers can cross several time zones in the course of their trip, I suggest carrying 4 watches. These can be bought very inexpensively. Keep the one you wear set at your home time zone and the rest on the other 3 zones for easy access. All appointments are generally set for the time zone of the shipper or consignee and it can sometimes get confusing.

## 2. TARGET FOR LAW ENFORCEMENT

There are many other issues to be considered! As an OVER THE ROAD truck driver you will be a target for many other agencies, businesses and law enforcement. For instance, trucks are viewed as 'cash cows' by most highway patrols, towing and repair shops.

Remember this! The first thing many highway patrolmen are going to ask you for is your logbook. It had better be in order or it will cost you money out of pocket. If you are too far behind, you may be put out of service for 10 hours and have to wait it out as well as pay a stiff fine. If you violate an out of service order the fine is $2,500 and your license may be suspended.

California comes to mind as one of the harshest states for truckers to travel in. The fines imposed for logbook violations are so exorbitant as to be ridiculous beyond belief. I have heard of fines approaching $20,000.00 and many cited drivers from out of state dare not return to the state because they could not afford to pay the fine and would be sent to prison if apprehended should they return and get caught. Seemingly, California is the most notorious of all states toward truckers. Maryland is another that comes to mind. No doubt there are others! Law enforcement is definitely necessary but it should be reasonable!

An experience I once had with California was related to the weight distribution on a 53' trailer. I was unfamiliar with the 40' kingpin to center of 1st trailer axle formula and adjusted the weight according to the 34,000# per tandem axle requirement. Although my axle weight was legal, the bridge formula caused me to have to move my trailer tandem ahead to comply with weight distribution requirements since the trailer was loaded heavy on the rear. This put 2500# more weight on the trailer tandem which then became overweight there (36,500#). The fine was over $200 and my company had to send another trailer to take the excess weight off my trailer because the California officer in charge at that weigh station would not allow me to take the load a mere ten miles to a terminal that could have unloaded and reloaded the pallets. This transfer at the weigh station involved hiring a wrecker service to bring a wrecker, forklift, chains and other material handling equipment to drag 2 pallets to the rear of the trailer and transfer them onto the other trailer. There was no loading dock or platform of any kind! Since the pallets were double-stacked bins of bulk Brussels sprouts, they tipped over and there were Brussels sprouts everywhere! What a mess! Anyway, this is an example of how bad it can get simply because that particular scale master at that particular California scale had made up his own rule about not letting trucks go anywhere to get things legal! I am sure there are many similar stories and worse that can be told by multitudes of other truckers about other incidents in other states as well as California! *Trucking is a tough and serious business!* No mercy!

*Law enforcement is unconcerned about the inconvenience and expense they are causing for the driver and his company. It is all about generating revenue!* Certainly if permits can be obtained for other heavy loads of excessive weight without equipment modification, safety is not an issue. It seems to me that a more lenient attitude could be adopted by state and federal agencies toward truck drivers and the companies they work for. The punishment should more fairly fit the crime rather than be so excessive as to be ridiculous as in these cases. After all, this is the United States not Nazi Germany.

These law enforcement officers need to be instructed to use more humane methods of handling violations that can be easily corrected without endangering the public. It just does not make sense that cranes or wreckers must be hired and additional equipment brought in at huge expense in cases such as this when an overweight permit could be purchased or a trip to a local loading platform would suffice, at reasonable cost. *The punishment presently goes far beyond the violation!* It simply is not right what is happening to OVER THE ROAD truckers out here! Unnecessary expenditures of this nature are ridiculous, bordering on corrupt!

Years ago I experienced another example of obnoxious behavior by the state police in the state of Vermont on my way to Brattleboro, Vt. from Albany N.Y., traveling on route 9 across the mountains. After descending a long 2-lane, winding and steep major mountain grade, I stopped at the bottom to let my smoking brakes cool while I went into a small local diner to calm my nerves and get breakfast. As I sat sipping my coffee, three highway patrol officers came in and sat across from me where I could not help but overhear their conversation. It was very unsettling to hear them laughing and telling how they had just been out all night 'harassing' (their word) the truckers, glancing my way occasionally and knowing it was my truck sitting across the way with the brakes smoking, since there were no other patrons. I gulped my coffee down and made a quiet exit before they finished their breakfast to escape the possibility of becoming their next victim. Not a happy event but a window into the mentality and attitude of the law toward truckers in that area. To them it seemed to be nothing more than a game and a fun thing to do, with *absolutely no compassion or concern for the anguish they were causing truck drivers!*

I just do not understand this kind of treatment of truckers! They are hard working people! They are United States citizens! They do not deserve this kind of abuse! The economy depends on them! There must be another way law enforcement can generate money rather than preying on and abusing truckers!

In the final analysis, when it comes to a truck driver needing money to pay his bills it makes no difference to anyone but him how much aggravation he has to endure to earn even a meager paycheck. It all comes down to money! If you cannot pay your bills, nothing else matters. It must be said again that this is a common problem in this career for many drivers! What a shame!

## 3. BROKER SKIMMING

Brokers and freight salesmen are literally skimming the cream off the top and putting exorbitant incomes in their pockets. I have witnessed this over the years and will explain how it works.

Many times I have seen groups of truckers huddled around outside the offices of truck brokers at truck stops in the morning, waiting for the brokers to arrive. At about 9 AM in dances an energetic, athletic young fellow in his mid-thirties or forties with his golf or tennis outfit on. He opens up and begins making phone calls to the various shippers he does business with. As the morning progresses he accepts dozens of loads to hand out to the anxious truckers standing by. From each of these loads, the broker will automatically deduct from 10 to 25 percent of the freight charge as his fee for handling these truckers' loads. This 'fee' can be anywhere from $100 to over $1000 per load, depending on where the load is going and what the rate is. It does not take too many loads to put several thousand dollars in the broker's pocket *in one day*. Then the broker closes up for the day at 4 or 5 in the afternoon and proceeds to play games with and wine and dine the traffic managers or freight controllers he does business with. Gifts of season passes to sports stadiums and other events are commonplace. Unlimited free use of vacation resort facilities is another enticement. *Everybody enjoys the fruits of the truck driver's efforts. Everybody that is, except the driver! Chances are he is barely making it from paycheck to meager paycheck!*

Freight salesmen for large trucking companies operate in a similar fashion. Visits to the finest restaurants, golf clubs, topless bars, sports stadiums and various other attractions are almost routine. Cost is no object because these salesmen have unlimited expense accounts with which to pay for these amenities to produce loads for their companies' trucks to haul.

I have knowledge of shipping clerks and traffic managers of large corporations being given riding lawn mowers, golf carts and even Corvettes. Private parties are thrown costing thousands to coerce shippers to use various trucking services! Money flows like water to everybody except the OVER THE ROAD truck driver or owner-operator who must struggle constantly just to make ends meet. *I have seen and plead guilty of participating in these events when I was in business!*

In reality, trucking companies utilizing owner-operators are nothing more than glorified brokers. The difference is that the trucking companies supply not only the loads but provide trailers to haul them on as well as operating authority, insurance and other basic legal requirements, simplifying entry into becoming a lease or owner-operator. In this regard, at least some of the revenue is being used to enhance the company's operations rather than going into the pockets of a high roller.

## 4. LUMPERS—LOADING AND UNLOADING FEES

There has long been a dispute or disagreement if you will, about who should physically load or unload the merchandise in the trailer; the warehouse employees or the truck driver. Since the warehouse has the option of routing loads by carriers that will abide by their demands, the truck driver has been caught in the middle and has been expected to do this work whenever demanded, until recent years. Laborers called 'lumpers' have now taken on this obligation. Not that using lumpers is anything new, only now the trucking companies no longer expect the OVER THE ROAD drivers to pay for lumpers out of their own pocket or do the work themselves, like it used to be. Too many good drivers have left the trade over this issue and many companies can no longer afford to lose good drivers.

When you arrive at your delivery point you will usually be asked whether or not you need a lumper (laborer) or if you want to unload the load yourself. Most drivers are not too excited about the thought of having to unload a trailer load of merchandise after completing several hundred miles in a run. This is usually a good time to get caught up on some rest. Even if a driver is well rested, many drivers choose to avoid the hassle and congestion of the receiving dock and use a lumper. The choice is usually yours. Of course, the cost of the lumper must be considered as well as several other things. Most receivers will let the lumpers use their power equipment but because of their liability will only supply a driver with a hand-operated pallet jack. The dock people tend to cooperate more with lumpers than a driver since they deal with them on a daily basis and lumpers are very familiar with how things are done. All this can be aggravating to a driver and may cost you money out of pocket but can be worthwhile if it will get you unloaded faster so you can get to your next load. Most of the time you are better off to stick with the customer's program.

Why are lumpers necessary? Who are they? Lumpers are independent laborers that load or unload trucks for an agreed upon amount determined by how much time and work is involved. They have no benefits, few rules and no regulations for the most part. They take on the duties of company paid warehouse workers in that they are present at these locations every day and have a working relationship with the warehouse or company personnel. They are usually allowed to use any company-owned power equipment necessary to accomplish the task. The cost to the shippers and receivers is nothing since the truck driver or his company must cover this charge. Anybody can be a lumper if they are physically and mentally capable.

Because it is difficult to retain the many new truck drivers coming into this field even without facing the unloading problem, most trucking companies have caved in to the shipper's and consignee's demands and agreed to pay these 'lumpers' to do this work rather than risk losing their drivers because the drivers refuse to do it.

Let us be honest about this. Should an OVER THE ROAD truck driver really be expected to load and unload the truck? Does an airline pilot handle the baggage onto and off the plane? What about a railroad engineer? And those occupations are a breeze compared with most truck driving jobs.

As explained before, should a truck driver decide to take on this chore for exercise or extra income, he will probably be expected to do it for far less compensation than a lumper would have gotten. The truck driver will also likely be required to use hand-operated, antiquated equipment that makes the job much more time consuming and physically difficult. Of course, this is to discourage truck drivers from taking work away from the lumpers. The lumpers depend on the company to provide enough work for them to make a living and the companies depend on the lumpers to accomplish their warehouse tasks at no cost to them. Everybody wins if the driver is able to catch up on his rest while the truck is being unloaded. Unfortunately, this does not put any money in the truck driver's pocket.

The simple unloading of a trailer involves more than you might imagine. There are many times dozens or even hundreds of different items that may have to be sorted out on separate pallets. The labels need to be facing out so the receiver can read them. The boxes cannot hang off the pallets or they will not fit in the pallet storage racks. The boxes must also be stacked or interlocked with each other on the pallet so they will not tip over or slide off. Each pallet needs to be strapped, taped or shrink wrapped by whoever unloads. Many different type loads have many specific requirements that the regular lumpers are very familiar with and an outside truck driver would have little idea about how to do. This is warehouse work, not that of a driver. Who do they think they are kidding?

Certainly the profitability of trucking companies is affected by this paying of lumpers, ultimately reducing the companies' profitability that in turn minimizes the possibility of driver pay increases. *This is another example of how everybody but the truck driver seems to be able to **demand and get** whatever they deem necessary for their time and efforts. And remember, all of these people go home every night and weekend!*

# 5. UNLOADING HASSLE

Upon arrival at a customer's facility to make a pickup or delivery there are usually several other truckers already there. Let us assume that all these drivers arrived during the night for an early morning appointment for pickup or delivery. If the customer opens at 7 A.M. and there are 10 or 15 drivers or more in some cases, the morning usually starts out as a 'free for all' as to who is going to get loaded or unloaded first. Everybody tries to get into the building ahead of everybody else, especially if it is a first come, first serve facility rather than by appointment only. This is quite prevalent in the refrigerated business rather than dry freight, although it can happen in any kind of trucking from time to time. When it comes to getting loaded or unloaded, unfortunately most OVER THE ROAD truck drivers have come to have little or no respect for other truck drivers. Crowding ahead and even bribing a receiving clerk to get unloaded first is not at all uncommon.

Getting to a customer at an appointed time is expected but if you are an hour or two early, some customers may tell you to come back at the designated time or have you park in a dirt lot with a portable toilet for facilities, if you are lucky!

Generally if all the drivers arrived during the night and are sleeping in their trucks, it is solely their own responsibility to wake up and check in with the receiver on time for their appointment, if they have one. Should they fail to wake up, chances are they will miss their appointment and may have to reschedule another one for later or even the next day. You snooze, you lose! Occasionally someone from a facility will come out and wake the drivers up. In any case, once the drivers get up and go into the building to check in it can get quite interesting.

Once inside, everybody stands around looking at each other, making small talk while waiting for the receiver to appear or open a sliding window that may have a note saying, 'Do not tap on window' (god must be inside). When the receiver (god) finally shows up he will usually be pre-occupied with other more important things than recognizing the presence of a bunch of unprofessional-looking truck drivers, such as rearranging pens and pencils, shuffling papers or pouring coffee. No eye contact or even the raising of a finger to acknowledge the drivers' presence. *Do not dare to interrupt him or her, as the case may be! God is busy collecting his thoughts.*

This waiting period may be 15 or 20 minutes or more and can have a demeaning effect on the drivers. After all, they *are* professional drivers who have just safely completed a run of several hundreds or even a couple thousand miles with a piece of equipment probably worth well over a hundred thousand dollars, carrying product worth thousands that had been ordered by the company where they are and the person in charge (god) will not even acknowledge their presence. Drivers are made to feel like a useless commodity, basically put on hold until convenient. This happens frequently! Prepare for it! This is not a pleasant part of trucking but I doubt if it will change any time soon!

When the receiver (god) finally gets around to communicate with the drivers as to the product they have on and any appointment times, a sour attitude is not uncommon. Then he will assign each driver a door and may ask if they need a lumper. If so, the driver must find the lumper and make arrangements for unloading and payment thereof. The lumper then takes over the load and gets it off the truck after the driver backs into the loading dock and secures his rig.

It can be very interesting to watch the confusion and impatience of these same (professional) drivers after they are assigned a dock to back into to get unloaded. I have seen them crowd ahead of each other, block each other's docks and generally cause mass confusion when trying to beat each other to the yard or dock. It can be a ridiculous mixture of seasoned and inexperienced drivers vying for position with no regard for one another, being totally unprofessional in their actions! Very embarrassing!

That is just one example. There are countless others!

By the time all this takes place and the driver is on his way to pick up another load, many hours without pay have been lost. Worse yet, if there are no loads available he may have to wait until the following day for his next load, without compensation. Additionally, all this time is expected to be logged as 'on duty, not driving' which means the driver will have that many fewer hours to drive and earn a paycheck. Last but not least, *the drivers have been demoralized and made to feel like second-class citizens for accomplishing their mission without compensation. Their attitudes are now in the toilet!*

Regulating trucking by the hour with logbooks while paying them by the mile is not unlike mixing oil with water. It does not work! *A truck driver's time needs also to be considered in the pay package!*

## 6. THE INVISIBLE MAN—MASKING YOUR EMOTIONS

Some people seem to have been born to make life miserable for truckers! It is surprising how many different people truckers must deal with who fail to even acknowledge the driver's presence upon arrival. As previously explained, many times there is no eye contact, nod of the head, raising of a finger or a spoken word; nothing! It is almost as if the drivers are invisible!

This takes place constantly at shippers, receivers and even your own company's dispatch window. Any facial expression by the driver indicating impatience, anger or frustration had better be totally suppressed! Shaking of the head, twisting of the mouth and other such negative contortions are not at all helpful and may slow things for you considerably. *Remember, your time is costing them nothing so they can jerk you around at their pleasure and keep you twisting in the wind indefinitely!*

You would do well to master the 'blank stare' expression of uncaring, even though you may be furious! Those in the window prefer a 'zombie like' attitude. Then, when they finally recognize your presence you had best have your thoughts and information in order or you will go back to the end of the line until you do.

I have no doubt that if these same truck drivers wore uniforms and it was common knowledge that they were paid professionally which included being paid for waiting around, they would be treated with much greater respect, just as UPS and Wal-Mart drivers are. Someone (god) would then become responsible for costly delays of drivers.

## 7. THE MOST DEMANDING PROFESSION

*NO OTHER TRANSPORTATION PROFESSION REQUIRES AS MUCH TOTAL CONCENTRATION AND IMPORTANT DECISION MAKING AT ALL TIMES OR DEMANDS SO MUCH IDLE TIME AWAY FROM HOME, MOST OF WHICH IS UNCOMPENSATED FOR. IN ADDITION, A TRUCK DRIVER IS*

*RESPONSIBLE FOR THE SECURITY OF HIS LOAD AND EQUIPMENT UNDER ALL CONDITIONS AS WELL AS THE SAFETY OF ALL THOSE AROUND HIM AT ALL TIMES. THERE IS LITTLE OR NO GUARANTEE OF COMPENSATION FOR TIME SPENT AND SERVICES RENDERED!*

*THE GENERAL PUBLIC SEEMS NOT TO REALIZE THAT A TRUCK CAN BE A KILLING MACHINE AS CAN ALL MOTOR VEHICLES, AND THE HIGHWAY IS THE KILLING ZONE. IT IS UP TO THE TRUCK DRIVER TO DO HIS BEST TO SEE THAT HIS RIG IS HANDLED SAFELY IN SPITE OF THE POOR DRIVING OF OTHERS. YOU DO NOT STOP AN 80,000 # VEHICLE ON A DIME AT ANY SPEED. MORE THAN ONE TRUCK DRIVER HAS DIED IN TRYING TO SAVE THE LIVES OF OTHERS BY AVOIDING A COLLISION WHEN THE OTHERS DID THE WRONG THING!*

How can you put a value on that? The answer is, it is all part of the job. It is what is expected of a truck driver regardless of all other circumstances *even if it costs him his own life,* which happens more than people realize.

The OVER THE ROAD truck driver must constantly deal with all other traffic and road rage as a professional and control his own anger, sometimes with near superhuman self-control. Drunk drivers and those on drugs, another multi-billion dollar industry, are a constant problem. Trucking is not an easy profession in that regard.

As a 48-state/Canada OVER THE ROAD truck driver you will see more cities, towns, villages and communities than you had any idea existed. You will meet people of all kinds more than in any other occupation. It can be very interesting, even after a lifetime of being in the trucking business. Everybody has to be somewhere all the time, doing something. Traveling around the country in a big truck, hopefully tucked safely (in your truck cab) away from smaller traffic and experiencing a bit of the lives of others, is not a bad option once you get used to it. There are also a great many interesting and friendly people in this land. It *can* be very enjoyable when things go well. However, you must know how to play the game. There are many dangers.

Becoming an OVER THE ROAD truck driver, you will have to deal with:

1. Yourself.
2. Your family.
3. Your company.
4. Customers.
5. Law enforcement.
6. Traffic.
7. Weather.
8. Other truckers.
9. The general public.
10. Many other things.

All of these play a major part in this field of endeavor and must be dealt with.

Yes, OVER THE ROAD trucking can be very, very good or it can be very, very bad. In the end, it all comes down to the earning capability, as in all professions. Attitude is directly affected by income, whether it is a pittance for doing something extra or overall financial reward, commensurate with effort, talent and time expended. *Clearly, those that are most satisfied with any profession are those well paid and vice-verse.*

## 8. CANADIAN CROSSING

Going into Canada can be a real thrill! Many trucking companies will not hire you if you will not or cannot go into Canada. Canada restricts anyone with a felony record from entering the country. Personally, I would prefer never to leave the borders of my own country in a commercial vehicle in which I am subjected to customs and laws that are foreign to those of the United States. *A United States citizen should not be forced to leave his country as a job requirement if he does not choose to do so!* Many customs officials in both the United States and Canada have attitudes that are in the toilet. Most truckers are usually treated with the utmost disrespect. Being treated otherwise would be the exception rather than the rule.

Since the 9/11 attack on our country, there has been some kind of 'quick pass' introduced to large, well-established trucking companies that frequent Canada, so that their drivers get priority treatment at customs. Those drivers come into the customs building and are allowed to go to the head of the line in front of dozens of other drivers who have been waiting. I have seen as many as a dozen or more drivers from the same company trickle in like this with the 'quick pass' and walk in front of dozens of other patient drivers (including me) that were waiting their turn and then were caused to wait just that much longer. Somehow this does not seem right but the customs officials could care less how the now further detained drivers feel about it and in fact seem arrogant, almost daring someone to complain about it.

Yes, I have crossed the international border into Canada and back to the United States countless times over the years and I still dread going there. *Canada has different laws regarding logbooks and ignorance of them can cost you big money!* In Quebec Province, it can be difficult to find someone who even speaks English rather than French. They appear to dislike Americans because even those that do speak English seem to ignore you. You had better have your directions down pat before going into Montreal since even the signs are in French. Getting lost there is very easy even with good directions. Additionally, speed limits and critical clearances on bridges are in metric, adding to the confusion.

Clearing your load through customs can be a challenge. *Communication in advance with the shipper and the person or department in your company that handles this is required and imperative!* Even then things can go wrong because the so-called 'Canada experts' in your company may not be so expert. *There is no way to know how things will go until you actually get to the border!* You are at the whim of the customs officials! Mile long waiting lines and longer of trucks are not unusual. Then, be prepared to be quizzed by a customs agent as to who, what, when, where, why and how. *Beware of those clerks with a god complex!* Customs officials do wield a lot of power. Some of the customs agents can get a bit carried away with their own importance at the expense of the lowly truck driver. Be sure to hone up on your 'yes sirs' and 'no sirs' and have your identification and paperwork ready. After convincing the agent you are not a terrorist or some other subversive, you then get to go to a 'customs broker' who will shuffle your papers and give them back to you to take to the 'godlike' immigration authorities.

A border crossing can take from a few minutes to a few hours, depending on how good your company prepared things for you ahead of time. *Usually, this is not a happy event and pays zero to the driver for all the aggravation, frustration and lost time. Some of these eight to five, no talent clerks can make a truck driver's passage miserable for no apparent reason.*

It is also important to know that due to new laws regarding national security, in order to return to the United States from Canada you must now have your birth certificate or passport with you or *U.S. Customs will not allow you to return to the United States! Do not leave the country without one of these documents!* This also includes going into Mexico.

Again, any time a driver is requested to cross the borders of the United States into another country, he should have the option to refuse. No one should be forced to leave his homeland as a condition of employment in these troubled times. If he chooses to do so, he should receive a substantial bonus to compensate for his lost time and forced aggravation.

## 9. HAZARDOUS MATERIAL (HAZ-MAT)

Hauling hazardous materials requires special training. The driver is supposed to be well versed in what to do in regard to proper loading, placarding loads properly, restricted routes, monitoring the load enroute and what to in case of an accident or spill. All drivers are provided with an ATA (American Trucking Association) handbook and a complete HAZ-MAT (hazardous material) handbook. The latter has a complete list of every hazardous product, labels and placards for each with specific loading instructions. These are small pocket-sized books in fine print that are jam-packed with all the federal rules and regulations pertaining to truck drivers. The details are complete but very confusing to a layman truck driver, who's other skills and responsibilities are already overwhelming. Nevertheless, should anything be amiss with a HAZ-MAT shipment that may at any time be inspected by any law enforcement officer or weigh station, the trucker will be held responsible and can be assessed huge fines, far beyond his earning capabilities.

For instance, if the driver inadvertently fails to comply with the laws regulating such activity, he is subject to fines up to $15,000! If a driver forgets to remove placards after the load is off the truck he can be fined $15,000, even if the truck is empty! To expect this penalty of underpaid OVER THE ROAD truck drivers at this time under present conditions is unreasonable! It does not even make sense!

No other industry imposes such horrific penalties on its professionals or even close! OVER THE ROAD truck drivers do not earn enough money to face that much financial risk, but they have no choice in whether or not they will haul such a HAZ-MAT load. It is all part of the job!

If the size of the fines indicates the importance of the employee's position, it surely is not reflected in his pay! He gets no additional pay for this responsibility!

*The fact is that the risk is the greatest and the pay is the poorest of all.*

## 10. ENGINE IDLING SHUTDOWN LAWS

Here's a good one! Many states have anti-pollution laws requiring drivers to turn their engines off after *five minutes* idling. I have experienced some *shippers and receivers actually enforcing this law on their own* when truckers enter their premises and expect truck drivers to sit in their vehicles *without heat or air conditioning* until their trucks are loaded or unloaded, which can take several hours, even overnight.

For example, I once had to pick up a load in northern New York and it was cold and snowing. There was high wind and the temperature was in the twenties. My student pulled into a service plaza on the New York State Thruway and we were greeted with a large sign stating that there was a 5-minute time limit for engine idling and any longer than that would result in getting a $300 citation. Since it was cold and we were only making a quick 'pit stop', we left the engine running, as did all the other trucks that were parked with sleeping drivers in the nearby parking area. Seeing a parked state trooper (in an idling car) monitoring the idling trucks, we promptly left and proceeded to the shipper in an isolated, country location. Having arrived the night before our appointment time, we checked in at the office and were told we could not get loaded until the next day. We parked in their lot and left the engine running with the heater on all night to keep from freezing to death while we slept.

The shipping foreman came out in the morning and the very first thing he did was to inform us of the New York State idling law. He said that New York's idling law requires that the engine must be shut off if the temperature is over 29 degrees. I would remind you that water freezes solid at 30 degrees or so. But how is it that a shipper is more interested in this law than getting us loaded?

I experienced a similar situation when making a delivery in California, which also has an idling restriction law. It was a brutally hot afternoon and over 100 degrees but that made no difference to the receiver who insisted on truck engines being turned off, leaving the drivers without air conditioning. The indication at that time was that an enforcer would be called if drivers failed to comply.

My questions are, 'What do they expect us to do to keep from freezing to death? How do they expect us to get proper rest if we have to restart the engine for 5 minutes to get some heat each time it gets too cold to bear?' Additionally, after being turned off for awhile, it takes considerably longer than the allowable 5 minutes just for the engine to get hot enough to generate any heat. Few people can tolerate 100 + degree temperatures to sleep in. Everybody voices concerns about driver fatigue but the lawmakers seem to have no consideration about it as indicated by these kinds of laws.

You can be sure the police that enforce these laws do not turn off their engines when they are sitting in their patrol cars if the outside temperature will cause them personal discomfort. In fact, they rarely ever turn off their engines!

In other instances, should a driver ask his supervisor about the company providing him with a motel during a layover to eliminate truck idling, he will be told that his motel is his sleeper berth on the back of the cab. Then the driver managers *will advise running the engine to keep warm or cool (in spite of the law) as circumstances may require,* since most drivers cannot afford to go to a motel on their own, while at the same time his company fuel department issues notices for the drivers to reduce idling their engines to lower fuel costs. *The dilemma is whether or not to run the motor!* One department says one thing and another department contradicts it! The fact is *the company prefers the driver to stay in the truck for load and equipment security reasons and to prevent motel expenses! Circumstances and common sense dictate that the engine must be run for driver comfort, safety and security, law or no law!* Let those that think otherwise get in a truck for two or three hours in 100+ degree weather without an air conditioner and *they will soon change their thinking!*

There is a service called *Idle-aire* that charges by the hour for heating, cooling and communication services designed to allow drivers to turn their engines off to save fuel due to idling while parked in some truck stops. While this is great idea, it is cost-prohibitive to a driver that is being paid on a mileage basis. This is another example of mixing mileage pay with hourly regulation of cost. If the companies are willing to utilize this service at company expense, I can see where it would then be feasible. Ironically, that cost is more than most companies provide as layover pay to their drivers.

What about train locomotives that never shut down in the winter because they do not install antifreeze in the engines? Ships in port must surely consume a considerable amount of fuel. Airplanes suck up fuel like it is going out of style. And of course, the millions of automobiles that clog the highways every day during morning and evening rush hours. These various and numerous fuel hogs are rarely even mentioned in regard to fuel conservation and pollution. It is the trucks that have, once again, been singled out for chastisement. It does not matter that the drivers are actually *living in the trucks* and need the constant creature comfort afforded to the rest of the population in their houses and office buildings, or that their *safe driving depends on them having this creature comfort to get proper rest!* Even buildings ultimately cause the consumption of some kind of fuel to generate electricity required to operate their furnaces and air conditioners. Could it be that truck drivers are an easier target for law enforcement to generate revenue from? It certainly seems that way.

## 11. SAFE DRIVING

Avoiding accidents through safe driving habits is one of the *most important functions* of this profession. It is one thing to cruise down an interstate highway where there are no traffic lights or cross traffic. It is quite another to have to utilize smaller country or congested city roads, winding through small towns and narrow city streets where you have never been before. The reality of maneuvering this huge equipment in tight surroundings can sometimes be overwhelming. In the winter, plowed snow causes even tighter conditions in all areas. *Continually adjusting safe driving methods to constantly changing conditions is mandatory! Sharing the highways with all other traffic of different types can be a real challenge. Preventing and avoiding accidents is at the top of the safety list and job responsibilities! Defensive driving is of the utmost importance!*

## 12. INTERRUPTED SLEEP, A MAJOR CAUSE OF FATIGUE

Be prepared to be awakened from a deep slumber, many times for seemingly unnecessary or miniscule reasons at the whim of a customer or even another truck driver knocking on your door seeking information. This happens constantly, almost on a daily basis. When working for a company that uses the sat-com system you will learn to live by the 'beep' of technology summoning you to the screen for unlimited and many times unnecessary 'fleet' messages. Nevertheless, communication between the drivers and company personnel, shippers and receivers is absolutely necessary. *The nature of the business requires drivers' sleep to be constantly intruded upon under current conditions.*

## 13. DRIVERS TREATED LIKE MUSHROOMS

Certainly, if OVER THE ROAD trucking was professional in the way drivers were paid, truckers could afford to be more professional in their way of doing things, as in all other professions. Additionally, everybody expects OVER THE ROAD truck drivers to perform on a timely basis but few timely things are done for them in return. Drivers frequently have great difficulty in getting home on time for special occasions or at all, for that matter. Some are gone for months at a time. They also have little or no say in whether they get a long run, short run or a local, regardless of their preference. Often an OVER THE ROAD truck driver may be heard to say, "I feel like a mushroom because I am kept in the dark and fed bulls—t" when it comes to getting dispatched, especially when it is time to go home.

I know for a fact that those in planning and conveniently 'once removed' from dealing directly with drivers, that these 'planners' may get angry if a driver manager attempts to coerce the 'planner' to send any particular driver to any specific destination. I was told this by several well-meaning and honest operations people whom I had done favors for after bailing them out of a potential service failure. This indicates to me that 'planners' are either over-worked, uncaring, unknowing or all of these things. Certainly they seem to be impersonal, adding to the aspect of drivers becoming 'just a number'. They think nothing of wasting a day or two in the life of a truck driver, knowing full well that the driver will not be paid. Sometimes it appears that you have been completely forgotten about.

## 14. FLEET MANAGER, DRIVER MANAGER, DISPATCHER OR LOAD PLANNER

'Fleet manager' and 'driver manager' are titles that basically mean the same thing, depending on the company you work for. Their function is to interface the driver with all the many departments of the company, including operations. Pay issues, overweight problems and time off seem to be their primary responsibility, along with student coordination when applicable. When it comes to driver complaints regarding low mileage, you will be informed that load planners coordinate dispatching loads in conjunction with information supplied to the computer by the driver, pertaining to hours available. This is a modern method of 'buck passing' that removes your immediate company supervisor or 'driver manager' from having to hear complaints of this nature. So-called *'load planners' are conveniently inaccessible to drivers* for the most part. It would seem that dispatchers do not exist any more, as such. The end result is drivers that usually have no one to talk to about how to get more miles, a driver's only method of generating a paycheck. *This is a source of constant frustration for most OVER THE ROAD truck drivers!*

## 15. POOR DISPATCHERS

Those load planners, who may have been hired from answering newspaper ads from trucking companies needing dispatchers, generally have no concept of what it is like to be an OVER THE ROAD truck driver. Most have never even been inside a truck. They are blindly attempting to provide loads for drivers by computer. They are simply computer 'button pushers', matching up available loads with available drivers. The aggravation and anxiety these inexperienced and inept people bestow upon the OVER THE ROAD truck drivers is sometimes abominable! Again, the reason this situation exists is that there is absolutely no incentive for management to be efficient with or concerned about a drivers' time, *other than that the driver may quit!* This seems to have become an acceptable conclusion for truck driver's careers with most companies.

## 16. REPOWERS

'Repower' refers to when two drivers swap loads with each other to accomplish various things such as home time or service problems. This happens frequently and many times, one of the drivers ends up with the 'dirty end of the stick'.

The mindset of dispatchers, driver managers, fleet managers or whatever you want to call them seems to be," Tell the driver whatever he wants to hear", especially if they want you to do a re-power of another driver's load so he can go home for a so-called 'emergency'. As the driver giving up your load, you have no way to know if it is a bona-fide emergency or if the other driver may simply be trying to rid himself of a bad load and get under a better load that takes him home. It seems as though when a re-power is requested this is sometimes the case. In addition, the details of the load you will be getting are usually kept a closely guarded secret, apparently for fear you may refuse to do it because of losing miles or getting a difficult multi-stop load that will take several more days to deliver with less overall miles. Been there, done that!

Then after the driver doing the favor accomplishes his end of the re-power and saves their bacon, if the 'promises' made to him are found to be not doable, he ends up holding the short end of the stick! Additionally, there may not even be any offer of deals or concessions to the driver giving up his good load to another driver. If push comes to shove and a driver refuses to relinquish his load to another driver, he will be reminded that this was one of the 'tucked away' conditions he agreed to upon employment! Yes, this is especially frustrating when the truck driver doing the favor gives up a high mileage load going where he also wanted to go, in exchange for a low mileage multi-stop load into some dead end place and loses another day or two because of it *with no additional compensation!*

## 17. HIRE FROM WITHIN

There are some driver-oriented companies that seem to be trying to overcome or minimize these problems because they try to hire dispatchers mostly from their own driver pool. The most common and surest way for truck drivers to determine which companies promote better conditions for their drivers is by talking with each other in truck stops, at a customer or over the CB radio. It is these conscientious companies that should prevail while the others fall by the wayside because of losing their drivers due to less than acceptable conditions. It is a sorting out process at this time in more ways than one.

Professionals expect to be treated as such, even in the (unprofessional) transportation industry! Failure to do so will eventually push most of them on to greener pastures.

## 18. SEAL RECORDS

Keeping an accurate seal record can be of critical importance to pinpoint responsibility should a shortage or damage occur. Simply by writing SLC (shipper load and count) on the bill of lading when signing your name will legally indicate that you have not counted or checked the merchandise and are not responsible for any discrepancies. Be sure a seal is installed on the trailer doors and record the seal number on all copies of the bill of lading, including the shipper's copy. If the shipper will not install a seal, do it yourself and again, get the seal number on all copies of the bill. Use a padlock, too.

Some shippers will not allow the truck driver to notate 'SLC' on the B/L since it *does* relieve the driver of responsibility for the count. The question is, why *should* the driver be liable for product he has not counted and everybody *knows* he has not counted it? The whole idea is for the shipper to count, stage and load the trailer, then put a seal on the doors and for the driver to take the load to the consignee where they record and break the seal, then recount the product as they unload it, leaving the driver out of it. Should this occur and the shipper insists that you sign a clear B/L, your only option is to tell them to take their product back off the truck because you will not be responsible for it. You will have to be very assertive about this! This will undoubtedly result in a call to your company and your company will either authorize you to comply with the shipper's request or suggest some other action. Just be sure that whatever you do, you will not be subject to paying for merchandise that may not be on the trailer. Also, be sure that the seal that is installed on the trailer door matches your paperwork. Be sure to get the name of whomever you talk to and write it on the bill.

Another frustrating thing about all this is that many times it is very difficult for a driver to get someone to acknowledge the seal being intact upon delivery. This defeats the purpose of going to the effort to do all this. The logical people to check seals would seem to be security guards upon entering or exiting a facility. However, most of them refuse and tell the driver to get the receiver to sign for the seal. This usually results in the receiver telling the driver to 'go ahead and break the seal and bring it in'. If the driver does this, and most do to avoid a confrontation with the customer, responsibility then becomes a bit fuzzy. As long as everything was shipped accurately and everybody is honest there is not a problem but should a receiver claim there is a shortage, it can be a less than happy event. The best thing to do is to notify your dispatch and let them decide how to handle things *before breaking the seal.* Sometimes just saying to the customer that you will have to call your dispatcher can result in a signature that the seal was intact. In any case it will get you off the hook if you first clear it with your dispatcher. Be sure to keep a record of who you talked with at your company for future reference. Very important!

## 19. MORALS

Regarding OVER THE ROAD trucking, the general population many times thinks of truck drivers as unfaithful, adulterous lowlifes. Undoubtedly, there are some of these types involved in this career. However, many airline pilots, lawyers, politicians and others are also involved in adulterous affairs but are still well respected. Could it be, once again, the lack of a professional image? Of course, basic moral concepts and individual upbringing have a lot to do with this.

Other factors come into play here in regard to a man's integrity and faithfulness to his wife and family. Being on the road exposes you to many temptations that must be resisted or it can cost you everything you are struggling for. Prostitutes, adult bookstores and topless bars are commonplace, not to mention casinos and gambling. Each person needs to know his own limitations and must face them and overcome them when necessary to preserve his family. This is a double-edged sword—the wife at home must also be faithful.

## 20. INFIDELITY AND DIVORCE

It is a well-known fact that the divorce rate among truckers is very high. Is it any wonder that someone who is deprived of the companionship of their mate may fall into infidelity? Being gone for weeks and even months at a time with layovers and long periods of waiting being prevalent is not conducive to a strong marital relationship. While the truck driver is exposed to many temptations to go astray while on the road, his mate may also be lead astray at the home front. Some wives of truck drivers are so affected by the poor income and sparse relationship with their husband that they abandon their marriage, divorce, run off with other men and even contemplate suicide.

*This is a career that can test even the strongest of family relationships!* This is why single, unmarried folks have an advantage since the long periods away from home base can be intriguing and adventurous for them and temporarily become part of their way of life, unlike the family man that is mainly concerned with supporting his family and longs to be with them.

## 21. SPORADIC ACTIVITY

Frankly, you may spend all day delivering a load, then pick up another load and drive all night getting to the next delivery. It may then take all day to wait to deliver that load before you can pick up another. If you want to maximize your earnings, you must stay on top of all pickup and delivery appointments and get broken rest whenever possible while being loaded or unloaded so that you can safely reach each destination. In so doing you will be utilizing any down time to your best advantage, since the only pay is for the miles driven between loads. *It is usually entirely up to the driver to work it all out!* Logbooks do not realistically provide for this.

## 22. LUMPERS—LOADING AND UNLOADING FEES

There has long been a dispute or disagreement if you will, about who should physically load or unload the merchandise in the trailer; the warehouse employees or the truck driver. Since the warehouse has the option of routing loads by carriers that will abide by their demands, the truck driver has been caught in the middle and has been expected to do this work whenever demanded, until recent years. Laborers called 'lumpers' have taken on this obligation. Not that using lumpers is anything new, only now the trucking companies no longer expect the OVER THE ROAD drivers to pay for lumpers out of their pocket or do the work themselves, like it used to be. Too many good drivers have left the trade over this issue and companies can no longer afford to lose good drivers.

When you arrive at your delivery point, you will usually be asked whether or not you need a lumper (laborer), or if you want to unload the load yourself. Most drivers are not too excited about the thought of having to unload a trailer load of merchandise after completing several hundred miles in a run. This is usually a good time to get caught up on some rest. Even if a driver is well rested, many drivers to avoid the hassle and congestion of the receiving dock choose to use a lumper. The choice is usually yours. Of course, the cost of the lumper must be considered as well as several other things. Most receivers will let the lumpers use their power equipment but because of their liability will only supply a driver with a hand-operated pallet jack. The dock people tend to cooperate more with lumpers than a driver since they deal with them on a daily basis and lumpers are familiar with how things are done. All this can be aggravating to a driver and may cost you money out of pocket but can be worthwhile if it will get you unloaded faster so you can get to your next load. Most of the time you are better off to stick with the customer's program. If you have a regular customer, you do not usually have to deal with this because things can be worked out in advance.

Why are lumpers necessary? Who are they? Lumpers are independent laborers that load or unload trucks for an agreed upon amount determined by how much time and work is involved. They have no benefits, few rules and no regulations for the most part. They take on the duties of company paid warehouse workers in that they are present at these locations every day and have a working relationship with the warehouse or company personnel. They are usually allowed to use any company-owned power equipment necessary to accomplish the task. The cost to the shippers and receivers is nothing since the truck driver or his company must pay this charge. Anybody can be a lumper if they are physically and mentally capable.

Because it is difficult to retain the many new truck drivers coming into this field even without facing the unloading problem, most trucking companies have caved in to the shipper's and consignee's demands and agreed to pay these 'lumpers' to do this work, rather than risk losing their drivers because most drivers refuse to do it and will quit if forced to.

Let us be honest about this. Should an OVER THE ROAD truck driver really be expected to load and unload the truck? Does an airline pilot handle the baggage onto and off the plane? What about a railroad engineer? And those occupations are a breeze compared with most truck driving jobs.

What's more, should a truck driver decide to take on this chore for exercise or extra income, he will probably be expected to do it for far less compensation than a lumper would have gotten. The truck driver will also likely be required to use hand-operated, antiquated equipment that makes the job much more time consuming and physically difficult. Of course, this is to discourage truck drivers from taking work away from the lumpers. The lumpers depend on the company to provide enough work for them to make a living and the companies depend on the lumpers to accomplish their warehouse tasks at no cost to them. Everybody wins if the driver is able to catch up on his rest while the truck is being unloaded. Unfortunately, this does not put any money in the truck driver's pocket.

The simple unloading of a trailer involves more than you might imagine. There are many times dozens or even hundreds of different items that may have to be sorted out on separate pallets. The labels need to be facing out so the receiver can read them. The boxes cannot hang off the pallets or they will not fit in the pallet storage racks. The boxes must also be stacked or interlocked with each other on the pallet so they will not tip over or slide off. Each pallet needs to be strapped, taped or shrink wrapped by whoever unloads. Many other different type loads have many other requirements that the regular lumpers are very familiar with and an outside truck driver would have little idea about how to do. This is warehouse work, not that of a driver. Who do they think they are kidding?

Certainly the profitability of trucking companies is affected by this paying of lumpers, ultimately reducing the companies' profitability that in turn minimizes the possibility of driver pay increases. *This is another example of how everybody but the truck driver seems to be able to **demand and get** whatever they deem necessary for their time and efforts. And remember, all of these people go home every night and weekend!*

## 23. UNLOADING HASSLE

Upon arrival at a customer's facility to make a pickup or delivery, there are usually several other truckers already there. Let us assume that all these drivers arrived during the night for an early morning appointment for pickup or delivery. If the customer opens at 7 A.M. and there are 10 or 15 drivers or more in some cases, the morning usually starts out as a 'free for all' as to who is going to get loaded or unloaded first. Everybody tries to get into the building ahead of everybody else, especially if it is a first come, first serve facility rather than by appointment only. This is quite prevalent in the refrigerated business rather than dry freight, although it can happen in any kind of trucking from time to time. When it comes to getting loaded or unloaded, unfortunately most OVER THE ROAD truck drivers have little or no respect for other truck drivers. Crowding ahead and even bribing a receiving clerk to get unloaded first is not at all uncommon.

Getting to a customer at an appointed time is expected but if you are an hour or two early, some customers may tell you to come back at the designated time or have you park in a dirt lot with a portable toilet for facilities, if you are lucky!

Generally if all the drivers arrived during the night and are sleeping in their trucks, it is solely their own responsibility to wake up and check in with the receiver on time for their appointment, if they have one. Should they fail to wake up, chances are they will miss their appointment and may have to reschedule another one for later or even the next day. Occasionally someone from a facility will come out and wake the drivers up. In any case, once the drivers get up and go into the building to check in, it can be quite interesting.

Once inside everybody stands around looking at each other, making small talk while waiting for the receiver to appear or open the sliding window which may have a note saying, 'Do not tap on window' (god must be inside). When the receiver finally shows up he will usually be pre-occupied with other more important things than recognizing the presence of a bunch of unprofessional-looking truck drivers, such as rearranging pens and pencils, shuffling papers or pouring coffee. No eye contact or even the raising of a finger to acknowledge the drivers' presence. *Do not dare to interrupt him or her, as the case may be! God is collecting his thoughts.*

This waiting period may be 15 or 20 minutes or more and can have a demeaning effect on the drivers. After all, they *are* professional drivers who have just safely completed a run of several hundreds or even a couple thousand miles, with a piece of equipment probably worth well over a hundred thousand dollars, carrying product worth thousands that had been ordered by the company where they are and the person in charge (god), will not even acknowledge their presence. Drivers are made to feel like a useless commodity, basically put on hold until convenient. This happens frequently! Prepare for it! This is not a pleasant part of trucking but I doubt if it will change any time soon!

When the receiver (god) finally gets around to communicate with the drivers as to the product they have on and any appointment times, a sour attitude is not uncommon. Then he will assign each driver a door and may ask if they need a lumper. If so, the driver must find the lumper and make arrangements for unloading and payment thereof. The lumper then takes over the load and gets it off the truck after the driver backs into the loading dock and secures his rig.

It can be very interesting to watch the confusion and impatience of these same (professional) drivers after they are assigned a dock to back into to get unloaded. I have seen them crowd ahead of each other, block each other's docks and generally cause mass confusion when trying to beat each other to the yard or dock. It can be a ridiculous mixture of seasoned and inexperienced drivers vying for position with no regard for one another, being totally unprofessional in their actions! Very embarrassing!

That is just one example. There are countless others!

By the time all this takes place and the driver is on his way to pick up another load, many hours without pay have been lost. Worse yet, if there are no loads available, he may have to wait until the following day for his next load, without compensation. Additionally, all this time is expected to be logged as 'on duty, not driving', which means the driver will have that many fewer hours to drive and earn a paycheck. You must realize that this is probably his only source of income. Last but not least, *the drivers have been demoralized and made to feel like second-class citizens for accomplishing their mission without compensation. Their attitudes are now in the toilet!*

Regulating trucking by the hour with logbooks while paying them by the mile is not unlike mixing oil with water. It does not work! *A truck driver's time needs also to be considered in the pay package!*

## 24. THE INVISIBLE MAN—MASKING YOUR EMOTIONS

Some people seem to have been born to make life miserable for truckers! It is surprising how many different people truckers deal with who fail to even acknowledge the driver's presence upon arrival. As previously explained, many times there is no eye contact, nod of the head, raising of a finger or a spoken word; nothing! It is almost as if the drivers are invisible!

This takes place constantly at shippers, receivers and even your own company's dispatch window. Any facial expression by the driver indicating impatience, anger or frustration had better be totally suppressed! Shaking of the head, twisting of the mouth and other such negative contortions are not at all helpful and may slow things for you considerably. *Remember, your time is costing them nothing, so they can jerk you around at their pleasure and keep you twisting in the wind indefinitely!*

You would do well to master the 'blank stare' expression of uncaring, even though you may be furious! Those in the window prefer a 'zombie like' attitude. Then, when they finally recognize your presence you had best have your thoughts and information in order or you will go back to the end of the line until you do. Their time is obviously far more important than yours.

I have no doubt that if these same truck drivers wore uniforms and it was common knowledge that they were paid professionally which included being paid for waiting around, they would be treated with much greater respect just as UPS and Wal-Mart drivers are. Someone would become responsible for costly delays of drivers.

## 25. COMMUNICATION—YOU NEED VOICE CONTACT

Communication plays a major role in trucking. How and with whom you communicate, as well as how often, can make a major difference in your earnings. Yes, most companies have some kind of instant communication right in the cab of the truck but unless you can actually talk to the people you are dealing with, a lot can be lost in the translation.

A mobile phone is mandatory!

Getting to a customer on time, then being told over a squawk box to go park your truck and wait for the next phase in your activity with no indication of how much time is involved and knowing you will be paid nothing for it is normal. Since everybody knows OVER THE ROAD truck drivers are on a mileage pay basis, including and especially the customers, nobody is concerned about delays of any kind because it costs them nothing. In fact, they take advantage of it! The only one who really cares is you!

Knowing how to speak Spanish or at least understanding it can be advantageous since many customers speak it and often (rudely) use it in your presence, seemingly (to them) putting you at a disadvantage or in an inferior position as they visit with each other while you stand by. This is very common and very inconsiderate. If someone is going to live and work in any country other than their own, they should learn the language. Most Mexicans are nice people but this is the United States of America, not Mexico! English is still the primary language, for now.

Rest assured that should you decide to take a nap while waiting, as soon as you get into a deep slumber someone will be knocking on your door to have you move to another dock or some other mundane thing. Getting loading or unloading completed usually only happens after three or four sleep interruptions unless you are lucky. This is being mentioned again because of the fatigue factor.

Should you miss your delivery appointment time, it can result in the customer rejecting the load or putting you on standby until last. Your company may also give you some kind of reprimand or 'black mark' on your record up to and including termination if it happens too often. This is why communication is critical should you get delayed for any reason. Updated ETAs (estimated time of arrival) via sat-com are very important to cover your tail should delays happen.

## 26. PARK AND SLEEP—BEWARE OF MUGGERS

Finding a suitable place to stop and sleep can many times be a challenge. Sometimes it seems like everybody hates or dislikes trucks. 'No Truck' signs are everywhere! Parking is often a problem. *But they all want what trucks carry!*

In any case, do not drive when tired! Park it and get some sleep! You will wake up refreshed and ready for action in a safe and rested condition.

For your personal safety, always try to find a well-lighted place to park such as a truck stop or rest area. These locations usually become more full as the night wears on. RVs and campers are becoming more of a problem taking up spaces in the designated truck parking instead of using the areas designated for them that can many times have plenty of room for RVs but are not conducive to trucks. Parking lots at Wal-Mart 24-hour Supercenters are becoming more popular with many OVER THE ROAD truckers because of the economy of acquiring supplies at a reasonable price and 24-hour rest room facilities access. Shopping malls can sometimes be utilized but facilities can be very limited other than simply a well-lit place to park a few hours.

There are many other supermarket chains that allow OVER THE ROAD truckers to stop, shop and park for the short term, most without after-hour facilities.

Most modern strip mall shopping centers are designed specifically to discourage big trucks from entering the parking area for automobiles. The lane openings are placed too close together to allow large trucks to maneuver into the parking area without running over the curbs or crushing shrubbery. Others have overhead barriers. It is obvious that trucks are not welcome.

When you are parked in an unfamiliar area not related to your getting loaded or unloaded, do not respond to any knocks on the door or even shouting to arouse you. It does not matter who it is as long as you are parked legally and out of the way. *It could be a thief, panhandler, druggie, mugger or some other unpleasant entity.* Since you are a total stranger to the area, it certainly will not be someone inviting you to a party. Usually nothing good can come from such a visit. Let them knock and shout and beat on the cab but do yourself a favor and do not make eye contact with whoever it is or they have you. The best thing to do is completely ignore them, roll over and go back to sleep.

In some states, should you park on an exit or entrance ramp to sleep, the highway patrol will wake you up and tell you to move or give you a citation, no matter how tired you are. What about safety now? What about no hours available in your logbook?

Generally, there are a few trucks periodically returning to the road from truck stops and rest areas that open up a few parking spots from time to time during the night. It sometimes pays to make a swing through the parking lot and find one of these. However, rest areas are usually parked so full with the trucks parked so close together as to prevent even passing between them on the right of way to return to the highway. I fail to understand what those parked drivers expect other truckers to do. In such a case, asking them to move can be the only option. West-coast mirrors are broken this way.

## 27. PARKING IN TRUCK STOPS AND CUSTOMERS

When entering a truck stop or customer parking lot at night it can be helpful to others if you douse your headlights as a courtesy to those who may be attempting to back into a parking spot. It is difficult enough to back into many of the tight spaces without being blinded by someone inconsiderate enough to leave his headlights on if his truck is aimed in your direction. Headlights glaring into your west-coast mirrors can also have a totally blinding effect, especially if the mirrors are dusty or wet from rain. We need all the help we can get out here. Being considerate of others and working together means a lot. Rude, selfish and uncaring people have no place in the transportation industry. This profession is tough enough without them. Unfortunately, they will always be present. The rest of us many times must struggle to maintain control of our emotions toward their ignorance and have patience with them. Hopefully, someday things will improve.

Finding a parking space in a truck stop after 6 PM can be a difficult search. In many areas, the truck stop parking lots start filling up in late afternoon and by nine or ten at night there are few if any spaces left. Generally, the reason for the few spaces that may be still open is that nobody could back into them due to space limitations. There are times when it makes more sense to find a shopping mall or supermarket nearby that allows truck parking.

# 13.

# TRUCKERS NEED A VOICE

As individuals, there are a great many truck drivers' complaining voices disappearing into thin air. *Without some kind of organized representation to funnel these complaints into one loud voice that can be heard by those that can effect change, it is going to be a long and difficult struggle to improve things.* Risk and responsibility does not begin to be commensurate with pay at this time, in most cases. For a person to commit his time and effort 24 hours a day, seven days a week to a company and trust that company to provide work and instead, his wife be in despair and crying because they cannot pay their bills, does not make any sense. This is commonplace and can sometimes be overheard in conversations in truck stop phone rooms as drivers talk with their spouses. *It is a shameful situation and totally demoralizing!*

Obviously, the government is concerned about the possibility of such a large labor force being in a position of shutting the country down with a work stoppage, and nobody else wants that to happen either. Deregulation seems to have been the remedy for preventing this by de-unionizing trucking, if you will. But what may have been considered good for government, big business and the public has resulted in going far beyond what was needed and/or intended in regard to truck driver pay and benefits. It has been a direct cause of the present dilemma in this field that we are now all facing; *truck driver shortage and safety on the highways!*

## 1. OWNER-OPERATOR INDEPENDENT DRIVER'S ASSOCIATION (OOIDA)

There is an organization called *Owner-Operator Independent Drivers Association* (OOIDA). This organization is based in Independence Missouri and represents many truck drivers and owner-operators in Washington, D.C. Possibly, if all drivers became members of this group, changes could eventually be implemented. There simply is no other representation I am aware of. The toll free number is 1-800-444-5791. Their advertisement is as follows:

> For 30 years the Owner-Operator Independent Drivers Association has been dedicated to protecting the rights of professional truckers—owner-operators, company drivers and small fleet owners.
>
> No other organization works harder than OOIDA to speak up for truckers' rights on regulatory and legislative issues and defend them from unfair treatment and violations of the federal truth-in-leasing regulations.

Your support and participation are vital in helping us achieve continued success. Join the nearly 120,000 members of OOIDA in giving truckers a voice.

This is the only large national organization that is actively supporting truck drivers, other than the Teamster's Union. Financial support of this organization to the fullest by OVER THE ROAD truckers obtaining membership might result in powerful representation of OVER THE ROAD truck drivers and dramatic improvement in conditions. However, OOIDA has been aware of all these problems for many, many years and although minor improvement for drivers has taken place in some areas, the major problems and causes of those problems regarding pay and conditions have been left intact. This organization specializes mainly in owner-operator concerns, not so much company drivers.

## 2. REPRESENTATION IS NEEDED

If the many unhappy and disgruntled OVER THE ROAD truck drivers all joined this OOIDA, it might result in some kind of positive influential representation. The key to doing this is getting *driver participation*. However, it is a well known fact that any two truck drivers rarely stick together on issues of this nature, or anything for that matter. This can also be very difficult since many drivers either simply cannot afford even the small dues involved to become a member or they are skeptical that it would do any good. The truck driver must somehow be made to realize the strength there is in numbers and that he needs representation if he is ever going to get a fair day's pay for a fair day's time and effort.

In my opinion, the Teamster's Union is not the answer. They have been shown to cause nearly as many problems as they resolve. Most unions get into nit-picking, childish situations that become very emotional and do not amount to a 'hill of beans'. There are too many rules and regulations for the average 'Joe' to even understand. Lawyers and arbitrators become routine, instead of working things out like adults and getting back to work without the threat of a strike or work stoppage. It becomes a war of wills and game of 'who has the most power'? The lawyers and arbitrators end up with the money! Everybody else loses.

Ultimately, there is no reason most OVER THE ROAD non-union truck drivers should be looked at as less than highly respected and well-paid professionals other than the greed and ineptitude of those controlling the money! Could it be that it is meant to be otherwise so that truck drivers cannot unite as a powerful labor group? Who is going to listen to a bunch of disorganized, rag-tag, sloppy looking truck drivers? The answer is, nobody!

Owner-operators are another story. However, those that are merely exchanging a company driver's job to be an 'owner-operator' or 'lease-operator' in name only need to look at things a lot closer before jumping from the frying pan into the fire.

## 3. THREAT TO SAFETY

Please understand I am not trying to unduly denigrate the trucking industry. Rather, I am hoping to provide information to help sort things out and somehow assist in eventually solving some of these ongoing problems by creating dialog. Trucking has been my life and it bothers me to see what has happened to trucking as a professional career in my lifetime.

*Deregulation of trucking has caused it to deteriorate into a career plagued by misfits, oddballs and degenerates behind the wheel of monsters on the highways that threaten all our lives!* It has surely become the 'unprofessional profession'. It seems as though deregulation has opened the door for multitudes of less than desirables to become truck drivers as an escape from becoming homeless vagrants or welfare recipients, in some cases. A big truck with a sleeper berth provides not only a place to live, but also an income. It can also provide a threat to the safety of all others on the highway if it is in the wrong hands!

## 4. OVER THE ROAD DRIVERS DOING CITY DELIVERIES

Present day OVER THE ROAD trucking is entirely different from the past. The drivers are generally assigned to a truck with a large live-in sleeper unit attached and are expected to maintain an RV (recreational vehicle) type lifestyle, combined with a job. Most of the time these drivers are required to single-handedly accomplish transporting loads from one location to another somewhere in the United States and/or Canada.

The drivers are also expected to become familiar with all the transportation laws and regulations related to nationwide U.S. and Canadian OVER THE ROAD transportation and comply with them. Most of the runs are irregular and the drivers must go wherever they are 'force dispatched' with little or no say in the assignment. If they get delayed for a day or two or three or even more, many times there is little or no compensation for time lost. Being away from home with little likelihood of getting there any time soon does not make it any easier. Law enforcement shows little or no consideration for the OVER THE ROAD trucker's plight. Instead, *they capitalize on the newcomer's lack of knowledge and expertise* by preying upon them to generate revenue if they should inadvertently violate some law.

## 5. BEAUTIFUL TRUCKS VS. PAY AND BENEFITS

In my lifelong experience as a trucker, most OVER THE ROAD truck driver pay has always been sub-standard except union pay, which is also borderline, but union drivers get many benefits that non-union drivers do not enjoy such as company paid-for pension plans and medical benefits. The downside for union drivers is that their trucks are usually of the stripped-down day-cab version, generally without frills or comfort and they must pull double and triple trailer combinations, which I consider very dangerous.

Now the deregulated companies can provide beautiful, ego-enhancing trucks, but offer few or no benefits for the drivers. It would seem that you cannot have it both ways. Many of these companies offer insurance, partially paid for by the driver and some provide 401K pension plans. All have far lower pay per mile, usually combined with no pay for down time. This has become accepted as standard, industry-wide.

Upon entry into the OVER THE ROAD driving profession, many *new drivers are more concerned with what truck they will drive and how fast it will go than what the pay will be.* However, as time goes by, they generally begin to realize that *pay and conditions are the things that matter most* and fast trucks cause speeding tickets that are very costly as well as jeopardizing their CDL.

## 6. EMPLOYMENT CONTRACTS

Some OVER THE ROAD trucking companies have employment contracts spelling out the many negative events that can happen and the driver's responsibility for preventing them, as well as the many tasks and job functions that must be performed, all *without any mention of additional compensation to the driver for doing these things!* In some cases, the driver is expected to pay partial restitution for any damage he may incur as a result of his activity. This can go into the thousands of dollars and will be deducted from his pay. I always thought this was considered a cost of doing business and do not think this practice is legal.

I can remember one incident where one of my new trainees tore the fenders and hood off another truck as he made a too-short turn when rushing into a service area, resulting in many thousands of dollars in damage. He became distraught and broke into tears, exclaiming that he just ruined his new career and would now be without a job. In calming him down, I reassured him that he not only did not ruin his career but would now be *assured* of a job so that he could pay his share of the damage. It was a bittersweet reassurance but factual. Unfortunately, this accident instantly put the other driver of the damaged vehicle out of work, probably without compensation until he could acquire another truck, however long that might take.

Something to consider is the recent upheaval in many states when the politicians got into a hassle with thousands of government union employees over their (bankrupt) budgets. There were riots in the streets in some states while in others, the news media barely knew there had been a problem. Some Governors were adept at dealing with the problem, others created near disasters by going head to head with the unions. I am not going to get into any details but the point is, under similar circumstances, the winners were those who communicated with each other in a reasonable manner and reached an agreeable decision. This is what is needed in trucking. Fair and reasonable negotiations to a satisfactory conclusion. We all know the tremendous problems that exist, now we all need to get serious about working on them.

# 14.

# OWNING A TRUCK

*Remember, driving a truck is one thing; owning one is quite another!*
Yes, there is a lot of money in trucking! But the thing to remember is that, as in any business, to be successful *you must take in more than you pay out!* And in trucking, there are so many variables that this can be very difficult to accomplish. You do not want to get into a situation where you are simply 'handling' a lot of money, taking it in with one hand and passing it out with the other. This happens all too often if you get into the wrong plan with many companies. *Before you realize what is happening, you are buried in debt,* 'robbing Peter to pay Paul', as the old saying goes. The truth is that the 'owner and lease operators' may be making the payments on the truck but it is doubtful that they will ever really own it because the deck is stacked against them.

For example, if you get a contract with a company to work for 80 cents per mile (CPM) and they run you 3000 miles in one week, it represents $2400. That seems like a lot of money. But if you need $1000 a week for your pay (which you can probably earn as a company driver), that only leaves $1400 for the truck payment, insurance and fuel, not to mention many other expenses. Fuel alone will eat up most of that. The money disappears rather quickly. Before you realize it, your operating expenses can cut deeply into your $1000 per week paycheck.

*Good record keeping is important!* Keep a daily record of all your expenses. A laptop computer can be helpful for this. It is important to resist the temptation to buy boats, motorcycles and other 'toys' until your business has proven to be successful. When the big checks start coming in you must realize that most of that money is already spoken for to make truck payments, buy fuel, insurance, maintenance and other mandatory expenses.

There *are* some profitable owner-operator trucking ventures but most are one on one and *require intense effort to succeed and continue to succeed.* The mistake most people make after they find their 'niche' is that they get tired of doing it themselves and hire a driver so they can sit back and enjoy the profits. This is when they lose control.

Nobody else is going to continually perform as good as you because it is not their truck or their business. They may do great for a while but eventually it gets boring for them too. Their personal life takes priority. They tear up your equipment. They have accidents. Soon, you are searching for another driver. Then another. Yes, it is usually relatively easy to find drivers for the classic style big trucks with long square hoods, big engines, high speeds and all the bells and whistles. But remember, it is *your* baby, not theirs. *You* will be responsible for making the monthly payments and performing the maintenance. Nevertheless, in the unlikely event you succeed it is all worth it!

These huge classic style 'dream' trucks are mighty impressive. They really are beautiful. *Owning and/or driving a big truck can be an ego trip! It is unlike anything else! It is an emotional experience!* As it turns out, many drivers are enchanted with the idea of 'owning their own truck' for many different reasons. And once they acquire one, it seems to become a part of them. No matter what happens, they do not want to lose it. It 'gets in your blood'!

Especially for those with pride of ownership who enjoy tinkering, cleaning, polishing and puttering. This becomes their hobby as well as their career. Trucks can be very cosmetic. Many times the income becomes secondary. This type individual is not concerned with how much money he can earn with the truck as long as he can meet all his obligations and still has time to frequent truck stops and swap yarns with his peers. Unfortunately, this attitude can eventually end up in financial disaster.

Some of the more successful owner-operators like to customize their 'dream machines' and enter them in truck shows and parades. Periodically, you will see some of them featured in trucking publications with pictures and background stories. This is America at it's best. It shows that the individual can still make a difference that all others can respect. Not getting lost in society is still okay; the free spirit still exists. These are a special breed and should be acknowledged as such. Many of these truckers are actually doing quite well, financially. However, it usually takes many years acquiring experience and developing customer relationships for this to take place. *It is not going to happen at 80 CPM!*

## 1. OWNER-OPERATOR AND LEASE-OPERATOR

Independent contractor, owner-operator and lease-operator mean basically the same thing. The driver is now a self-employed entrepreneur and responsible for everything previously paid for by the company with no guarantee of income. *This frees the trucking company of all obligations to the driver as an employee and to the truck as to costs for maintenance and repairs.*

A former student of mine in our company indoctrination (training) program told me the following story about entering the field of trucking. After schooling and training with his initial company by passing through the brief two-week training school period and three weeks on the road with an OTR trainer, they coerced him to go immediately into their lease-operator program in partnership with another first-time driver. Together, they *consistently averaged 7000 miles per week* at 80CPM with a brand new truck. To their disappointment, *the bottom line was only a few hundred dollars each per week,* hardly enough to justify the time and effort. They both gave up the truck and quit their jobs after a four-month attempt no hope of success.

What's concerning about this is that so many people seem to be intrigued with the idea of being not just a truck driver but also an owner-operator, *and know nothing about it!* It is very easy to disillusion yourself as a company driver that becoming a lease or owner-operator there will be better conditions and you think you can make more income. There are many expenses that must be considered. Yes, you should make considerably more *gross* income but *it is the net income, or what is left after expenses that matters!*

In these times of driver shortages, high maintenance costs and soaring fuel prices, most trucking companies have found it is to their advantage to encourage drivers to "own" or "lease" their own truck from the company and thereby more or less 'lock them in' as drivers for an agreed upon period of time. The need for good, dependable drivers has far outstripped the supply of people willing to put up with the pay and conditions of OVER THE ROAD trucking for any prolonged length of time. *This has led to the many owner-operator programs designed to entice people with an entrepreneurial spirit to 'come on in suckers, the water's fine',* thereby entangling them for the long term.

This puts the driver into a self-employed category whereby he now must realize that his company benefits change dramatically! *Basically, he does not have any now!* It is for these very benefits, regular pay and steady work that most people hire on as company drivers.

## 2. DRIVER SHORTAGE MAKES IT EASY TO BUY A TRUCK AND GO BROKE

Presently, many of these trucking companies desperate for drivers are encouraging those who stumble in to become involved in a lease or owner-operator program, regardless of their background or qualifications. If they can pass the preliminary requirements (warm body), the company will usually sign them up to 'buy' or 'lease' a truck, no credit check! These companies provide the training, the truck, the financing and everything else necessary to comply with the various state and federal requirements. They really have made it easy for the unwary individual to become deeply involved before he realizes what he has gotten himself into. All this would be fine if the reward justified the effort. But this is not usually the case. Many of these unsuspecting individuals have gotten into deep financial trouble over this and many others have had to go bankrupt. It all sounds real good up front but beware!

An interesting item I heard on a radio talk show stated that ten percent of the State of Illinois' work force consisted of truckers. It also said that thirty nine thousand (39,000) owner operators from Illinois were quitting, regardless of a five to seven cents per mile fuel surcharge that was coming into effect. The increase just was not enough for them to be able to make it!

## 3. TRUCKS ARE EXPENSIVE TO OWN

The idea of 'own your own truck, be your own boss' can become a burning desire if you have never tried it. These big trucks are beautiful and have fantastic visual and physical appeal, especially to someone who has never earned a lot of money and may have thought such a purchase was out of the question. These folks tend to see only what they want to see and ignore the fact that there are many huge financial responsibilities connected with such an obligation, many of them 'hidden'.

Many of the modern trucking companies have made it *too* easy for these people to get into a truck lease or purchase plan if they are simply willing to drive the truck. Forgive me for belaboring the obvious, but the trucking companies are trying to shift responsibility and efficiency of operations from themselves to those who have little or no experience in such matters and whether or not they fail seems to be of little or no concern to those in management.

By doing this, the company has solved several major problems. They have assured the company of a driver, obligated him for the truck payments and maintenance and a myriad of other savings to the company become automatically effective in the process, most at the expense of the new 'owner'. *Now the obligation for the truck payment, insurance and fuel lies squarely on the driver who is totally dependent on the company to provide enough work to be successful, with no guarantee of any kind!*

When no credit check or down payment is required for such a high cost item, a bright red flag should go up to the driver. Use your common sense! The advice of a lawyer, accountant or financial advisor is definitely in order *before signing!*

## 4. ROUTINE FLEET MAINTENANCE GOES UNNOTICED

It is important to realize that as a company driver, you may pull the company truck into the safety lane at the company repair facility and get the truck checked out and serviced, things repaired or replaced, then be on your way. All you generally experience is a break in your activity as a driver while all this is being done, at company expense. Tires and batteries are replaced, oil changed, grease job, defects repaired, brakes and clutch adjusted and many other preventive maintenance tasks taken care of without a driver's concern. Magically, almost, everything is fixed or maintained at no awareness to the driver as to the cost. Warranty issues are handled with the power of fleet ownership.

This is the advantage of fleet maintenance, buying in bulk or large quantities, and having your own mechanics rather than the sixty to one hundred dollars per hour of a public garage or truck stop. As a company driver, if you are driving a new company truck with low mileage, it may seem that it seldom if ever has any problems. This, of course, is the way it should be if you work for a successful, up-to-date company with a good maintenance program. However, even these new trucks require considerable preventive maintenance. And it is all done in a routine manner that is hardly noticeable to the driver while he is in the office taking care of driver clearance procedures or watching movies in the driver's lounge.

As a company driver, when it comes time to take a week or two off, he can put his personal things in storage and turn in his truck for someone else to drive. When he returns, he will be issued another fresh truck, many times brand new!

## 5. OWNER-OPERATOR HAS TO PAY

Everything changes if you become a 'lease' or 'owner-operator'. Suddenly, the maintenance and repairs become noticeable because now they are going to come out of your pocket! All those 'little things' that went unnoticed before as a company driver are suddenly being deducted from your settlement check. They now take on new meaning! *It is not free after all!* Additionally, you will now forfeit all personal insurance, benefits and any paid time off for vacations or holidays! You will have to provide your own workmen's compensation, or it's equivalent. To put it bluntly, you are 'running bare' until you provide all the necessary benefits, *at your expense!*

*You* must now pay for the tolls, the fuel, and the wash jobs, as well as countless other small things that may have never entered your mind as a company driver. These are just a few of the things that must be looked at now, so that you can be made aware that it is a whole new ball game once you sign your name on the dotted line and leave the umbrella of company employment.

I suspect that when the company shop does work on their lease or owner-operator's trucks that there may be a profit of some kind there for the company also. Since they are hiring full time mechanics by the hour to maintain the company fleet, why not charge 'outside' trucks similar to a public repair shop? Not only does it provide more work for the mechanics, but helps increase the overall profit picture of the company. If the hourly rate to 'in-house' trucks is less than an outside repair shop, everybody wins.

Several times I have seen two or three owner-operators talking to each other in truck stops practically in tears because they were not making it. This is a tough business! I overheard one owner-operator say he had been successful in every business he ever tried but trucking was just too much for him!

On the other hand, some of the more realistic programs may work if the driver is willing and able to fully commit himself and his time to become completely engrossed in his truck as an 'investment'. This can be a very difficult thing to do, especially if they have a young family depending on them to be present at special occasions and events, unless they have other sources of income. Individual circumstances make a big difference. *A working wife with family medical benefits or additional income from a pension from a previous job can make all the difference!* It is also a big advantage if there are small or no car or house payments. All these things must be considered! Otherwise, you can end up working for just a few cents per mile because most of the earnings can go to pay for benefits and truck expenses.

Look at it like this. As a company driver you can usually earn from 30 to 50 cents per mile, depending on who you drive for and how long. Benefits such as insurance, workman's compensation, Social Security, medical, vacation pay and usually several others are at least partially provided as part of the pay package.

However, as an owner or lease-operator that takes in 80 to 90 cents per mile in most cases, you are generally required to pick up all these costs and more. Because of the variables, it is impossible to put a cents per mile number on what most of these plans *really* pay to a driver. If you figure just 30 CPM for your pay and add in the cost of fuel, the truck payment or lease, not to mention maintenance, insurance for yourself and the truck plus countless other obligations, the margin of profit has got to be mighty slim. Many of these truckers are hanging on by a thread, trying desperately to keep from going broke or bankrupt. If you give up a job that pays 35 to 40 CPM or more, you will definitely suffer a severe pay cut! A good share of the money that would have gone into your pocket will go to pay truck expenses, leaving you with whatever is left, if anything.

Additionally, as an owner-operator, any prolonged time off for vacations or family obligations can cut deeply into the necessary time required to produce income. *This is a long-term obligation and your life now belongs to the trucking and finance companies for the duration of the contract.*

An important thing to remember when leasing or buying a truck is that there are only twelve payments in fifty-two weeks when making payments by the month whereas there are fifty-two payments when made by the week. This means the lender has gotten an additional (month) payment from you each year since twelve times four weeks would only be forty-eight weeks.

For example, if the monthly payment is $2000 a month, that would be $24,000 per year. If the payment was made weekly at $ 500 per week, it would total $26,000 a year. Making weekly payments would cost you $2000 more per year. Easy money for the lender with less risk, since if weekly payments get behind, the lender has more time to enforce payment collection instead of waiting for a whole month or two to pass.

## 6. TRUCKS REPOSSESSED

I heard on the radio that after the price of fuel escalated in early 2001, *close to a billion dollars worth of trucks were turned in or repossessed by finance companies that year for non-payment.* Imagine all the lives that were negatively affected by that!

If the profitability of a trucking operation hinges on the price of fuel, it may not have been very stable to begin with. Fuel surcharges may be assessed to help compensate for these increases but they usually are not enough and take awhile to become effective, during which time the trucker must absorb the cost. Additionally, although a fuel surcharge may be assessed to compensate for higher priced fuel, some companies pass little or none of the surcharge on to their owner or lease-operators. It is important to monitor your settlement sheets very closely and keep on top of things. The profitability of your business depends on it. Since truckers must be on the road constantly, staying on top of paperwork can be a problem unless you have a regular run that will get you to your mail often or have someone you can trust to handle it. Again, a laptop computer can help here, especially if your company of choice utilizes computer payout records.

## 7. BREAKDOWN ON THE ROAD

Something else to consider is a breakdown on the road. Should this happen, you may be required to call a wrecker to take the disabled unit to a repair shop. This cost is usually around $150 per hour from the time the wrecker starts out until he returns to his point of origin or up to $10 per mile or more, with a minimum charge of $150 or more. The rates at the repair shop will run from $60 to $100 per hour. Take a look at the list of labor rates and prices in any truck stop repair shop. It can be very disheartening to see the mechanic go to the time clock, punch in on your job, then in slow motion head for the coffee pot as he lights up a cigarette. Cab fare to a motel, motel charges, meals and unproductive time can eat a big hole in your overall profitability. *Trucking is a high cost business and the expenses continue on, no matter what else happens!*

## 8. REDUCING OVERHEAD

Of course, many single OVER THE ROAD drivers may still live at home with their parents or live in the truck, not having to be concerned with rent, buying a house and all that goes with it. These people have a definite advantage and a much better chance of being successful. As long as they have some spending money they are not interested in how much they earn per mile or any other way. They just enjoy riding down the road in their 'dream machine'.

Others that have a working spouse may not have to pay for health insurance benefits if the spouse acquires coverage through their employer. This is definitely a major cost-saver. All of these things and more figure into the profitability of an individual's OVER THE ROAD trucking operation. In a way, assistance of this nature can be looked upon as subsidy and at only 80 to 90 CPM you will need all the help you can get. Frankly, I feel *there is something very wrong with a profession or business that cannot stand fully on it's own merit.* Living with parents or income from pensions or other personal resources should not be necessary for the success of any business.

## 9. CUSTOM MADE TRUCKS ARE SAFER

Years ago, size of equipment laws severely restricted the overall length of truck-trailer combinations. This resulted in the development of what was referred to as COE (cab over engine) trucks that could comply with the laws and were more maneuverable in tight quarters. However, most truck drivers preferred to drive (long nose) conventional trucks for comfort and safety reasons. With the advent of deregulation, length laws were relaxed to attract more badly needed OVER THE ROAD drivers into the industry to assist in reducing driver shortage and excessive driver turnover. This ultimately resulted in companies and owner-operators changing over to longer wheel-based tractors with far more comfortable living quarters for use in long haul trucking operations.

Custom-made trucks for owner-operators definitely have a more solid, sturdy feel to them, especially if they are of the good old 'classic' style with a long hood and oversize steering wheel. They handle better and are safer to drive because they do not 'wander' like most company trucks of today. The larger, thicker steering wheel holds the truck on a truer track and affords much better handling. It only makes sense that the smaller the steering wheel, the quicker and shorter the steering action will be which can cause the driver to lose control. Many of today's company trucks sport smaller steering wheels due to the power steering. *This causes the drivers to be constantly 'steering' the truck rather than the truck hugging the road on track, if you will, 'holding it's own'.* Only those that have driven both kinds realize the difference.

Power steering in trucks is one of the modern engineering designs that I feel has been somewhat counter productive in regard to driver enjoyment and safety in trucking. A quick jerk on the steering wheel in an emergency situation can result in loss of control whereby the truck may run off the road or even roll over from a sudden shift in weight. Should a steering tire drop off onto the shoulder of the road, it can cause instant loss of control. *I fear today's power steering, to appease new 'modern age' truck drivers such as the 'weaker sex', if you will, may have caused another safety problem.*

Most of the current 'owner-operators' acquire their trucks through a driver purchase or leasing plan involving aerodynamically styled fleet equipment, rather than the classic style custom-made trucks ordered through a dealer from the factory. These are usually company drivers that have been coerced to 'take over' their fleet truck as an owner or lease-operator at a less than realistic rate of pay. There are even a few trucking companies that provide the much-desired custom-made trucks to drivers, indicating that they understand more clearly the emotional attachment this type equipment has for a driver. I heard one driver say he could hardly wait to get back in his truck because he enjoyed driving it so much. I will have to agree, it is a great feeling with that style truck. Unfortunately, most company trucks in large fleets do not generally produce that feeling. It becomes 'just a job' with no 'pride in your ride'.

*The fact is that the engineers designing fleet equipment are themselves four-wheeler drivers and probably have little or no idea of the feel of a big truck.* These new trucks are increasingly looking and handling more like a smaller vehicle. There is very little of the necessary intimidation factor needed for the safety of the general public. 80,000# trucks look like 'just another vehicle' instead of the huge monster they really are.

Part of the reason for this is that, due to the extensive driver turnover, most beginner drivers, especially women, are more comfortable with the aerodynamic style of truck that looks and handles increasingly like an automobile. Better fuel consumption is also a consideration.

The custom-designed classic style truck with the long hood causes everyone to realize that this is over-sized heavy equipment and must be treated as such. There is a more solid and true feel to it on the open highway. This type of truck requires more skill and awareness in limited space such as backing into tight spots, maneuvering in city traffic and making pickups and deliveries. The turning radius of the steering is usually much greater to prevent wandering on the open highway. These trucks are designed with OVER THE ROAD trucking and handling in mind. They handle beautifully on the open road but can be very difficult to maneuver in tight conditions due to the wide turning radius of the steering. They look and feel like the heavy piece of equipment they are and command the respect of other traffic because of their intimidating appearance. *This image might be looked upon as safety enhancement because of the 'scare' factor that just might stop some crazy 4-wheeler from doing a suicidal pullout. 'Headlights on for safety' has a similar affect and is always a good idea.*

Unless you have driven both types, you have no idea of the difference but I can tell you that the old style rack and pinion with a large steering wheel was a genuine pleasure to drive. Today's engineers do not seem to realize that we are dealing with eighty thousand (80,000) pounds and you simply cannot jerk this much weight quickly about with power steering without consequences. These modern trucks are not such a pleasure to drive. That enjoyment is being engineered away. *They are becoming more dangerous, in many cases.*

## 10. USED TRUCKS ARE A GLUT ON THE MARKET

Something else to consider is that there is a tremendous glut of used OVER THE ROAD trucks all over the country. Acres and acres containing thousands of used OVER THE ROAD tractors can be seen throughout the country, awaiting disposition.

One reason for this is that most of today's new OVER THE ROAD drivers will *initially sacrifice income to drive a new or faster truck.* It is highly motivating! New vehicle warranty is also undoubtedly a consideration as well as tax depreciation benefits. This kind of thinking has resulted in most large trucking companies replacing their trucks after only three to five years so that the equipment remains attractive to the many new entrants coming into the transportation field. This type of commercial equipment can be completely depreciated for a complete tax write-off in this short period of time. When the warranty is gone and the depreciation used up, the trucks are traded in for new ones. Our 'throw away' society has reached solidly into the heavy equipment category and it seems that it may be presenting another problem; what to do with all the used trucks? This has resulted in various owner-operator plans at cheaper prices, designed to get some of this equipment back into circulation.

When the economy of the world is good, there has been a market for much of this equipment in third world countries. Some of it may also be disposed of for use in local and short haul operations here in the United States. But presently it appears that since thousands of new trucks have been continually acquired for many years that it may have reached a saturation point.

It seems the endless supply of new trucks to entice people to become OVER THE ROAD truck drivers has resulted in more used trucks than can readily be disposed of. Truck dealers and trucking companies have come up with creative financing and leasing plans that enable even those with bad or questionable credit to obligate themselves to pay for a used truck that may have already been paid for or depreciated off, as a further enticement for drivers to get more deeply involved in trucking as an 'owner-operator'.

Trucking companies desperate for drivers are actually *giving trucks away to any drivers willing to endure present income and conditions* over a prolonged period of time. This helps to solve two problems at once, *acquiring drivers and disposing of used trucks.*

## 11. NO STATISTICS ON FAILURES

Trucking is a very high cost industry and it is easy for even an experienced trucker to underestimate all the expenses of operating a modern big truck. Statistics relating to the success and failure of those who have "given it a shot" are very elusive. I suspect the reason for this is not to discourage anyone willing to do so because:

1.  The federal government realizes the constant daily need for trucks to move merchandise across the nation without interruption. This fact was punctuated during earlier years when most OVER THE ROAD trucking was controlled by the Teamsters Union. It was shown that nationwide work stoppages in the transportation industry due to contract and labor disagreements resulted in crippling the nation's economy and brought government and industry management to their knees. It appears this labor problem was the main reason for deregulation of trucking, which in turn resulted in nearly all truckload and specialized hauling to go into non-union operations. This, in turn, resulted in the loss of OVER THE ROAD truck drivers to have anyone to represent them in regard to benefits and income provisions. *It seems to me that any industry that affects the country to this degree should have appropriate labor representation instead of the one-sided free-for-all policy that now exists.*

2.  Deregulation of trucking caused newly developed truckload carriers to wage rate wars which resulted in *drastically lowering freight rates, thereby reducing one of the most costly aspects of trucking; driver's pay, benefits and working conditions.* Ultimately, this drastic reduction in cost of truck driver labor and benefits resulted in dramatic *savings* to shippers, manufacturers and industry in general. This in turn seems to have helped produce a generation of top executives in other (shipping) industries benefiting from all this, competing with each other in a game of 'Which CEO makes the most money'? This is beyond ridiculous! This super-pay for top executives had to come from somewhere. Most of it undoubtedly came from savings in trucking at the expense of OVER THE ROAD truck drivers! The 'Trickle-down' theory for labor appears to have resulted in a 'Trickle-up' effect for top management! That management should be awarded such unrealistically high bonuses while the millions that actually do the physical work live paycheck to paycheck seems grossly unbalanced to me. *How much is enough for these top executives?* Consider this. If one million *truck drivers* earn one dollar a day less than normal, that would be $365 million dollars a year. Suppose *three* million drivers earned $10 a day less than a union driver. This comes to $10,950,000,000.00 a year. That is *ten billion, nine hundred fifty million dollars!* This is perhaps an over simplification, but I think you get the idea. To look at it another way, let's break things down by the hour.

An OVER THE ROAD solo driver is on the truck twenty-four hours a day, seven days a week. There are 168 hours in a week. If the driver's pay rate is 30 CPM and he drove 3500 miles in a week, he will earn $1050.00. Dividing 168 hours into $1050.00 you come up with a little over $6.00 an hour for his time and effort. Not too impressive!

Okay, let us take 8 hours a day out for sleeping so now you have 168 minus 56 hours (8 hrs X 7 days) a week spent sleeping which leaves 112 hours a week. Dividing 112 into $1050.00, you still come up with less than $10.00 an hour for all the hours committed. Still not very impressive!

Additionally, since his logbook only allows the driver to drive 70 hours a week, this means the deck is stacked against him up front. It is *guaranteed* that he will be idle 112 hours minus 70 or 42 more hours a week. And that is if he is able even to *get* 3500 miles, which is not likely, week after week. There will probably be many weeks with far fewer than 3500 miles, which will further erode his check. *The driver has little or no control about how many miles he will get.* There may be times when a driver will only get as few as 1500 or 1800 miles, even though he was available and begging for work but no loads were available or possibly the truck broken down. It happens! It happens too often!

In spite of this, a solo OVER THE ROAD company driver may still earn from 30 to 60 thousand dollars a year which seems like a respectable income compared to many other occupations, if you do not consider that the time involved can figure out to minimum wage or less. No provision for overtime. Teams and driver trainers can earn considerably more *if* the miles and trainees are available. Those are the important unknown factors that make all the difference. Remember, there are *no guarantees*! I can remember reading an article years ago in a trucking management magazine that said, "Give truck drivers a big shiny truck loaded with chrome and all the bells and whistles and pay them little." There is more than a shred of truth to this! Trucking companies are capitalizing on truck drivers' ego and pride, but it does not last long if benefits and a livable income are an issue.

3. There seems to be an unending procession of people who are willing to take a chance on becoming an "entrepreneur" by obligating themselves to take on the risk and responsibility of becoming a so-called "owner-operator". In reality, most of these people are merely exchanging a position as a company paid driver with benefits for the marginal existence of now having the responsibility of paying for and maintaining a piece of equipment that can cost as much or more than some houses. He may find himself reaching deep into his own pocket to keep his head above water and find he is actually working to support his truck with no money left for himself and his family.

4. Truck dealers and manufacturers constantly paint a rosy picture to assure themselves of buyers for their "dream machines". Creative financing and leasing programs have been designed to make it possible for nearly anyone to "own your own truck" if you

are willing to devote your time and effort. Poor credit background and bankruptcies are overlooked in many cases. This helps to assure the trucking companies of drivers for their trucks and buyers for truck manufacturers and dealers.

I did hear that there is about a 7% success rate in being a long-term owner-operator. Does that mean a 93% rate of failure? Not a good risk, I would say!

# 15.

# ONLY THE STRONG COMPANIES
# WILL SURVIVE

Great changes are taking place in transportation, mostly unnoticed by the public. Oil prices are among the biggest influence causing changes at this time. Small and medium sized trucking companies are having a tremendous struggle to maintain a profit and many are folding up every day. According to some of the latest news articles, *only the strongest will survive and should become stronger as they take over the business of the failed companies.* This may or may not be true.

Just as there are now only a handful of surviving union trucking companies, probably most of the deregulated companies will eventually fall by the wayside also for many different reasons, mainly inadequate freight rates. There will be buy-outs, mergers, bankruptcies and liquidations. This should eventually result in higher freight rates and ultimately, higher driver pay.

Drop trailers figure into this significantly! As previously mentioned, many large trucking companies can provide virtually an unlimited number of trailers to a shipper for loading convenience or to a consignee for 'free storage' of product until needed. This greatly reduces the need for warehousing which is extremely costly. The trailers have become portable 'mini-warehouses'! Shippers and receivers benefit from free warehousing and trucking companies benefit in return by securing loads to haul.

The large shippers and consignees are in tune with large trucking companies that can provide trailer pools as needed. Even the drivers can benefit if they are able to quickly drop their load and pick up another with a minimum of waiting time.

The only small companies that may survive will be those in 'niches' or specialized hauling that require personalized service or handling at premium rates.

Eventually, this transition *could* result in the need for more genuine *independent* owner-operators rather than the variety that signs on to a 'mother' company and settles for less than realistic compensation. In this case the owner-operator will many times deal directly with the customer, one on one. These are the *true* owner-operators that own one truck and drive the truck themselves. This may require obtaining operating rights through what is known as an ICC practitioner for authority to do business throughout the United States and Canada.

However, some owner-operators prefer to operate on the rights of a broker or company that can provide loads for ten percent or so of the revenue. This seems to work quite well for all concerned in many cases. It seems worth ten percent of the revenue if the broker provides loads, permits, base plate and insurance and does all the fuel tax filing. In any case, when the owner-operator gets a larger share of the revenue, *his chances of being successful are much greater and it creates a more stable environment.* This is more in line with the way it should be!

## 1. TRAILER POOLS

The fact that many large trucking companies can afford to provide large pools of trailers to shippers and receivers to be used as storage and staging loads indicates that *funds are readily available for THAT purpose.* Yes, trailer pools do benefit everybody, including the OVER THE ROAD truckers that can perform a simple drop and hook, rather than lose a lot of time waiting around to be live loaded or unloaded. But how is it that there are funds available to *buy* these large trailer pools? Clearly, *lower driver compensation and no pay for the many millions of hours spent waiting **every day** by multitudes of truck drivers across the country, has been a major factor in making funds available for companies to buy these extra trailers.* It does not take a financial genius to figure this out. This drastically reduced driver income and unpaid waiting time no doubt adds up to billions of dollars of benefit to all these long haul trucking companies every year.

## 2. PRIVATE FLEETS REDUCED

The fixed costs of private companies using modern OVER THE ROAD common carrier fleets have also been a determining factor in reducing or eliminating many private corporate fleets because they can now get their product moved somewhat cheaper with an outside trucking company than they can do it themselves, without the headaches. Once again, *the underpaid OVER THE ROAD truck drivers are the overwhelming cost saving factor!* This type of JIT (just in time) trucking also saves millions in warehouse costs, as explained in my first book. The trucking companies are now able to provide trailers to shippers to hold their product on until needed.

Of course, much of the increased profits from the savings realized goes toward the huge salaries and bonuses of top management of those companies, where else? Meanwhile, the hundreds or thousands of truck drivers that those companies previously employed *now must find another job,* seek another career, or join the ranks of the unemployed.

## 3. TEAM DRIVERS

There are also team drivers and husband-wife teams. Team combinations are very much in demand these days to satisfy the service and logbook requirements of today. Some people actually sell their homes, put their belongings in storage and live exclusively in the truck. They can definitely save a lot of money that way if that is their goal. *Compatibility is of utmost importance in team operations!* Being with another person in such close quarters 24/7 can eventually become a problem. Especially if those involved are strangers as with during training and come from different walks of life. Other than husband-wife teams, very few others last very long.

*Team running is a poor choice for most people!* You are sacrificing being able to get somewhat quality sleep while the truck is parked as a solo driver for trying to sleep while moving down the road in all kinds of rough going and weather conditions. It can be difficult for drivers to drive so that the other can get proper sleep. Braking, rumble strips, unscheduled stopping, curves, horn and radio usage can be less than helpful for the driver trying to sleep. In addition, you are splitting the pay with another person and must cover twice as many miles just to earn as much as running solo. Granted, you may get longer runs and maybe a couple cents per mile extra to help compensate for it but generally *it simply is not enough*. Two people sharing the same space for prolonged periods of time must be more than compatible. I repeat, it rarely works over a long period of time.

On the other hand, teams consisting of husband and wife can generate income far beyond any other combination of company solo drivers if they can develop a successful system of routines. Routines are very important, since when both team members share all the chores, responsibilities and inspections equally, while one is in the driving mode and the other is in the rest mode, they both can be confidant that all the necessary duties of operating to maximum capacity are being performed by the other.

Realistically, for a team to have to drive 6,000 to 8,000 miles a week, as is now sometimes being done to make it worthwhile as a lease or owner-operator for several years with minimal time off, is not only outrageous but also inhuman and unacceptable to most who attempt it. Additionally, the safety of the general public must be considered in this situation. For two people to continually push themselves to the limit of their endurance and beyond, driving an enormous 80,000# vehicle across the country in a tired condition definitely puts the public at risk no matter how you look at it. Team running is not conducive to getting good rest! Most of the roads are miserable to try to sleep on and construction all over the country does not help any. Sleep interruptions happen constantly. Fatigue is ever present!

## 4. OVER THE ROAD TRUCK DRIVERS MAKING CITY DELIVERIES

One of the biggest safety and pay issues existing presently is in regard to an OVER THE ROAD truck driver making city deliveries and/or pickups. At this time there are few companies that adequately take this fact into consideration.

> There are city delivery drivers.
> There are OVER THE ROAD drivers.
> And then there are those that do both. Let us analyze this a bit.

Most trucking companies that specialize in city deliveries as a primary function of their operation have things well sorted out, whether or not they are union. The tractors are small, two-axle day cabs (no sleeper) that pull short trailers for maximum safety and maneuverability in the limited confines of most cities. Local drivers work on 8 to 10 hour shifts every day and go home every night. This allows them to be well rested every morning so that they are prepared to safely face the rigors of dealing with all the difficulties involved regarding city deliveries. These drivers are paid strictly by the hour and are usually provided with health, welfare and retirement benefits. It is high risk of having an accident and constant hustle to make deliveries and pickups on a timely basis. Another safety advantage most of them have is that these drivers usually cover the same areas in the same cities every day so that they become familiar with traffic, one-way streets, short cuts and directions to all the deliveries as well as detours around on-going construction projects and many other things of that nature. These drivers generally have weekends and holidays off at home as well as being home every night. They are usually paid time and a half if they work overtime and double or triple time for holidays.

OVER THE ROAD truck drivers for these same companies report to the local terminal they are domiciled in and in most cases have more or less regular runs that they have previously bid on, determined by seniority. The equipment can vary from using a day cab to a full-sized OVER THE ROAD tractor with a sleeper berth, depending on the type operation their company is involved in. A mechanic or local driver generally prepares their equipment (hooking the tractor to multiple trailers) in advance so that when they arrive, all they have to do is get in and drive off. They usually take their trailer or trailers to another company terminal where another mechanic or local driver takes over. They are then taken to a motel for their 10-hour rest break before returning to their starting point. There are many variations of this but the point is that city drivers do city work and OVER THE ROAD drivers drive OVER THE ROAD, resulting in safer conditions for *all* the drivers. These OVER THE ROAD truck drivers are also paid by the mile and if they perform any additional functions en-route such as dropping off a trailer and picking up another, there is a pay provision for each such function. They are provided with the same benefit package that city drivers get. Regular time off is pre-determined, as are paid holidays and vacations. Con-way trucking comes to mind as one of these companies.

However, today's non-union OVER THE ROAD truck driver that this writing is about has been stripped of most of the benefits and safety advantages of the previously described operations. These drivers rarely have any idea where their load is going to go or where they will be going after they get there. Every load assignment is an adventure in OVER THE ROAD trucking. Simple docking maneuvers can be major problem. The satellite communicator generally presents their trip plan to them and it is up to each driver to accomplish his assignment on time to the best of his ability. Usually there is ample time. If the entire load goes to one delivery, not too much can go wrong other than getting lost or making a few wrong turns while trying to locate a customer.

*It is when there may be multiple drops that can include downtown city deliveries that things can get challenging!* The OVER THE ROAD driver must then drive his oversized OVER THE ROAD monster rig into any given city of any size and try to locate the customer. The huge tractors of today, attached to oversized 53' long, 102" wide trailers, were not designed to be making city deliveries on streets that barely accommodate smaller city trucks designed for that purpose. In addition, most OVER THE ROAD truck drivers are relatively newcomers in trucking and do well simply to make it safely from one point to another. Accidents are imminent! Drivers of smaller, private vehicles duck and dive around these big rigs like ants on an anthill. If the truck blocks their path, impatient attitudes quickly produce horn blowing and middle fingers in the air showing their displeasure with such ungainly equipment being in their way. Many +allowed on the highway and in this case, I agree with them. City streets are no place for OVER THE ROAD rigs with inexperienced drivers, *or any truck drivers unfamiliar with the area, experienced or not!*

OVER THE ROAD trucks should be restricted or limited from making city deliveries whenever possible. *They are simply too big!* Most of the OVER THE ROAD drivers are too inexperienced anyway! *This is a very poor combination!* Of course there are exceptions but whenever possible, sending inexperienced OVER THE ROAD truck drivers (or experienced, for that matter) into cities with OVER THE ROAD equipment should be avoided for the sake of safety. Once again, the risk, skill required, time spent and frustration to the OVER THE ROAD truck driver are barely compensated for, if at all. The way I see it is that if an

OVER THE ROAD truck driver must do this, the **compensation should match the risk and responsibility.**

## 5. RELAYS AND SHUTTLES

A few years back there was talk of eliminating all long runs by implementing relays and shuttles every 500 to 600 miles with drivers going out from a central location and coming right back (hub and wheel concept). There are undoubtedly operations that would not be conducive to this scenario but as time goes by and OVER THE ROAD trucking companies become larger and fewer, most of them will see the advantages of doing this. Again, this reverts back to the way things were done prior to deregulation.

This would result in a driver domiciled in his hometown taking his load to a relay point, swap trailers and then return home. He would thereby be home every other night and possibly on weekends. This seems like a feasible solution that would make worlds of difference in regularity and safety to drivers that wanted to participate. Those that did not could be utilized by 'running the board', or basically continue on as it is now, traveling all over the country, possibly at a higher rate of pay. Some actually like to do that. Once again, something for everybody. Surely it would take some preparation and coordination but the end result could benefit drivers *and* management with some kind of regularity and greatly reduce driver turnover if properly implemented. Some trucking companies have already implemented this on a limited basis.

It seems to dovetail with increased utilization of the railroad to piggyback the longer runs moving coast to coast. Eventually, I can see rail utilization happening on a much larger scale than it already is. The only thing slowing it from happening sooner is poor and/or limited rail service. Increasingly, large numbers of trailers belonging to large trucking companies can be seen on trains. J.B. Hunt, Schneider Transport and UPS (United Parcel Service) sometimes have entire trainloads. This obviously saves on fuel, reduces the need for more drivers and relieves some truck congestion on the highways.

## 6. COMMUNICATION—BACK BURNER MENTALITY

On weekends, nights or holidays, it can be very challenging to try to talk with a dispatcher on the phone. *These companies absolutely own you and trying to talk to a live person can be in some cases not only very frustrating but also infuriating.* In large trucking companies, the sat-com has nearly replaced the telephone completely in regard to driver-management communication after (and even during) normal business hours. Most trucking companies reduce their staff to a skeleton crew after hours, since few people like to work during these times. *Only truck drivers are expected to do that!*

With adequate compensation for waiting time, this problem would undoubtedly be greatly reduced or eliminated. Lazy or unresponsive office personnel might be replaced with someone that properly recognizes the drivers' plight and knows how to get the job done on the driver's behalf, or at least try. Presently, drivers are simply shuffled onto the back burner and seemingly forgotten about until they are needed. Kind of like a hold button. *Getting put on hold for the weekend results in a very unhappy mileage-paid driver, not to mention his spouse!* Even during the week, since a fleet driver manager may have 50 to 60 trucks or more to monitor. It is as if there is a multi-burner stove with most of the trucks simmering on the back burners and the hot burners in front with problems getting all the immediate attention.

A good example of this would be if there is need for a re-power and you are the only truck available, or so they say. If you are already on a good load you do not want to give up you are immediately put on the front burner until you agree to do so. Half-promises are made and partial agreement to any of your (futile) demands are met to coerce you to cooperate. The pressure is intense! They try to stop just short of blatantly lying to you. But when it is all over and the dust settles it can be a very different story trying to collect on the 'promises'. You have just given up your load and been shuffled onto the back burner. *Do not expect any extra pay!*

## 7. DISPATCHERS IGNORE PHONES

Trying to talk to somebody on the phone can be a real challenge with large companies. If you are fortunate enough to get a receptionist or operator instead of being put on hold, this may simply be a starting point. Next you may have to work your way through a voice mail system that generally results in you being put on hold again and again. Dropped calls and cutoffs are commonplace. Although in this day and age some of this might be expected, the length of time on hold can be up to a half an hour or more while you hang on the line with a problem or question. Weekends are the worst! Hopefully, you are not at an outdoor phone booth in sub-freezing, rainy or blistering hot, desert conditions. If you happen to have your own mobile phone service it had best be one with unlimited no long distance, no roaming charges. Otherwise, prolonged periods of time on hold with limited minutes to conduct company business at your expense can get very costly on a mobile phone when the phone bill comes in.

In the past I have stood at the dispatch window and witnessed night and weekend dispatchers gossiping on the phone with their wives or girl friends while the driver call-in lines were ringing off the hook and totally ignored. Other times I have seen after-hour people huddled together telling jokes and laughing and somewhat indignant when they had to break things up to attend to the business of a driver or two standing at the dispatch window, peering in. The supervisory eight to five segment of management had gone home for the night or weekend. Nobody seemed to care. In talking with drivers from various other truck lines, this seems to be commonplace. *'When the cat's away, the mice will play'.*

What matters to most people is being treated with dignity and respect! Being totally ignored and not even acknowledged as a professional is prevalent in this occupation. Having to wait on hold longer than 10 minutes is unnecessary and inconsiderate but not unusual. *It indicates either an inadequate or an uncaring staff.*

## 8. GATHER INFORMATION

Nevertheless, unlike other professions or businesses focused on producing a product, providing a service or managing people, there are simply unlimited possibilities and goals that can be explored in trucking. An excellent way to satisfy your curiosity is to actually visit with drivers that are involved in the type of trucking that you think you are interested in. In doing this, try to do it during a time when the driver is in a 'waiting mode'. In other words, not under pressure, so that he can give you his undivided attention and answer all your questions. All areas of the country have huge grocery warehouses, factories and distribution centers that ship and receive product that comes from all over the country on trucks. Many times, these drivers may be available to talk to you while they are waiting on the street at a company entrance gate to go in and get loaded or unloaded. Truck stops are always full of drivers, especially at night. Many of them are very candid and like to talk about their work. They too, had to start somewhere. Just remember some of these drivers are happy with the profession and their company and some of them are not. Be sure to ask which of these emotions is theirs. Get both sides of the story from as many drivers as you can. *Keep accurate notes!* Be sure to include specialized hauling because it pays more and is not likely to be put on the railroad.

## 9. CUT YOUR LOSSES

Over the years, I have trained many people to do this, or try to do it. I have also witnessed others in training with other trainers. *My experience has been that most of these students had a pre-conceived idea about trucking that was entirely unrealistic!* Many of these disillusioned people are weeded out in the first few weeks of training. They were smart enough to cut their losses and go back where they came from. Unfortunately, others have either obligated themselves for a training school loan or paid for schooling some other way, for which there is no reimbursement. Very sad, but true! The people that stay can become vulnerable to the many programs and schemes designed to entice them into obligating themselves to 'give it a shot, what do you have to lose?'

While some of these plans to enter the trucking profession are somewhat realistic and might work for someone with the right attitude and experience, many people are getting themselves in deep water, heading for a drop-off. It troubles me to see all these folks blindly coming into an industry that can and probably will suck them into the whirlpool of activity and send them down the wrong path when they could better spend their time and money pursuing a profession more acceptable to them and their family. Not to mention the fact that some of these unsuspecting people will undoubtedly become involved in minor and major truck accidents that could dramatically alter their lives and others, maybe forever. It happens every day, unfortunately. As mentioned before, this is a dangerous profession with one of the highest fatality rates.

In addition to the large number of truck drivers killed in accidents annually, I read where an additional nearly one thousand truck drivers were killed in the year 2000 from muggings, hijackings and robberies. This aspect of OVER THE ROAD trucking is minimized or not even mentioned during orientation but is nevertheless a distinct problem. Truckers are targets for thieves, muggers and hijackers of high value loads. In large metropolitan areas, the underbelly of society has come to the realization of driver vulnerability and targeted the large, nationwide trucking companies as having 'greenhorn' drivers who are totally unfamiliar with the area and usually confused as to where to go. Unscrupulous thieves take advantage of these truckers' unfamiliarity and offer to 'assist' them in finding their destination, then take the trusting and confused greenhorn trucker down a blind ally where more muggers are laying in wait. The results can be disastrous! You must be aware of this possibility along with many other dangers constantly. Con artists also frequent truck stop parking lots, trying to sell shoddy or stolen merchandise.

Don't get me wrong; trucking has been very good to me as a career all throughout my life even though I suffered some major setbacks myself as an owner of trucks. Hopefully, I can help someone else avoid those pitfalls. There are many unknowns in trucking that can alter the profit picture quickly and dramatically.

## 10. PROFITABILITY—COMPANY SURVIVAL

There are many different types of trucking and it can take a long time to sort it all out so that an individual can choose what he thinks is best for him. It is better if you can *begin* with the company or type of trucking that you think fits you best right from the start. There are virtually thousands of companies to pick from and they all have a different plan for their drivers.

There are advantages of staying with the same company rather than trying out first one, then another, looking for the 'best' one. A lot is lost in each such transition, including delays in medical insurance coverage, vacation time and rate of pay increases. Company stability should definitely be a consideration. Many of these truckload companies are going bankrupt or selling out to other ones and the end results are a bit fuzzy, many times not very good. Remember, only the strong are going to survive during these troubled times!

What makes the difference for one company to be a survivor while others fall by the wayside seems to be a combination of good management, good drivers, good equipment and good accounts. Let us take a quick look at each of these.

Good management. People who have first hand knowledge of actually performing the daily activities of OVER THE ROAD trucking should be able to better understand the needs and limitations of the drivers that are committed to performing these tasks. If they have not forgotten the reality of what life on the road consists of and make decisions accordingly, it will be obvious to an experienced driver. *Treating drivers with respect through good communication with operations that enhance his productivity are of great importance.* It is the overall feeling of accomplishment by a driver combined with adequate home time that make this career acceptable, as opposed to inadequate income due to low mileage and weeks or months away from home, seemingly forgotten about. If a company can provide these things, it will have good retention of experienced drivers! Being lied to by dispatchers is a real turn-off and unacceptable. Unfortunately, this is commonplace.

Good drivers! Responsible drivers with experience and common sense are a valuable and necessary commodity in OVER THE ROAD trucking. Being a self-starter combined with dependability, patience and endurance is also needed. In addition, while being service oriented is important, drivers must first be aware of the greater need for safety at all times. Safety has become a leading issue in this 'revolution' because of the tremendous turnover of inexperienced drivers that are 'trying it out' and experiencing accidents. *Retaining safe and experienced drivers is part of the challenge to management.*

Good equipment. New equipment with an adequate maintenance program is necessary to prevent down time and therefore increase productivity. *High mileage without breakdowns* depends on reliable, well maintained tractors and trailers.

Good accounts. Twenty-four hour a day, seven days a week capability combined with drop trailers are among the type customer base that is needed to provide OVER THE ROAD drivers with adequate mileage to make it worth their time and effort. Drop yards are definitely a big advantage. *Excessive waiting time at customers is a major problem!*

149

# 16.

# SAFETY IN TRUCKING (and all vehicles)

Having been a lifelong trucker, I have a pretty good idea of what is safe and what is not in regard to sharing the highway not only with the general public, but other trucks. Right or wrong, my thoughts certainly should not create animosity in anyone and that is not my intention. The idea is to ultimately reduce accidents, increase safety and save lives through professional compensation and driving methods.

Unfortunately, many people look at trucks as an obstacle in their way to wherever they are scurrying to. Trucks are something to be gotten in front of, even at the risk of their own lives. To them, trucks are a hateful nuisance and should be banned from the highways or only allowed to use city streets at night. They are vehicles to be used for advancement in heavy traffic because there always seems to be a space in front of them (safety zone) that somebody can rudely jump into. Wherever the frantic-paced eight to five citizen is going is always far more important than being concerned about what the truckers are doing or where they are going. Slamming on the brakes after passing a truck or diving across three or four lanes of superhighway traffic in front a truck to make a split-second exit seems to be an acceptable way to drive for many people. *Only after an accident do they realize their stupidity, if they survive!* Some of these idiots are clearly on drugs!

I think another reason for this lack of respect for big trucks is because of the aerodynamic designs that cause many modern designed trucks to appear much smaller and less intimidating than they really are. What people do not realize is that the 80,000 # monster is still present but appears no more ominous than a large pickup truck!

Most of the super-slabs are obsolete due to the increased amount of vehicles since they were built, and lack of maintenance. Interstate highways were designed and built over fifty years ago with two lanes each direction but due to the increase in traffic, many are now being upgraded to three or even four lanes each way in many areas. A minimum of three lanes each direction would enhance safety on the highways immeasurably. Left lane for fast and/or through traffic, center lane for casual driving and right lane for slow travel and/or entering and exiting.

Nobody has all the answers to safety on the highways but maybe, by everybody who is genuinely concerned working together to solve the most glaring problems, safety and accident prevention being on top of the list, the injury and death tolls can be significantly reduced.

Most new drivers are timid and unsure of themselves in their driving for the first several months, and rightly so. It is important that the more experienced and seasoned drivers understand this so that chances of a mishap are lessened. Impatient and discourteous driving on the part of more experienced drivers can result in not only anger and frustration on the part of the newcomer but also unnecessary accidents.

'Lights on for safety' is not only a good idea but also mandatory many times and places. When you see signs saying 'This is a driver safety corridor', what it means is that your headlights must be turned on or you may get a citation. Headlights on is always a good idea, especially on 2-lane roads.

The fact is that just *being* an OVER THE ROAD truck driver can sharpen skills that will bring about an awareness of safe driving habits that usually escape not only the general population but even law enforcement.

## 1. AGGRESSIVE DRIVING

Most OVER THE ROAD truckers have the attitude that the sooner they get to their destination, the quicker they will get unloaded and under another load to increase their income. This is a dangerous scenario and although many times true, causes unsafe driving habits, speeding, sparring for position and leap-frogging in traffic, resulting in accidents.

The point to be made in regard to this is that the anger and frustration suffered by the overworked and underpaid trucker can many times be evidenced in the way they drive! There is a lot of suppressed anger amongst truck drivers due to the many unfair conditions. Possibly, this 'don't give a dang' and belligerent attitude is how some of them choose to protest. As far as I am concerned, they are making a bad situation worse!

Nobody likes looking in the west-coast mirrors and seeing that other trucks are right on your tail with no following distance. *How much worse must it be for the driver of a smaller vehicle to experience this common occurrence?* OVER THE ROAD truckers especially must realize this and compensate for it constantly rather than join in and be one of them. This is part of what makes a professional. This is what the OVER THE ROAD truck driver is paid to do and expected to do.

The days of roaring down the highway 90 to 100 MPH with a loaded truck, loud or no muffler and an engine break that echoes valley to valley waking everybody up in the middle of the night, are numbered. There are still too many egomaniacs in fancy trucks that think they own the road and drive like it. These drivers are on an ego trip in their 'super-rigs' and think everybody else should get out of the way. 'King of the Road', if you will. A heavy foot on the throttle is not good. Speed is a killer!

These things can cause non-truck drivers to have a hateful attitude toward big trucks and even drive in dangerous ways that in turn make the trucker's job tougher and safety much more difficult.

The truth is that there are many ignorant, less than intelligent, haphazard drivers of all kinds of vehicles on the highways that lack common sense and good judgment, are angry, over-aggressive and ignorant in their driving. I guarantee that drugs and stupidity are constantly present. As a professional driver you have to be on your toes every minute, realize this and deal with it. Discourtesy and failure to perform simple functions such as using turn signals is increasing. *No signals indicate a gross lack of respect among drivers!* Over-aggressive driving in congested areas and construction zones also seems to be increasing even when highway patrols are present. Bad attitudes and anger over the CB radio are on the rise. *Road rage is always present!*

Why are many truck drivers over-aggressive?

1. Late dispatch, trying to make up for lost time.
2. Gain safe following distance by passing.

3. Improve visibility with front position.
4. Avoid poor or inattentive driver ahead.
5. Avoid smoking vehicle ahead.
6. Get ahead of boats, RVs and campers (sight-seers and tourists).
7. Preparing to climb a grade or mountain.
8. Keep up momentum.
9. Outrun bad weather coming in from behind.
10. Beat big city rush hours.
11. Meet pickup and delivery appointments.
12. Avoid or reduce spray or slush onto the windshield from other traffic.
13. On the way home after several weeks or months on the road.
14. Just like to drive fast (ego).
15. And the big one, being paid only by the mile.

*If only for the sake of safety, we have got to take the 'hurry' out of trucking!* It is this aspect of OVER THE ROAD trucking that has become so dangerous. *OVER THE ROAD truckers should be compensated fairly so that they can afford to hurry, 'slowly'!*

Oversize loads can present something of a hazard when they go careening down the highway behind powerful tractors that will go as fast or faster than other traffic. These drivers are usually restricted from traveling after dark and on the weekends in most states. Therefore, they try to make up for lost time by getting in more miles during the hours they are allowed to operate by using excessive speed. This can be a scary and dangerous scenario when there is barely room to pass, due to a wide load. They should have to travel slower or at least slow down temporarily to allow other traffic to get on around them quickly, *without having to race with them!* These drivers usually will not give an inch, believe me! Common sense on their part could be a big help here.

Maybe the highway patrol should concentrate more on writing citations for over-aggressive and discourteous driving, poor or no following distances and failure to use turn signals or dim high beams, instead of being so overly concerned about catching somebody traveling a few miles an hour over the speed limit at 2 or 3 AM in rural areas where no other traffic is present. Smoking vehicles in need of engine repair should definitely be included. Controlling problem drivers during busy times would make more sense to me than raising the general revenue by 'cat and mouse' methods many times presently used in small towns during night-time hours on graveyard shifts. They would still have plenty of tickets to write. The revenue would still be there and maybe it would result in safer driving by everyone. There is no shortage of violators of this type.

In congested urban areas, it is another story due to aggressive, impatient drivers. Speed control there is definitely necessary. It is there that passing and following distance should be more heavily enforced. Too many idiots will pass and then pull right back in front of the passed vehicle and immediately slow back down, completely eliminating the safety zone of the truck that was passed, even causing him to hit the brakes. Sadly, many truck drivers are guilty of this poor driving practice too.

## 2. TRUCKERS SAVING LIVES

A large part of a truck driver's job is saving other people's lives when those people do the wrong thing, especially when carrying a load that could shift or tip over with sudden braking, or swerving to miss someone unaware of the danger they are causing. These things are best learned from long-time experience on the road and retained through long-term drivers of the profession. However, it is this safety aspect of OVER THE ROAD trucking that is disappearing due to all the many excessive demands that are not only inadequately compensated for, but also expected to be done without pay of any kind. Experienced truck drivers are becoming fewer and fewer.

If the number of big trucks on the highways doubles in the next ten years as is predicted by the experts, some major changes will have to be implemented in regard to driver retention for safety's sake! *'Safety must come first!'* If a reasonable, workable solution can be introduced whereby all OVER THE ROAD truck drivers will be able to produce a guaranteed living wage, which at the same time would reduce accidents and fatalities on the highway, *it must be utilized.* It is a matter of life or death!

## 3. DORMANT RAILROAD CROSSINGS

There are many abandoned railroad crossings that cause drivers of trucks carrying hazardous material (HAZ-MAT) and buses to comply with laws requiring a complete stop before crossing them or risk paying thousands of dollars in fines. Many unsuspecting drivers following in private vehicles are not aware of laws governing trucks and buses and being unprepared, can collide with the rear of commercial vehicles stopping at these dormant crossings in their haste to scurry blindly toward their destination. Simply requiring the railroads to remove crossing signs and posting exempt signs could solve this problem very easily.

## 4. TURN SIGNALS

Turn signals are one of the few ways traffic can communicate with each other. In my opinion, failure to use turn signals for any reason should result in a citation and/or reprimand. It is hard to understand why so many drivers, many of them truckers, do not use turn signals. It is effortless to engage turn signals. This is one of the most important requirements of any driver, especially a trucker, and one of the most often not done. *Regardless of any other circumstances or conditions, turn signals are always necessary.* Failure to use them indicates disrespect not only for others but also for yourself. Why is this not enforced more by the highway patrol?

Should you come upon a major traffic slowdown or stoppage, engage your 4-way hazard signals immediately to warn other fast-moving traffic behind you that cannot see what is happening in front of you. This simple action could easily prevent a disaster behind you and may even prevent someone from rear-ending you.

## 5. FOLLOWING DISTANCE—THE BIG ONE

*The single, most effective way to improve safety is to constantly maximize following distance so that if anything should occur there would be ample time and space to avoid a collision!*

I preach this constantly to my trainees and you will see it many times in my writings. It is up to the truck driver to take it upon himself to realize that this *lack of understanding* by the motoring public exists and compensate for it. It is not going to go away. A good method for determining adequate following distance is for the truck driver to drive as if the truck has no brakes. Especially in winter weather and rush hour traffic. It works! It is safe! It feels good! It is 'no accident'! If you think this kind of caution will cause unnecessary delay, consider the lost time an accident will result in. What's the big hurry? A feeling of being somewhat in control results in peace of mind instead of straining to gain every foot on the bumper of other traffic. *Fatigue and stress are also greatly reduced with better following distance!*

For example, one day I was coming out of Long Island and through New York City during the afternoon rush hour and was being followed by another trucker. After following me for about five or six miles in this heavy traffic, the other driver came on the CB radio and told me my brake lights did not seem to be working. I told him they did when I hit the brakes but I kept enough following distance so I did not need to brake. I noticed his following distance soon increased also. This works best if you are behind another truck because then most traffic will not jump into the 'safety zone' you have created since they are not anxious to get behind another truck.

## 6. TOP SPEED RESTRICTION

Most large fleets have restricted their trucks' top speed for safety reasons demanded by insurance companies and this has caused these trucks to have limited passing capability which can cause passing problems. Smaller fleets and independents generally let their trucks go less restricted to retain drivers and keep their drivers happy. Truck drivers for large companies are completely at the whim of hopefully well meaning people in management, many who know nothing about the actual driving of a big truck because they never did it. It makes a big difference how fast the truck is governed.

What most of the public do not seem to realize is that the speed of a big truck is determined by what is called a governor, which controls fuel flow. It is a little known fact that *all* trucks have the capability of reaching triple digit speeds, but for safety and economy, these governors can be set by the truck's on-board computer to travel at any speed deemed necessary for the operation of any individual truck. With few exceptions, the faster a truck goes the more fuel it will use. Insurance companies also provide better rates for trucking companies that set their trucks at lower speeds. This is why some fleets have trucks that seem to be slower or faster than others and 'turtle races' take place.

This speed restriction can result in traffic backups when a driver attempts to pass another vehicle going just a little slower than his truck and the vehicle being passed speeds up just enough to prevent the pass but not enough to allow the passing truck back safely in line behind him. Following traffic can become impatient and sometimes angry in situations such as this. Much of this problem is caused by the lack of understanding by private citizens in regard to truck speed limitations. They apparently do not realize that the truck is already traveling at the top speed set by the governor and wonder why the truck does not get on by. I have talked with many private citizens and that was what I was told. They are aware that it is a dangerous situation but not that they were causing it by tapping their cruise control to go a little faster. They blame the truck driver for not slowing a bit and pulling back in behind them.

What they also fail to realize is that to pull back in behind them, a big truck needs a safety zone in front of it of several hundred feet at highway speeds and pulling back in close to the rear bumper of their automobile will not allow for it. Should the trucker pull behind them too soon, they complain that the truck is on their back bumper, following too close and of course it is so, because the auto driver caused it to be that way. Many times the truck driver should continue to slow down to gain back his following distance and let the other traffic go ahead. It may surprise you to sometimes see how soon all the other traffic seems to disappear. Good common sense comes into play here.

Some automobile drivers will stay behind a big truck to avoid a speeding ticket but keep changing lanes to maintain maximum vision ahead. This can be very annoying to a trucker, especially if he is waiting for traffic to clear so he can make a slow pass of another truck going only a little faster. It is also very dangerous for the auto driver should a tire blow out and throw off a heavy recap into his car. Additionally, the truck driver may also be concerned about becoming boxed in since most private vehicles do not want a big truck pulling out in front of them and will try to prevent it by speeding up when he signals a pass.

Yes, many times an auto will ride along behind the truck in the passing lane without passing, then speed up when the trucker signals intention to pass. *Riding alongside or even near a big truck is a poor option, especially if you have any other choices!* Should a smaller vehicle come *even in slight contact* with this heavy equipment, the sheer weight difference can throw the smaller vehicle totally out of control, possibly causing a rollover or worse. A fully loaded truck can weigh up to 80,000# or more, while the average private vehicle weighs only 2,000# to 4,000#. Even the new large pickups and SUVs do not come close in weight. *Drivers of these vehicles need to realize the imminent danger of being only feet or inches, many times, away from these huge trucks, moving at highway speeds.*

What most 4-wheeler drivers do not even think about is that every truck driver knows what it is like to drive a car but few of them know what it is like to drive a big truck.

One thing to keep in mind if you are a truck driver trainer or team driver is that should an accident involving your vehicle occur, be sure whoever was driving at the time is still behind the wheel when the highway patrol arrives because *that is the person who will be cited should there be any question of responsibility!* I know of an incident where the trainer got cited for a student's accident because he changed seats before the police came and then the student denied responsibility when the officer asked who was driving. You can be sure they had a personality conflict going before and after the accident occurred. Not a happy event.

## 7. SUBMIT TO OTHER TRAFFIC

If you do not want to get a traffic citation or be involved in an accident, *the best prevention is to submit to all other traffic.* Remember, you are the professional driver and are not expected to maneuver like a sports car. Additionally, a big rig handles vastly different when it is loaded from when it is empty. It is best to overcome the temptation to 'compete' with smaller traffic when your trailer is empty just because you now have more acceleration capability. People do not expect it and it is dangerous.

You might also keep in mind that there are a number of devious auto drivers that may *want* to collide with a truck so they can collect on the trucking company's insurance. Lawyers can be seen on television every day advertising that they can collect an insurance settlement from a big commercial truck-involved accident! Keeping adequate following distance is the best preventive measure here.

## 8. OVERSIZED EQUIPMENT IS DANGEROUS

The modern day equipment is so huge and ungainly that safety has become more of a factor than ever before. The 'powers to be', bureaucrats, money people, or whatever you want to call them, have influenced lawmakers to allow transportation equipment to increase in size so that more product can be shipped at a cheaper price *with no additional pay to the drivers.* However, it seems nobody took into consideration the fact that most of the city streets, highways, truck stops and industrial shipping and receiving docks were designed for the much smaller equipment of the past. The result has been an undetermined increase in the number of minor accidents and a dramatic increase in major ones. In fact, minor accidents are now many times referred to as 'incidents'. Maybe this makes them more acceptable. It sure does not help the truck drivers.

## 9. SAFE PASSING

Many so-called 'Super Truckers' are in reality 'Stupid Truckers' in the way they drive! Yes, it is a great feeling to drive a big, classic style conventional across the country, hauling the nation's goods of one kind or another and the feeling of 'King of the Road' does exist! But this does not mean that everybody else must 'step aside' so that the 'super (stupid) trucker' can exceed every speed law of every state they travel through, endangering the lives of everyone they come in contact with, just because the truck driver may be on an 'ego trip'. There is no doubt that these big rigs have the capability of high speeds well into triple digits, but the highway is not a racetrack. People in other vehicles, large and small driving at the posted speed, have equal rights of safe passage on the highways and should not have to be worried about some monster truck suddenly roaring up behind them and try to force them out of their way in a threatening manner. As a lifelong trucker, I have traveled the highways in my personal car as well and have experienced this 'road hog' style of truck driving with my family present. It is a very scary, almost terrifying event when this happens and there is nothing you can do about it as the driver or passenger of a smaller vehicle when the all lanes of the highway are full and there is no place to 'get out of the way'.

Even while driving an eighteen-wheeler, I have experienced other eighteens roaring up in the right lane in an attempt to pass me on the right while I was in a 'passing mode' with my slower truck but not going fast enough to suit them, even though it was obvious there was not enough space to complete their unsafe pass on the right. What can they be thinking? Who in the world do they think they are, driving like that?

If you are in the right lane and other traffic is passing you, even though you may be driving over the speed limit, you probably will not be cited. But, if you are in the left lane passing other traffic and on the bumper of an automobile, you are a prime candidate for a traffic ticket. Roll with the flow! Keep your following distance!

Another extremely dangerous inside passing scenario is when someone moves into the left lane to compensate for a 'sitting duck' and an impatient or stupid driver takes that 'opportunity' to pass in the space between the two, that was meant to be a safe zone. The prevention for this is to only move ½ a lane over, thereby not leaving enough room for an inside pass, then return to the right lane when it is safe. Many states now have laws requiring traffic to move over in such instances.

Generally, *brake lights and turn signals are the only means of communicating with other traffic,* other than using a CB radio. Your turn signal should have blinked at least once and preferably two or three times before changing lanes for any reason, especially when passing. While this may sometimes seem like an invitation for a stupid and ignorant automobile driver to speed up to get alongside of you, changing lanes at the same time as signaling can result in a collision if someone behind decides to pass you at the same time. In heavy traffic it is always a good idea to signal your *intent* to change lanes in advance as a warning to others that you want to do so rather than waiting for a space to open up. Many times, a courteous driver will open up space for you to come into if he knows you want to come out but *he cannot know to do it unless you signal first!*

Other times when a truck is in a fast passing mode and already in the passing lane, passenger cars and even other big trucks ahead but in the slow lane, will pull out in front of the passing truck, causing some pretty fancy brake work and repositioning of equipment (as well as an attitude adjustment) to prevent a rear-end collision by the passing vehicle. If the passing truck is too rapidly overtaking, he may not be able to slow down quick enough to prevent an accident caused by the pullout. It could force him off the road. *Many drivers of smaller vehicles may not understand how dangerous it is to pull in front of a passing big rig but there is no excuse for another truck driver to do it!* This is poor driving of the worst kind. A lot of common sense is needed here on everybody's part since accident prevention is a far better choice than accident involvement. In an accident everybody loses. *Once again, what the hell is the big hurry? Drive professionally or park it!*

In rain or snow, many times traffic will speed up as you attempt to pass because they obviously do not want the truck to throw spray and slush on their windshield and cause them to lose their vision. They may be scared, rude or over aggressive, but since you are the professional, you will have to sort out the safest thing to do, even if it means slowing and falling far back behind them. *Things change rapidly in traffic and soon you will be out of the situation and the possibility of being involved in an accident!* Be patient, courteous and professional. It will pay dividends in the long run. Many drivers of smaller vehicles are scared to death of big trucks and do not know how to properly share the road with them. It is best to use any available bypasses around large cities to avoid local traffic whenever possible, especially during rush hours and bad weather.

When you know you are going to make a turn or use an exit coming up, passing and then pulling in front of, then immediately slowing quickly in front of the vehicle you just passed to make your turn or exit makes absolutely no sense and is very dangerous. It is best to slow down and *fall in behind other traffic* well in advance in preparation for your next maneuver. *This is heavy equipment and the faster you travel, the less control you have over it!* Take a look at all the evidence of exiting too fast on the exit ramps. Skid marks into the ditch and crushed guardrails are commonplace nationwide.

Merging and yielding are also major causes of concern. Different situations call for different methods of joining other traffic. When trucks are prohibited from left lanes, it causes entering traffic to force themselves into a solid line of large, heavy trucks. When merging in slow-moving heavy city traffic, it is usually best to alternately take turns with other vehicles, each allowing the other to merge and yield dovetail fashion, as necessary. *Common courtesy and common sense play a large role here!*

High-speed merging calls for a different method, since the variables may be far different. In-coming traffic should do their best to get up to speed in the acceleration lane so as not to cause main-line traffic to slam on their brakes or force a lane change abruptly, which could cause a sideswipe or rear-ender. Adequate following distance is extremely important in all cases because it results in a safe merge for everybody. Being inconsiderate and trying to squeeze other traffic out is a formula for disaster. *If you try to think of other drivers as if they were friends or family, it can improve your driving considerably!*

I would describe a safe pass on the open road when only two vehicles are involved as follows. The overtaking vehicle coming up behind the slower vehicle in the same lane should first engage his left turn signal while still at least a hundred yards or more behind, then a few seconds later execute a gradual change into the left lane. A glance and friendly wave at the other driver while passing shows respect for him. After clearing the front of the other vehicle the driver of the passed vehicle might douse or give a flash of headlights, one way or another. Any signal should be taken as a courtesy gesture and appreciated with a blink or two of the clearance lights or 4-ways which says 'thanks'.

Then, if no other traffic is pushing to pass the passing vehicle, that driver should remain in the left lane for a reasonable time and distance so as not to return unnecessarily close in front of the passed vehicle thereby blocking that driver's line of sight. Even if there is other traffic anxious to get by it is totally inappropriate for the passing vehicle to jerk the steering wheel sharply to the right and barely miss colliding with the passed vehicle. At least a truck length of distance would be considered a bare minimum safe distance before returning to the right lane. *What's the hurry?* Again, be professional! Be safe.

Too many times passing vehicles cut closely in front of the one they are passing, just barely missing them for no other reason than lack of understanding that it is dangerous. I sure do not enjoy having a truck pull squarely in front of me so that the rear trailer doors are close enough to count the rivets, especially if there is no other traffic around. That is not professional driving. It is dangerous and unsafe driving! If a dog or some other animal should run in front of the first vehicle and he slammed on the brakes there could be a disaster. It happens!

## 10. COURTESY SIGNALING WITH LIGHTS

Unfortunately, the general public as well as many truckers, seems to have the misconception that the idea of passing is to cut as close as you can in front of the vehicle being passed without hitting him. You can see it in the way they pass, swerving unnecessarily into your safety zone. This may have been necessary years ago when there were no interstate highways. In those days, trucks were mostly struggling, underpowered units traveling on dangerous 2-lane highways. When passing each other or other traffic, many times head-on collisions occurred because of the extremely limited space for passing. There were no 2-way CB radios for driver communication, only light signals. It was in those days that truck drivers developed passing techniques using light signals for letting the other driver know he had safely cleared and could return to the right lane, many times avoiding collisions with oncoming traffic by inches. Due to the modern super highways and powerful tractors of today this type of driving is no longer appropriate. There is generally plenty of time for passing safely.

Much of the old time courtesy signaling by using headlights and clearance lights, basically as saying 'Thank you' and 'You are welcome' has gone 'out the window', so to speak. It used to be almost a ritual for truck drivers to assist each other when passing by using appropriate signals with their lights. These are very basic signals that even the general public could understand as simple courtesy gestures both by those passing and those being passed and are still present today, although on a much smaller scale. Even many of the general public sometimes participated in this signaling procedure and some still do today. However, as mentioned before, ignorance and lack of courtesy in driving habits have increased dramatically in recent years and this includes the age-old light signaling of the 'good ol' days'.

Courtesy signaling with lights is not a law. Most rookies have no idea how this practice came about. Some old time truck drivers have stubborn thoughts about how this procedure should be utilized but I feel they should be flexible in their thinking. Courtesy signaling with lights today is simply a show of respect of truck drivers for one another and should be considered as such, not complained about if someone thinks it should have been performed differently.

In my experience, most truck drivers appreciate a signal used when passing that can be seen. They want to know they have been signaled rather than wonder about it with apprehension. Although many find high beam signals offensive, personally, I prefer the quick flash of headlights that leaves no doubt that I am clear of the chance of a collision. However, it is getting more 'why bother?' with light signals because most truck drivers don't respond anyway or flash a spotlight in your eyes at night to let you know they prefer headlight dousing to a flick of the high beams. I consider these ignorant drivers, living in a world of their own. I figure if someone took the trouble to signal me I should respond, whether or not I like the method they used. Common courtesy. Looks professional!

## 11. ENTRANCE RAMPS

Why do trucks not always move into the next lane so a 4-wheeler can come off the entrance ramp into mainline traffic? One reason is because afterwards, many 4-wheelers ride alongside the truck in the blind spot instead of getting up to speed so the trucker can return to the right lane. Another reason is that every time you make a lane change there is increased risk of a side-swipe accident. In addition there simply may not be enough space to move into and still maintain safe following distance. In a split speed limit state whereby trucks are limited to 55 MPH, pulling out into the next lane where traffic is moving at 70 MPH can be disastrous! It is not such a simple matter to perform lane changes with a big truck as people in private vehicles may think. The driver's CDL and safety record are constantly at stake. Any experienced highway patrolman will acknowledge that it is up to the ramp traffic to affect a safe merge, not the mainline traffic. *It is up to incoming traffic to either quickly get up to speed and get safely into line or fall back and come in behind.* It is imperative that each person must use his own judgment and common sense for a safe merge.

Most, but not all of the time, incoming 4-wheelers onto the super-slab have three choices:

1. Step on it to get up to speed.
2. Fall in behind.
3. Bounce alongside mainline traffic on the shoulder because you did neither.

However, many choose to try to force trucks into the next lane and then ride alongside the truck indefinitely in the blind spot, unknowingly risking a mishap to himself and frustrating the trucker. Most automobiles can accelerate from 0 to 60 mph in just a few seconds and can accomplish getting up to speed with ease. In my view, the safest thing the trucker can do is hold his ground and leave it up to the auto driver to do one of the above obvious choices. *Of course there are common sense exceptions that need to be dealt with on an individual basis. Nothing is worth having an accident!*

When nearing exit/entrance ramps and you are not exiting, prepare to move into the left lane well in advance. Then, if someone ahead is exiting you are less likely to be affected by their slowing to do so. In like manner, if someone is coming on, you have already prepared for them. Remember, much of the general public drives as though *you, the trucker* must yield to *them*. Accidents are imminent! Be prepared to yield if you must! It is not worth causing an accident, no matter who is at fault.

When there are sometimes three lanes in congested areas, the center lane is usually safest for trucks unless trucks are allowed in the far left lane, in which case that lane would be the safest, in my opinion. However, 'no left lane for trucks' continues to be a popular idea for lawmakers who simply do not understand about trucks.

## 12. EXITING

Sometimes a big truck needing to exit can get trapped in the left lane by heavy traffic that will not allow an opening for him to change lanes to exit. Get that signal blinking and leave it on well in advance of your exit. If you see that the traffic you have been traveling with will not submit, slow with a show of brake lights with your signal still blinking and someone will have to open a space before you come to a complete stop in the left lane. If you miss your exit in a city you are unfamiliar with it can be a real bear to get turned around and find your way back. Many times the return to go the other direction is not accessible. *Trust me, you do not want to get lost on downtown city streets anywhere!* This is when things can *really* go wrong! Citations and accidents can result when trying to find a suitable place to turn around. Muggings are possible.

Should you miss your lane change or route connection on an interstate, it may be possible to use the highway you got on by mistake as an alternate route that will bring you back to the road you were trying to stay on. This can happen in heavy traffic when you are unknowingly in the wrong lane and get 'side tracked'. Keep your road atlas where you can grab it quickly and look for other connections that will route you where you need to go. Interstate 'business route' signs can sometimes cause you to exit by mistake. If you do exit inadvertently, it is sometimes best to follow the 'business route' signs and eventually they will direct you back to the interstate. However, some business routes will take you into heavy downtown traffic and/or miles out of your way. Each incident is different and must be handled accordingly. Missed or wrong turns are frustrating but they will happen on occasion. It is best to expect it and be prepared for them by having a road atlas handy and open to the area you are driving in if you are unfamiliar with it.

Be sure you are down to posted speed or below before entering the curve on exit ramps or you may find yourself over the bank, lying on your side. It happens all the while. A rollover will cost your company a minimum of $15,000.00 in repairs and could cost you your job, maybe your career. Take heed, slow down well ahead of time. Larger or better placement of signs could be of great assistance here.

## 13. ENTERING MAINLINE TRAFFIC

Another major factor in safety is to use great care when pulling into traffic from a dead stop at an intersection, especially with a fully loaded rig. Patience is very important here since it may take quite a few minutes for an opening to occur that will allow a safe entry. Then, it will take another half a minute or so to get into your lane and get up to speed. Just remember it is better to lose five or ten minutes waiting for a safe break in traffic to enter into rather than spend hours or days involved in an accident that *you* caused by being too impatient. Eventually a space will open up, one way or another. Pulling out in front of fast-moving, impatient traffic can result in a run-under, decapitating the other driver. You will be held responsible!

Anybody, truck or car, that would pull in front of an approaching, fast-moving eighteen-wheeler, especially in front of a loaded 80,000# truck rolling downhill, and once in front of the monster, jam on the brakes is either;

1. Insane!
2. Stupid!
3. Or has a death wish!

I have seen this occur many times and have had it happen to me. No amount of following distance can help in a case such as this. If some impatient driver decides he can squeeze into traffic and let everyone else bear the consequences, there is little you can do except try your best to maintain control of your rig and try to get some identification on the offender should he cause an accident and keep on going. Forward momentum of 80,000 # is a factor that drivers of private vehicles either do not understand or simply ignore in their haste. Drivers that cause accidents for others while they speed merrily on their way should always be reported if at all possible. Hopefully, law enforcement will know how to deal with them and take appropriate action.

## 14. SOMEONE IS ALWAYS BEHIND YOU

Remember this! No matter where you are or whether it is day or night, there will almost always be someone in a vehicle behind you, be it a car or truck. Do not let this cause you to be in a bigger hurry than you should be because you may think you are holding them up. Oh, it is okay to be as considerate as you can under present circumstances but do not let them push you beyond your turnoff or other location you may be looking for. Chances are, if it is a truck, they could be looking for the same turn or location you are and if you miss your turn you will then be behind them and maybe have to wait a couple of hours for them to get loaded or unloaded because they became first in line. Keep your CB radio turned on so you can communicate with anyone willing to assist you with directions.

Sometimes, another driver or even a customer will spot you searching as you are proceeding slowly down the highway and chirp in to help you. Missing your turn can once again, result in an accident or at least difficulty in finding a place to turn around. Unfortunately, it is every man for himself out here. First come, first served. Often, you will find other truck drivers taking advantage of your unfamiliarity with an area by jumping ahead of you knowing now you will have to wait for them instead of vice-verse. This has become more and more prevalent as well as more obvious in recent years. Courtesy and respect for the other driver seem to have diminished considerably. Many times even appointments are not even honored by the customers to load or unload. It has become pretty much of a 'free for all'. This is the cold, hard truth, like it or not.

## 15. WEIGHT AND SPACE MANAGEMENT

Most of the general public has no idea of the weight and space management of a fully loaded truck or the limited braking capability. Even an empty rig is hard to stop, since without weight to hold it down, harsh braking can result in severe bouncing and sideway movement of the rig, as well as jackknifing.

Of course, driving slower is good whenever possible, but it is best to travel with the flow of traffic. Most other drivers have enough common sense to realize that they must be patient and do the right thing. It only takes a couple seconds to become involved in an accident that can change your life forever. Use caution. One slip of the wheel or inattentive moment can result in ending your career. Always drive so that you feel comfortable and in control. Your life and the lives of others depend on it. Always try to leave yourself an escape route or a way out. Scan your mirrors constantly. Remember, auto drivers *never* want to get stuck behind a big truck and will take *death defying chances* to prevent it! Some of them may be under the influence of drugs or alcohol!

## 16. FOUL WEATHER

When bad weather cannot be avoided, once again do the safe thing. Park it! A few hours waiting for conditions to change can make a big difference in whether or not you reach your destination. Again, 'better late than never'! There is no shame in parking your truck in bad weather. Think of the alternative!

In winter season it can be helpful to carry a bag of cat litter and/or a bottle of bleach for traction purposes in case you get stuck. That's right, Clorox. Pour it on your tires and it will make them stick to the snow, providing traction.

Remember that snow blows off a cold windshield but sticks to and freezes on a warmed one and will eventually build up ice so that the windshield wipers cannot wipe properly. Therefore, it is sometimes better to keep the defroster turned off until absolutely necessary. Adding rubbing alcohol to the washer fluid will remove most ice. Rubbing alcohol is also an inexpensive additive to help prevent fuel gelling in sub-zero weather.

Rain-X for water removal and ice prevention on windshield in winter driving works great. Hand-held 12-volt defrosters are available that plug into the cigar lighter.

Snow has a hypnotizing effect, especially at night. Use low beams.

When there is no other traffic on the road during a snowstorm, there will be no visible white lines to guide you and no tire tracks to follow so that you know where the highway is. The safest thing to do is park it ASAP in a safe place, such as an exit/on ramp and leave the clearance lights on to prevent someone from hitting you. Try to communicate with someone over the CB as to driving conditions coming from the other direction. In like manner, upon encountering fog, rain or snow, many times you can get out of it if you keep going at a steady pace. These conditions can be patchy or regional in nature due to passing clouds and wind. Talking to oncoming traffic over the CB can be helpful to find out how things are where they have been and how widespread bad conditions may be. If it gets too thick, park it!

Fog is a killer! When fog moves in so heavy that you cannot see much more than a truck length in front of you, you had better get parked ASAP. It is already too late to be safe, should you be driving. Most multi-vehicle accidents happen in dense fog because there is no safe way to drive in it. Traffic is always in a big hurry and when blinding fog is a factor, it can be disastrous. I have seen fifty-plus vehicle pileups and it is not a pleasant sight. Autos are crushed underneath huge trucks, trucks are jackknifed, and vans opened up like a ripped open soda can, people injured, dead and dying everywhere. Mass chaos, total havoc, and ultimate disaster! Park it! Fog is the worst. Whiteouts due to heavy snow can also be disastrous.

When foul weather begins to overtake you, it is sometimes possible to outrun it if you are traveling the same direction it is coming from and are ahead of it. Weather usually moves much slower than a motor vehicle and staying ahead of a weather front may avoid a shutdown caused by snow or icy conditions moving in behind you.

Headlights on in rain, fog and snow so other traffic can see you coming is important. In many states, it is the law.

Be also aware that some modern-designed trucks have protective headlight coverings also intended to increase streamlining for increased fuel mileage. This design has resulted in snow buildup on the headlights since the shield creates an insulated airspace that remains too cool to melt snow when it hits the headlight covering. The snow buildup then causes extreme headlight dimming to the point of being dangerous. The remedy for this is to install fog lights or running lights that have no such covering and will melt the snow as it hits or stop and brush off the snow.

Innovative winter wiper blades can also be very helpful to prevent snow and ice buildup on the wipers. This type blade has a loose rubber covering that effectively causes the snow and ice to fall off as the wipers go back and forth.

In freezing weather when it is raining or the road is wet, watch the conditions carefully to determine if the water is changing to 'black ice'. If you can see spray coming off your tires when you scan your mirrors, you are still safe. However, when the wet road stops producing spray and reflects the lights from the vehicle ahead like a mirror, you are traveling on 'black ice'. Going from daytime to nighttime or a change in altitude can cause this situation because hills and valleys quickly affect air temperatures. An incoming weather front can also cause this. Apply the 4-way hazard signals! Avoid hitting the brakes and coast into any possible parking area slowly to avoid a jackknife or sliding out of control into the ditch or into other vehicles. *This is extremely dangerous and it is mandatory to stop as soon as you locate a safe place to wait for the 'salt and pepper shaker', as the highway sanding crew is known.* Remember, bridges freeze first!

Yes, there are times when the most prudent decision is to park and wait for the highway road crews to plow, salt and sand before you continue on. In most places they are very efficient and many times you may see highway crews waiting in the median before a storm hits in preparation for immediate action. Consider this a warning and be prepared to find a safe place to park. As soon as possible, check your CB radio for being on and the volume turned up so you can hear any reports from other drivers. This is an advantage of having meteorologists issue advance warnings to the public. We are a nation of motorists and need all the help we can get. Knowing where the storms are and when they are going to hit is a big advantage. Sometimes you can reroute yourself.

Other times, if you take notice of the oncoming trucks and see that the sides of the trailers are plastered with road slush and the undercarriages are loaded with snow and ice, it may be time to stop and see what the road conditions and weather look like where those trucks have been, since you are probably going to be there soon if you continue on. Talk to them on the CB! Stop at a truck stop and inquire. Call truck stops ahead on your route and ask about their weather.

Accumulate as much information as you can before charging blindly into the face of an oncoming storm. It might be a good time to take a break, make phone calls, get some sleep or something to eat. The alternative could be a parking spot buried in snow in the middle of some highway. It happens. Carry some canned food, just in case. You may be unexpectedly shut down somewhere for quite a while. A large candle can provide your only heat for quite a while. Remember to crack a window for fresh air. Winter weather can get real bad, real fast, anytime.

Smoke from fires and dust storms out west can be just as bad or worse than fog.

## 17. CHAINS

If you are in mountain country where chains are required, constant checking on conditions ahead is necessary. It is mandatory to carry chains in several western mountain states even if you do not intend to use them. Most trucking companies do not allow their drivers to chain up! They feel that if the roads are that bad, it is too dangerous to be on them!

This seems to be another revenue generating scheme for state and local governments to, once again, fleece the truckers. Admittedly, when conditions are severe and the roads are so bad that accidents are imminent, the highway department should restrict or stop all traffic to prevent or minimize the possibility of an accident. However, if someone chooses not to install chains or company policy will not allow them to, I do not see why it should be necessary to have to spend all the money on them simply to 'show and tell'. Especially if there are check points to assure that vehicles going beyond that point have chains installed, why should it matter if there are hundreds of other trucks and cars that choose to 'wait it out' until the roads clear? Maybe someone has figured out that this is a pretty neat way to put some more money in their kitty. Big money! The fine runs into hundreds of dollars if you do not carry chains in a big truck, regardless of whether or not you ever use them. The seeming proof that it is a revenue game is that on occasion, an official will actually come out and make drivers un-bag their chains so they can count them to make sure they have the required number of sets even though the official has been told the chains are not going to be installed. Additionally, they will sometimes open roads that required chains to traffic one way but not the other, tricking the drivers on the unopened side into proceeding without chains and citing them when they do. Games police play! I have seen this happen. Again, the trucker pays. Be sure you carry chains where required. You, not the company, will pay!

In regard to pay, installing chains on a big rig can be quite a chore. If chains are not properly installed they may do severe damage to your equipment. The chains can also come off and get lost if not tightened properly. Chains are expensive and the drivers are accountable for them. Sometimes there are people that will put chains on for a nominal fee per axle. Then, after the truck gets over the mountain or area requiring chains, a chain uninstaller will take the chains off for another charge. This shows that doing this deserves getting paid extra to install chains but I am not aware of any companies that will pay their drivers or anybody else to do it, for that matter. The driver must either bear this cost, put the chains on himself or wait until the conditions improve enough not to require chains. If chains are required I do not want to be driving anyway.

## 18. PICKUP TAILGATES DOWN OR MISSING

Pickup trucks with the tailgate down or missing altogether should be ticketed, fined and proof of the tailgate being reinstalled should be included. An alternate means of preventing loose items in the bed of a pickup from sliding onto the highway might be acceptable, such as a custom fitted net or bars of some kind. It seems that these drivers have the idea that with the tailgate fastened in the upright closed position that the airflow against the tailgate causes increased fuel consumption so they think they are saving gas with the tailgate down. This may or may not be true, but I know for sure that many items have slid out of pickups into the path of following traffic which has no time or space to avoid running into or over them, causing damage to their vehicles and even accidents in trying to avoid these unexpected obstacles. Spare tires, some mounted on rims, ladders, construction supplies such as screen doors and heating ducts; I have seen them all and more in the center of interstate highways, with traffic moving at high speeds and no way to know of the danger ahead. There needs to be a law that addresses this major problem. In my opinion, this practice is far more dangerous than a vehicle traveling a couple miles an hour over the posted speed limit at 2 AM and should be vigorously enforced by the law.

## 19. SIGNS

Observe unusual traffic warning signs posted, especially on non-interstate highways. Usually there is a good reason these signs were deemed necessary; probably repeated accidents. Be responsive to the advice of these signs and grateful that the local officials were concerned and intelligent enough to post them.

When approaching exits be aware that some identical exit signs have different meanings. By that I mean that sometimes when a sign says 'next exit', it may mean the one you are immediately approaching or it could mean the exit after that. I have seen it both ways, so a bit of caution and a lot of common sense is in order here. This is a nationwide occurrence with great irregularity. When a sign says 'this exit' it leaves no doubt that it means the one you are approaching. This would seem to be a better posting. Such confusion can cause some unknowing motorists to slam on their brakes at the last second so as not to miss their exit.

I think the various federal, state and local highway departments have done a phenomenal job for the most part, of posting signs nationwide to help motorists locate the many different routes, exits, cities and towns, warnings and countless other things that are necessary to travel around this great country. In spite of this there are still many places that need additional signs for sooner warning of approaching exits, towns and cities, for safety's sake. The sooner someone knows his turnoff is getting close, the safer everybody is for obvious reasons. As mentioned before, last minute darting and diving to avoid missing an exit can result in tragedy. Drivers that continue passing at the last minute even though it means cutting the passed vehicle off so they can make their exit, are inviting disaster. Nobody wins, everybody loses! Look for this to happen and be prepared to back out of it to allow the confused driver to make his exit without colliding with you. Be professional! Do the right thing. You must always expect the unexpected!

Another thing that should be considered is to position signs at a height that does not block a truck driver's view of on-coming traffic when at an intersection or entrance to main-line highways. Many signs are installed at the trucker's eye level. Clearly, no one has taken this aspect into consideration in many locations and it sometimes causes great difficulty for a truck driver to make a safe passage into traffic when trees, bushes or other signs block their line of sight.

It can be more dangerous for a big rig to move at the slower truck speed limit of 55 MPH and cause faster (65 MPH) automobile traffic to back up and struggle to pass rather than allowing the truck to roll with the flow of traffic at the higher speed.

It is the same with restricting trucks to only the right lane when climbing steep grades. It would not make sense for an empty or lightly loaded truck traveling at 65 MPH climbing a hill not to pass a heavily laden big rig struggling at 25 to 35 MPH in the slow lane, to slam on the brakes going uphill just to comply with 'trucks use right lane only' signs. Changing the signs to read 'Slower vehicles keep right' would make more sense.

Apparently, this law was written due to loaded trucks slowly climbing hills trying to pass each other at slow speeds and thereby blocking both lanes to following traffic. I call this 'turtle racing'. This of course, is sometimes caused by poor judgment on the part of the passing truck driver. He should realize the problem he is going to cause and not try to pass if he cannot do it on a timely basis. The reality is that most truck drivers try to squeeze every ounce of power out of their vehicle when approaching and climbing grades to maintain momentum. Highway patrols use this aspect as a tool to catch truckers speeding and therefore produce revenue.

The solution for this might be best handled by citing the slow truck in the passing lane that did not have quite enough steam to get quickly by and failed to drop back and fall back in line. In effect, the law does result in this but leaves fast moving trucks vulnerable to a citation for simply using common sense and rolling uphill with the flow rather than jamming on the brakes to avoid a rear-end collision *going uphill* just to comply with such an unrealistic law.

Some of these laws for truckers are archaic. These and other outdated laws relating to big rigs need to be updated and improved. Conditions have changed considerably over the years in relation to increased engine power, size of equipment, traffic and highway conditions.

Fortunately, most law enforcement officers use good common sense relating to most issues rather than adhering to the strict letter of the law. Usually it is the rookie officers that are unrealistically strict, trying to develop a reputation and lacking the wisdom and compassion that usually comes only with experience. Instead of signs reading 'Trucks Right Lane Only' or 'No Truck Passing', the signs should say 'No lane Blocking'. This is far more accurate and applies to everybody, not just truckers. Albuquerque, N.M. has signs posted saying, "NO VEHICLES LEFT LANE UNDER 65 MPH", evidence of their awareness of the problem and positive attempt at a realistic solution.

Personally, I usually feel much safer telling trainees to drive just a little slower than everybody else and refrain from passing unless absolutely necessary. In explaining to trainees this method of 'rolling with the flow', I am confidant I am doing the right thing rather than to allow new drivers to believe there are no 'gray' areas in traffic enforcement. Causing a traffic blockage is always dangerous and usually results in impatient drivers passing unsafely, especially on a two-lane highway.

The way the laws are presently written it sometimes seems to truck drivers as though it is all about generating money from truckers and 'safety be damned'. This can also be seen when some of the state DOT weigh stations allow the trucks waiting to enter the station to back up into the travel lanes of the highway. Many states would rather risk a rear-end collision on the highway than miss an opportunity to fine a trucker or two for being a few pounds overweight. There *are* exceptions in some states that post signs whereby truckers are allowed to bypass scales when the ramp is full. *I am sure they arrived at this procedure through hard learned lessons!*

Remember this! In large metropolitan areas such as Los Angeles, Chicago and New York to mention a few, 4-wheelers have no fear of big trucks. They take unbelievable chances, risking their lives and the lives of others.

If you are a rookie truck driver and unfamiliar with the big cities as previously mentioned, avoid going into them prematurely. Advise your fleet manager of your fears and use key words or phrases such as 'scared', 'nervous' or 'unsafe', and 'never been there' or 'afraid of an accident'. *They must react to these comments!* If they do not, call your safety department. I guarantee that if they are qualified personnel, they will see it your way and get another driver to relieve you of the load if they value their job. Do not go into these huge cities until you are confident and ready to meet the challenge.

Always lock your doors and windows to prevent muggings, break-ins or robberies. This is a common occurrence. Truck drivers are not allowed to carry guns, knives or other weapons for self-defense. Only murderers, cutthroats and thieves can do that. Mace and pepper spray are illegal too but wasp and hornet spray are legal and can be an effective deterrent and will reach up to 30 feet with a blinding stream.

## 20. SAFETY ZONE

*Do not jump into my safety zone! I left that space in front for me!* If you feel the need to pass, go on ahead several hundred feet to where you are not creating a hazard for those you are passing before you pull back in. Barely missing the passed vehicle's front bumper makes no sense on an interstate highway. Otherwise, stay back in line and be professional enough to leave yourself a safety zone. What is the big hurry, anyway? You will just be pulling off shortly to do something and then be back out here passing all of us again, causing another hazard.

## 21. JACKKNIFE

Pulling abruptly into the safe following distance of an eighteen-wheeler on slippery highways can result in what is commonly know as a 'jackknife'. What this means is that when the truck driver suddenly applies the brakes harshly, the trailer begins to slide sideways and moves alongside the tractor, more or less folding together as a pocket jackknife. As this is happening the trailer is going into other lanes of traffic and it will be on a fatal collision course. There is very little that can be done to pull out of this as it is occurring. An event such as this can block an entire highway for many hours. Driving too fast or braking too hard when stopping or turning on slippery pavement usually causes jackknifes. They can also occur when accelerating on a curve when on slippery pavement, braking when coming down a hill or harshly braking to regain your following distance. Going too fast on slippery roads when cornering to enter a ramp to get on an interstate from a crossroad can also cause a jackknife. Weather can be a big factor here.

## 22. LEFT LANE DRIVING

Lawmakers and the general public seem to be primarily concerned about why big trucks drive in the left lane on interstate highways. Many states and municipalities have passed laws restricting trucks from left lane driving. However, there are many common sense reasons for truck drivers to utilize the left lane. It is really very simple, if you are a truck driver. For one thing, it seems like the natural thing to do when you are piloting a monstrous 80,000# vehicle in congested areas where smaller traffic darts about indiscriminately, unconcerned and unaware of the hazard they are causing or the danger they are in.

Driving in the left lane in highly congested areas eliminates the concern for traffic in blind spots on the left side of the truck. The driver can now concentrate his attention on adequate following distance and right side blind spots. The ease of traveling through these heavy traffic areas is greatly enhanced and driver stress for the trucker is greatly reduced with traffic now on only one side of the truck and in front, where the driver can maintain nearly full control. The possibility of an accident caused by other poor drivers is now nearly eliminated.

Occasionally, an irritated 4-wheeler driver will jump in front of the truck and slow down to indicate he does not approve of having a truck staying in the left lane, showing that the auto driver is ignorant of the safety factor. This is more indication that the public needs to be more educated with an awareness of how to share the highways with heavy equipment. An 80,000# truck cannot stop on a dime or even brake enough to prevent a rear end accident in all these cases. Individuals in their private vehicles have no business trying to 'educate' truck drivers or each other for that matter. These 4-wheelers are causing a hazardous situation and creating ROAD RAGE. They are dangerous!

I think the biggest reason big trucks stay in the left lane is to maintain a safe following distance, also known as a 'safety zone'. When traffic causes a passing situation for a big truck, it is important that the driver maintains a safe following distance as much as possible. Due to the immense weight of the vehicle, safe following distance for a truck is far greater than an automobile and therefore the driver must stay in the passing or left lane until a large enough space in the right lane opens up for him to pull back over and still maintain this safe following distance from vehicles ahead of him. Since the general public does not realize this, they drive alongside the truck or just enough ahead of it in the right lane so that the truck driver would not have an adequate safety zone should he pull back into the right lane.

This also happens when a big truck attempts to pass a smaller vehicle and the driver being passed speeds up just enough so the truck is stuck in the passing lane, as explained before. Since the trucker needs several hundred feet of following distance before he can safely return to the right lane behind the smaller vehicle, he must run the left lane indefinitely while the other driver fails to realize the problem he is causing. Following traffic sees only that the truck is blocking the lane they want to use and naturally blame the trucker. Lack of understanding is prevalent.

Highway deterioration is a large factor. First of all, if there are two drivers on a truck, one of them needs to get some sleep for his turn to drive. Some of the interstate highways are so old that the right lanes have deteriorated to the point of being so rough that a vehicle will bounce and jounce the occupants badly about inside, making rest impossible. Many times the left lane is much smoother and this is why a driver will sometimes use the left lane so that his co-driver can get some rest and therefore not fall asleep at the wheel when his turn to drive comes up. This is especially true in the states of Missouri, Louisiana, Oklahoma and Arkansas, although there are others.

Extreme high wind can also cause a truck driver to use the left lane if the wind is coming from that direction, so that his truck leans into the wind thereby helping to prevent getting blown over on his side, since highways are usually built high in the center so the water will drain properly each way. This situation happens more than people realize because these huge trailers catch a lot of wind.

Left lane driving is also many times done by 4-wheelers that do not want to pass and therefore become 'bear bait', but want more visibility. Then, if the truck driver overtakes other traffic in the right lane and signals his intention to pass, the auto driver speeds up to block the pass. Very unsafe and very irritating to the trucker! They should either get on past the truck and disappear in the distance or fall far enough behind so they can see around the truck without hanging in the left lane, looking as if they want to pass, but not doing so.

Center-lane driving on 6-lane interstates in congested areas is another common dangerous practice. Since big trucks are sometimes prohibited from driving in the left lane, that leaves only the center lane for passing and the right lane for entering and exiting traffic. However, 4-wheelers many times continually ride in the center lane, blocking the big trucks and knowing full well what they are doing, but nevertheless failing to utilize the left lane intended for them to alleviate the situation. This is definitely a problem that highway patrol should monitor. I-95 in Connecticut is the first one to come to mind. This is probably the worst place for this because it is ever-present, 24 hours a day. It is almost as if these drivers of smaller vehicles are trained to drive obstructively. And again, the far left lane is usually empty because the general driving public is afraid to use it for fear of getting a speeding ticket. The right lane is usually blocked by incoming and exiting traffic.

Diving from the far left lane across the other two lanes to exit at the last second is another major problem with many 4-wheelers. What in the world they are thinking of is beyond my understanding! Seems like they need to plan ahead more and not be in such a big hurry. Their lives are at stake! How can they drive so crazy? Surely, most that do this are local drivers that know their exit is coming up. Are they on drugs?

## 23. LEFT LANE FOR TRUCKS IS USUALLY SAFEST

There are many cities across the country that have major interstate highways going straight through them. These are usually three or four lanes wide in each direction in the congested areas. The scenario here is usually that local traffic tends to stay in the two or three right lanes in preparation for exiting and through traffic can utilize the far left lane for ease of passing. If the left lanes are not posted, trucks can greatly benefit from staying in the far left lane. I think most law enforcement will agree that it is safer to keep the huge trucks away from all other traffic whenever possible.

I believe most seasoned truckers will also agree with me that everyone would *feel and be* safer with trucks traveling in the far left lane instead of *creating a barrier* in the right two lanes on many congested and multi-lane highways. *Forcing local traffic to struggle through two solid lines of big trucks in the right two lanes simply does not make sense!* Sideswipes and shoulder accidents are a direct result of this practice, as well as rear-enders. Somebody needs to wake up and smell the coffee on this one. Decades ago when these laws were first enacted, underpowered trucks had trouble keeping up to speed in the left lane but most of today's high-powered trucks do not have such a problem.

There are few cities in California that allow trucks in the left lane. In fact, trucks are required by law to stay *out* of the left-most lanes throughout the state unless it is posted otherwise, as when going through Stockton and Sacramento on I-5. To me, these exceptions magnify the fact that *even California recognizes it is safer for everybody when trucks travel in the left-most lanes in some congested areas.* For the Republic of California to admit to this by actually posting signs for trucks to keep left is significant since this state has rigid laws regarding truck traffic. Again, California is by far the leader in writing citations for truckers. Trucks are treated as a necessary evil there.

Anyway, I believe trucks should be encouraged to stay in the far left lane of multi-lane highways in congested areas, away from the other traffic whenever possible. This would greatly reduce the continual sparring for position with cars and would likely reduce the accident rate in large metropolitan areas. Someone seems to be missing the boat here when instead trucks have been banned from many left lanes in many states.

It would be nice if when automobile drivers noticed weigh station signs or truck stops coming up, they would have presence of mind enough to *move into the left lane to allow more access for the trucks to maneuver into and out of the weigh stations.*

Believe it or not, Ohio got it exactly right when they designed the I-271 Cleveland bypass. Ohio included two far left separate express lanes, away from local traffic and allows all traffic, including trucks to utilize them. *This, in my opinion is the most innovative, up-to-date bypass highway in the country and should be used as an example* for all other highway planners to study before spending billions more on the obsolete patterns of fifty years ago or the ridiculous tolls roads proposed for truckers only as in Virginia.

## 24. MAKING WRONG TURNS OR MISSING TURNS

One of the biggest problems for truck drivers on a continuing basis can be trying to locate a shipper or receiver that they have never been to before. *Making wrong turns or missing a turn requires finding space enough to turn around safely with this huge equipment.* This is always a challenge! For a truck driver who barely speaks English, it has to be even more difficult. *Safety is definitely an issue whenever a turn is missed! It happens often!*

Time spent getting lost due to poor or no customer directions is just part of the job and not even mentioned by anyone. Again, logging it will reduce your available driving time to earn money accordingly, with your logbook.

Taking shortcuts to avoid congested areas can result in huge fines if you get on a weight or size restricted highway. Interstate highways are always the safest to avoid this. Rand-McNally Motor Carriers' Road Atlas for truckers is very useful for locating most restrictions of this nature. The highways with no restrictions for trucks are highlighted and there is information on each individual state listed separately in the front of the atlas.

## 25. NON-TRUCKERS ARE BECOMING MORE EDUCATED

Hopefully, the one big positive aspect about all this 'trying out' of trucking has been that there are now far more ex truck drivers in private vehicles now that *should* understand a bit more of how to share the nations highways with big trucks. Maybe this will ultimately result in a few less accidents and a more courteous atmosphere on the highway from time to time. Sure hope so!

Those in management positions in the trucking industry should be included in this line of thinking. There are many of *them* that simply have no idea of the reality of what it is like to be an OVER THE ROAD truck driver. I guarantee that if they took the time to get out here and experience just a small portion of what they are setting policy for, *their thinking would change dramatically!* This is the kind of information that cannot be learned from management literature or sitting behind a desk; the feel of driving a big truck or even riding in one. Not to mention uncompensated-for waiting time in the confines of a truck, away from friends and family. Unfortunately, I doubt if this understanding will ever take place to any large degree. Too many other problems take priority such as recruiting new drivers.

## 26. EVIDENCE OF DANGER

If you visit any large trucking company you will almost always see not one, but many wrecked trucks sitting around somewhere. This is stark evidence of the danger involved with OVER THE ROAD trucking. Some of these wrecks represent fatalities of either the truck driver or those that he came in contact with. Just the fact that there are usually many wrecks at most trucking companies should make it obvious that there is a serious problem with OVER THE ROAD truck drivers out here. Mangled wrecks can also be seen at many junkyards and towing companies all over the country. Each one has an unpleasant story!

I continually warn my trainees about the danger of following too close and tell them to back out of it when somebody cuts into your safety zone and slows down. Turn on the headlights to let the offender know. Make him aware he is too close in front. Turn on the headlights when going through any congested area or construction zone. Fog lights or running lights are really great for this purpose. Bright lights on large vehicles have a necessary intimidating effect and may even prevent accidents.

Remember, lawyers advertise on TV to represent people involved with big trucks in an accident, knowing that they will most likely be able to obtain huge settlements from a trucker's insurance company.

## 27. SITTING DUCKS

Whenever you see a vehicle of any kind parked on the shoulder of the road, also known as the 'breakdown lane', try to immediately work your vehicle into the next lane away from it. These 'sitting ducks' have been the cause of countless tragedies over the years. Some vehicles are unattended but many have people moving around them that may step inadvertently into the path of oncoming traffic. I have seen others pull right out in front of fast moving on-line traffic, causing frantic braking and juggling for position of all other vehicles to avoid collision. Such stupidity is difficult to understand.

I feel strongly that only those in an emergency condition should be allowed to pull onto the shoulder. If it is a commercial vehicle, the driver knows that he must get out his triangle flares and display them in the appropriate positions designated by law. 'Sitting ducks" are especially dangerous after dark because you can come upon them suddenly without any warning. Since you have no time to work your way into the next lane, you are only inches from a possible disaster, particularly if they have no warning flares set up. If there is no emergency and the driver could have gone on to an exit ramp or rest area, he should be issued a citation and given a stiff fine for public endangerment.

Highway patrol should be included in this since they *constantly* create an unnecessary hazard. They are some of the biggest offenders! They are supposed to serve and protect, not scare and endanger. I fear these officers sometimes get a bit carried away with their own importance and rely too heavily on the visibility of their 'disco lights' to protect them from harm. Unfortunately, many of them are killed each year because of this.

Recently, some states have enacted laws that require traffic to move into the left lane if there is an emergency or police vehicle on the shoulder. I think most people *already* try to move over but it is not always possible in high speed, bumper to bumper heavy traffic. You simply cannot see them in time. In a dual speed limit state, to expect a 55 MPH truck to pull into the left lane in front of a 70 MPH vehicle is not only ridiculous, it is stupid.

What will it take to make law enforcement wake up and realize this imminent danger they are causing? How many more patrolmen must die? How many more accidents must they cause? Why do they not take their 'catch' to the nearest exit ramp or other safe place to write them up? Is citing a motorist for going slightly over the speed limit worth a patrolman's life? I think not! Lets be sensible and end this slaughter on the highways!

## 28. SHARK'S TEETH IN GRILL

There has been a new obnoxious development in the appearance of trucks themselves. Somebody got the bright idea to install shark's teeth images in the grill so that when they approach traffic from the rear, it will intimidate the drivers to move over and let the 'vicious monster' by. I wonder what the general public must think about this. It surely does not look very professional to me. It seems to me that the truck driver image is poor enough already without promoting an obvious negative impression such as this. Could this present the idea that truckers are speeding, obnoxious road hogs?

## 29. CB RADIO

The citizens band (CB) radio has been one of the most helpful tools for modern day truckers. They are used by truckers to get directions, warn each other about accidents, weather-related road conditions and countless other dangerous situations that can help prevent accidents and promote safety on the highways. Sooner or later, every trucker adopts a CB name, or "handle'. Each individual having a handle is a way of truckers talking to each other without revealing your real identity to a total stranger. Many times, drivers develop a CB 'voice' which they use to pass the time away talking to another driver or drivers. Kind of a 'hidden identity' to be someone else for a time.

Many customers require drivers to monitor a certain CB channel to gain access to their facility or to let them know when they can load or unload. It is very much taken for granted that all truck drivers have a CB.

CBs are also helpful to keep truckers from getting traffic citations by notifying each other if a highway patrol (speed cop) is present or hiding to catch those exceeding the speed limit as they try to make up for lost time.

Unfortunately, CB radios are abused by a few obnoxious loudmouth truck drivers that choose to use foul and unacceptable language over the airwaves and once again, create a less than acceptable image for the trucking industry. This activity is very difficult to control by law enforcement! However, many times the truckers themselves can monitor this unacceptable activity and admonish the culprits. It is not a pleasant experience to listen to how some of these ignorant people carry on over the CB radio. Most of the time, no response is the best response and the culprits get the message and shut up. Unfortunately, many times a traveling family with children may be exposed to this less than desirable verbal abuse. This is unacceptable! There are also base stations operated by people at home all around the country and automobile drivers that are guilty of this practice.

## 30. DUAL SPEED LIMITS, SOME STATES

As mentioned before, some states have dual speed limits that allow autos to travel at higher speeds than trucks, and also allow the auto drivers to use radar detectors that are illegal for truckers. While automobiles may have a speed limit of 65 or 70mph, commercial big trucks sometimes have a speed limit of only 55 or 60mph on the same highway.

In my opinion, a speed limit for big trucks of only 55mph presents a major safety issue. In heavy traffic areas, it has created a situation similar to a demolition derby on the highway with everybody sparring for position. It causes an attitude of lead, follow or get out of the way! Leap-frogging is a common occurrence and is very dangerous. Interstate 70 through Ohio is a good example of this.

For a professional truck driver to be restricted to a lower speed *under present conditions*, while allowing smaller traffic to drive faster over hundreds of miles, it also causes the following problems:

1. Boredom and monotony.
2. Fatigue and tiredness.
3. Sleepiness.
4. Stress.
5. Logbook problems.
6. Reduced income.
7. Speeding tickets.
8. Traffic bunching.
9. Tailgating.
10. Leap-frogging.
11. Reduced following distance.
12. Cut-offs.
13. Racing to get ahead.
14. Dangerous braking.
15. Sideswipes.
16. Rear-enders.
17. Bad attitudes.
18. ROAD RAGE.
19. Discourtesy.
20. Poor or no turn signal usage.

For these reasons, the CB radio has long been a necessary tool to help truckers avoid getting traffic tickets which can result in loss of license and lively-hood, as well as increase the insurance rates on their private vehicles, as mentioned before.

Since OVER THE ROAD truckers travel ten times or more than the mileage of private citizens, maybe there should be an adjustment in the number of citations or points allocated as penalties. The deck is definitely stacked against truck drivers and always has been. It is unfair and is not getting any better. Increasing the fines significantly without imminent loss of license might make more sense. Professional compensation would surely result in safer driving.

## 31. TRAFFIC CITATIONS

Speed limits are definitely necessary in all busy and congested areas. They are also necessary in all construction zones and secondary roadways. Interstate highways need speed limits in open country and in congested areas. There are 'recommended speeds' in mountainous or unusual terrain. However, some states and municipalities have taken the opportunity of using speed limits to generate revenue from the public to supplement their budget. Truckers seem to be favorite targets for this generation of revenue for many reasons. An OVER THE ROAD truck driver is totally alone in his mission when it comes to citations and the resulting fines. It is their responsibility to continually drive at a safe and prudent speed according to constantly changing conditions! This is all the more important because of the enormous amount of weight involved regarding this heavy equipment. There is definitely a safety issue.

Trucks are an easy target for law enforcement because of their size. Trucks can appear to be going much faster than they are and this illusion encourages the public to support law enforcement against big trucks. The fact that most long distance truckers do not have regular runs or schedules so they cannot appear in court on a specific date to defend themselves allows law enforcement to write tickets that they know will probably not be challenged.

As previously mentioned, one of the most obvious methods used to single out truckers as 'cash cows' is establishing a 55 MPH speed limit for trucks in areas where 4-wheelers have speed limits up to 70 MPH. The way this works is that whenever law enforcement feels the need to increase revenue or citation activity, all they have to do is sit at the bottom of a hill and wait for the trucks to either try to get a head start at the bottom to pull their heavy rig up the grade or catch them 'letting it roll' past the allowable speed when rolling down a grade. California, Oregon, Pennsylvania and Ohio are great for doing this.

On the one hand, I consider this a form of 'entrapment' and feel it should not be allowed due to common sense driving. On the other hand, uncontrolled, maniacal downhill running at high speeds with a heavily laden 80,000 # rig is dangerous and unacceptable. Engine brakes with mufflers should be mandatory and reasonable tolerance allowed for maximum downhill speed control and safety.

In any case, once a citation is issued, the underpaid truck driver must then take steps to either contest the ticket through one of the many trucker legal services available or simply accept the citation, pay the fine and let the points go on his license which will probably increase his personal automobile insurance premiums for years to come. The fines can be several hundred dollars. Failing to respond to the citation can result in loss or suspension of his driver's license, even jail!

If the trucker chooses to contest the ticket, the legal services also usually cost several hundred dollars and the court costs could be several hundred more, especially in California. But it may be possible to get the citation reduced to a lesser charge that will not affect your license or insurance cost. Some states allow you to take a safe driving course to dismiss the ticket if it is the first one received in their state and have internet traffic school.

If a trucker should get a citation for what is classified as a 'serious violation', it will put his CDL in jeopardy.

'Serious violations' are as follows; one speeding ticket 15 MPH or more over the speed limit, which puts a truck driver on probation for 3 years. A second ticket over 15 MPH will result in a 60 day CDL license suspension and a 3rd will add on another 120 days. This is also the penalty for reckless driving, improper lane change, following too close or driving without your CDL on your truck, which also includes a $2500 fine. Professionals are expected to play by the rules, regardless of the many unprofessional conditions they must endure. The penalties can be financially crippling and many times far outweigh the offense!

I once read that there are 425,000 tickets *a month* issued to *truck drivers* nationwide, and that in the next three years one out of three drivers will lose their CDL licenses. *That figures to well over five million tickets a year!* If each ticket was a fine of only $100, it comes to over *half a billion dollars* in fines, not to mention attorney fees and court costs.

## 32. GETTING DIRECTIONS TO GO TO THE CUSTOMER

It is always a good idea to do a map study of where you are going and *write everything down in detail before starting out.* Include highway route numbers, towns where you must change routes, exit numbers, approximate distances between route changes and any other pertinent information that is available to you in advance. When getting directions by phone, any landmarks such as convenience stores, churches, cemeteries, gas stations and countless other things can be very helpful.

This is one of the most important and sometimes difficult parts of trucking. Many accidents and lost time can be prevented simply by acquiring exact directions to avoid taking wrong turns or getting lost and having to find a place to turn around and go back. It can be very frustrating, even dangerous!

There are several ways directions can be acquired.

1.  Your company may provide them by including them in print with your bills of lading. These are generally the most accurate, since they can be perused and upgraded. Not very many companies use this method in this computer age. Too archaic! But it works because it is physically visual to the driver and can be corrected manually something changes.

2.  Your company may provide directions with an onboard satcom (satellite communicator). These can be very good or not so good, depending on how persistent a company is at upgrading wrong and out-dated directions. Most OVER THE ROAD trucking companies have a satellite computer macro for their drivers to send in updated directions for stops that have none, or are wrong. Some of these directions are poor or even incomprehensible. Abbreviations should only be used if they are clearly representative of what is meant. For instance, LT can mean left turn or it can mean light. It can become very confusing when someone gets carried away with their own

idea of shorthand and can become counter-productive. Broken or misspelled words can also cause confusion. These directions are usually sent in by other truck drivers after making pickups or deliveries. Many are not too good.

3. Calling the customer by phone. When doing this, be sure to ask for landmarks and distances between turns or streets. When they are finished, always repeat the directions back slowly to the person providing them so they can re-think what they have told you. Many times in doing this, they will discover a left or right turn was the opposite of what they said.

4. Getting a customer's recorded directions by phone. This can be a hassle if the recording goes too fast or is difficult to understand for various reasons. These are sometimes the worst directions because there is no way to quiz a live person if you have a question. Occasionally, they can be excellent!

5. As you near your destination, many times you can use your CB radio to ask for 'local information'. There are sometimes people on base stations in different areas that enjoy assisting truckers locate their customers. Use caution here, though, since there are those that prey on truckers and may direct you into a mugging.

6. Stop as you approach the customer and ask someone at a truck stop, gas station or convenience store. Some truck stops have a wall map of the largest nearby city or a book of directions to most customers in their immediate area. If there are no truck stops available, you may have to stop at a business of some kind where you can safely park your truck to ask for directions. Usually you will find the customers more helpful than a busy store clerk.

7. Global Positioning Systems (GPS). I can see where this could someday be the ultimate solution to this problem. I am sure all vehicles will eventually have a GPS that will be immensely helpful in finding locations one has never been to before. This will surely enhance safety and assist countless OVER THE ROAD truckers and the public, in their travels. Some mobile phone services already have GPS programs. Everything is presented step by step and turn by turn as you progress toward your destination. Each and every turn is given aloud to you in advance to prepare you for them.

In spite of all these methods, there will probably be times that you will get lost or confused anyway. Everybody does, sooner or later. Having a mobile phone is a great advantage.

Having a powerful handheld spotlight is mandatory for locating street signs and numbers on buildings after dark.

Incomplete load pickup information is another problem. Sometimes, if the information provided does not include a trailer number or pickup number, the driver can be stalled indefinitely until he can produce it.

## 33. PROFESSIONAL APPEARANCE GAINS RESPECT

I realize this next opinion is not going to be a very popular segment of this writing for many that are already OVER THE ROAD truck drivers, but I feel it must be said. It takes a certain amount of intelligence, talent and common sense among other things, to be able accomplish the demands of this profession. Even though these drivers come from all walks of life, it is important that they enhance their image for the sake of self-respect and maximum compensation.

Truck drivers do not have to act like pigs and look like slobs. They choose to be that way!

A professional OVER THE ROAD truck driver should show by example and look professional in their driving habits and appearance. Like it or not, we are constantly in the public's eye.

In writing books about the trucking profession, it has caused me to more closely scrutinize my 'fellow drivers' and much of the time it has been very disappointing. Could it be that the unprofessional and often slovenly appearance of these drivers has an affect on how they are paid and how they are treated in other circumstances? Oh, there are a good many very presentable drivers also, but the majority looks unprofessional, bordering on riff-raff. How can drivers that do not have any respect for themselves expect to gain respect from others? In like manner, if the drivers do not even respect themselves, why would they respect others?

Surely, today's OVER THE ROAD truck drivers have brought a lot of disrespect from the general population upon themselves not only in the way they drive, using no signals as they wander lane to lane or when exiting and making turns, but also in their appearance.

As I said before, I am sure this appearance has something to do with how truckers are treated when waiting to get loaded or unloaded. Undoubtedly, truck stop personnel also look upon many of these unkempt drivers with disdain.

Yes, there are quite a few rough looking, slovenly characters driving trucks these days and always has been. And unfortunately, the public has a way of putting all truck drivers into the same category. Recently I read of a woman truck driver that visited her local public grade school and asked the children how they pictured truck drivers. She was shocked when told they are big, fat, hairy, dirty people. I cannot deny that this type of driver exists, because there are many like that. Fortunately, this lady trucker took the time to explain she was a truck driver too, and invited the children to inspect her truck. This is the kind of awareness and education that should be promoted on a much larger scale.

In another incident, in talking candidly with a friendly lady truck stop fuel manager of four years experience in the trucking industry who had previously been manager of a major chain restaurant unrelated to trucking, I asked what her first impression was of dealing with drivers of big trucks. Her immediate comment was, "Oh, my god!" I then asked her what her opinion was of most of the truck drivers she came in contact with. She answered with one word, "A—holes!" This manager was obviously an educated and intelligent professional whom I had never met before, answering a spur of the moment inquiry. Unfortunately, this opinion seems prevalent throughout the industry.

More and more people with higher education *are* entering this field and it will be up to them to help improve the overall image of truck drivers and improve the pay and benefits. Trying to escape from society and becoming a 'hermit in a truck', looking like Rip Van Winkle or Blackbeard the Pirate will not benefit the cause, although this certainly is an option. Unfortunately, these are usually the type to 'let themselves go' and 'do their own thing'. I realize that some of these people purposely look like this in protest for poor pay and horrible treatment from those they come in contact with but this does not solve anything. Nevertheless, there *is* room out here for everybody and that is the American way. *God Bless America!*

Being a truck driver, you get to see a whole lot more of the big picture than the clock puncher. Because of being away from home, friends and family for prolonged periods of time, trucking allows someone to release the real person inside, good or bad. There is a lot of solitude and opportunity for soul searching in this profession. Maybe this has something to do with how a person either decides to cave in to slovenliness and a slothful appearance or maintain a socially acceptable image.

A person ought to have a little self-respect when it comes to wearing dirty clothes with holes in the knees and underwear showing. This may be fashionable for movie stars but certainly does not enhance the truck driver's image to the public. Filthy apparel and smelly body odor are not only unacceptable, but also unhealthy and unnecessary. Is it any wonder these types are treated as second-class citizens? Every truck stop provides free shower facilities after fueling and most have laundromats available.

Of course, there are also a good many clean, professional looking truck drivers. It is entirely up to the individual how he maintains his appearance. There is no reason to appear like a bum. Some of the large trucking companies do have a dress code to adhere to. UPS is a good example, although that is a bit extreme at this time. Personally, I would like to someday see a similar image out here for all truckers.

Anyone who intends to try to develop a business as an independent owner-operator will stand a much better chance of doing so if he looks more like a professional businessman than a burned out hippie from the sixties. People in a decision-making capacity are going to be a lot more receptive to someone that blends in with the rest of society and cares what their customers think about a driver's appearance.

Let me put it like this. Suppose you were at the airport to catch a commercial flight and could look out into the cockpit of the plane you were going to board, which is sometimes possible. If the pilot and co-pilot were sitting there wearing skull caps and cross-bone muscle shirts, sporting scraggly beards and long unkempt hair, holes in their clothes, rings in their ears or nose and tattoos plastered everywhere, would you feel good about getting on the plane?

Shorts that look like underwear, sweatpants that look like pajamas and muscle shirts exposing hairy armpits are not appropriate attire anywhere in public. When the general public sees truck drivers that look like that, how do you suppose they feel about it? What about shippers and customers you are delivering to? Do you think it makes a difference? How about the people you work for?

Maybe if an employer looked in his driver's lounge and saw only drivers with a professional image, he would feel more inclined to pay and treat them more professionally. Maybe! What do you think?

Wal-Mart drivers in uniform look professional. Most Teamster Union drivers are also generally more professional in their appearance and safer in their driving. So are all company truck drivers in uniform. Nobody ridicules them! They are treated with respect! They drive safer! They appear safer! They are safer! It is demanded of them and they respond to this demand because they value their job and the company they work for. They are paid professionally! They act professional! They are professional!

Unskilled! I don't think so!

## 34. PRIVATE VEHICLES ARE A BIG PROBLEM

For sure the CDL was a big step in the right direction but the solution to safety on the highways goes much deeper than that. What the government seems not to have taken into consideration is the fact that most drivers out here are not driving eighteen-wheelers. They are driving their own personal pleasure vehicles and these drivers are totally unregulated other than the credit-sized card in their wallet that indicates they passed a minimum requirement driver's test to get permission to drive a motor vehicle called a 'driver's license'. Certainly, they are not required to use a logbook to record their activity.

This is where a good share of the problem concerning safety lies. These millions of drivers of all sizes of underpowered and overpowered personal vehicles are for the most part totally unaware of the danger of being around eighteen-wheelers. Proof of this is the fact than they endlessly ride alongside these huge eighteen-wheelers for mile after mile, oblivious that a tire could blow out or a wheel come off and change their lives forever. These small vehicles seem to trust the ability of the truck driver to hold his position indefinitely as though the truck was riding on rails. Rutted blacktop highways, dips in the road, high wind and other factors can cause a truck or any vehicle for that matter, to swerve or 'walk' into the next lane. If they only realized that many times a truck driver does not even know the smaller vehicle is there because it is in a blind spot, maybe they would drive differently. Many times they find out too late, only after an accident or near-accident occurs. Of course should this happen, the first one to get blamed is the truck driver.

It seems that everyone concerned about highway safety relating to truck accidents has been concentrating on how to improve the truck driver's ability and skills by requiring the CDL and most recently, up-grading federal guidelines for logbook rules and regulations to combat fatigue. Surely these things are important.

But what about the millions of automobile drivers that do not have a clue as to how they should be functioning when they are sharing the space near a large heavily-laden truck traveling down the highway at high speeds and totally at the control of a mere human being that has been hopefully, fully trained as a professional to 'watch out' for his 'little brother', if you will. These 'oblivious millions' are a large part of the problem when it comes to placing responsibility for a good share of these truck-related accidents. Anyone who believes otherwise is simply not thinking.

It is these millions of drivers that are allowed to work all day at their regular profession and when they are done working, jump in their personal vehicle with friends or family and drive however long it takes to get to their place of 'rest and relaxation'. Additionally, many of these folks have acquired large buses, RVs (recreational vehicles), camp trailers, boats and countless other vehicle combinations and bring them blindly into harm's way onto the 'super slab' without a lick of training or experience.

It really does not occur to anyone that all this is going on until you take the time to stop and think about it. Is it any wonder there are so many accidents and incidents every hour of every day out here. We all seem to have a lot riding on this 'safety push'. Maybe someone will enlighten the 'powers to be' and get them interested in working on this part of the problem. Of course, it is much easier to concentrate on the truck drivers since there are fewer of them and a much easier target as well as a source of guaranteed revenue.

When you are in your personal car, stay as far as you can away from all big trucks. If you are in a passing mode, get it done as quickly as you can and proceed ahead of the big trucks far enough so that they have their safety zone back sooner, rather than later. You do not want them anywhere close to you very long. If the 'super truckers' traveling twenty or thirty miles an hour over the speed limit overtake you, you should back out of it and let them go. Many times the big trucks seem to travel in packs and if they are overtaking you, simply slow down and let them all pass. Falling far behind them insures your safety and increases your visibility as they get further and further ahead. You will probably pass them later as they are parked alongside the road dealing with the highway patrol. Better them than you. You may also see them tipped over further on down the road.

# 17.

# TRUCKING CHOICES

Basically, we have seen four types of trucking. To fully explain each would fill another book. This is a brief description.

1. Union company trucks -50+ CPM with full benefits and pension, completely paid by the company. Most pull wiggle-wagons, drive 60 to 65 MPH day cabs and stay in motels, when needed. The drivers usually wear uniforms and usually look, act and drive more professionally. Earn from 50 to 70 thousand per year. Home weekly.

2. Non-union company trucks -24 to 45 CPM with partial benefits co-paid by company and driver. These can be dry vans, refrigerated, flatbed, tankers or specialized equipment, almost always with sleeper berths for overnight stays. Few get home weekly, are mostly home monthly or semimonthly, as the case may be. A few partial uniforms, mostly casual apparel. Earn from 30 to 120 thousand per year, depending on driver training capabilities and load availability.

3. Lease and owner operators -80 CPM and up with the driver bearing most or all of the cost of benefits and all expenses and responsibility. Home time is the same as # 2. Gross earnings from 75 to 200 thousand per year depending on whether team or solo. Net income is variable, usually not very good. Some tax advantages.

4. Independent owner operator -1.00 to 10.00 per mile depending on each individual circumstance, with the driver bearing 100% of benefits and expenses. These are generally the 'dream trucks' with plenty of chrome and all the bells and whistles that go up to triple digit speeds, thereby achieving 3 or 4 miles per gallon. Gross income from 100 to 300 thousand dollars per year or more, depending on individual circumstances. Net income can be very good with good tax advantages.

## 1. IMPORTANT CONSIDERATIONS

Remember, the three most important things to consider if you choose to become involved in long haul OVER THE ROAD trucking of any kind are:

1. Adequate compensation.
2. Frequent home time.
3. Good equipment.

As an entry level OVER THE ROAD truck driver at this time, be prepared to perform many tasks and obligations without compensation. Expect to spend a considerable amount of time in truck stops waiting for your dispatcher to get you a load. Waiting to load and unload for hour after hour without pay is commonplace with many companies. Be prepared to miss or reschedule appointments with doctors, dentists and many other personal events. Traveling around the United States and Canada without a dedicated run is not conducive to meeting your own personal schedules and appointments. Expect to face fog, blizzards, torrential rain, floods, hailstones, snow and ice as well as other environmental happenings such as high winds, tornadoes and forest fires.

An OVER THE ROAD truck driver must learn to be patient, courteous, cooperative and docile as opposed to impatient, aggressive, overbearing and obnoxious. You will be dealing with people that can be helpful and friendly or make your job and life miserable. Most of this attitude exchange depends on the truck driver and how he handles the many situations and problems that develop every day. It can sometimes be a real challenge. Bite your tongue and count to ten. It usually pays off in the end.

However, with the experience you gain, you should eventually qualify for almost any local truck driving jobs that are available in your hometown area. You should never have to be concerned about unemployment as long as you maintain good health. There are OVER THE ROAD truck drivers out here in their seventies and older, truckin' on down the road. It does get in your blood and can be a very enjoyable and educational profession in spite of all the shortcomings. You should always be able to earn a decent living, whether OVER THE ROAD or local. The need for trucking has existed since the beginning of time and will continue to exist in some form forever. If you follow the tips and advice in this book you can have a long and successful career.

## 2. PUBLICATIONS

It is commonplace that, apparently to help alleviate the on-going truck driver shortage, much of the trucker media sugarcoats the fact that today's OVER THE ROAD trucking career is far less than acceptable to a normal person of today's society. It is commendable that others in this same media present things as they really are. Exposing the latter information is the only way things can change.

Some of the leading transportation publications that are presently available to truck drivers are *NATSO TRUCKER NEWS*, *THE TRUCKER* newspaper and *NEWPORT"S ROADSTAR*. They all seem to be very driver friendly and dig into many of the crucial problems facing the OVER THE ROAD truck driver from the driver's viewpoint. Some of the editors are or were themselves truck drivers and are therefore highly cognizant of the many ongoing problems. These publications delve deeply into the needs and complaints of truckers and the transportation industry as a whole.

Other very informative trucker publications are *AMERICAN TRUCKER ON THE ROAD*, *LAND LINE* magazine and of course *ROAD KING* and *OVERDRIVE*. All of these are excellent publications and are staffed with people who seem genuinely concerned about what is happening in today's transportation industry.

*TRANSPORT TOPICS* is an older publication that is popular with management because it focuses on the industry from a management viewpoint.

These monthly publications that are available at no charge at most truck stops.

# 18.

# SUMMARY OF OVER THE ROAD TRUCKING

In spite of all the shortcomings, a career in trucking can nevertheless be a most mentally fulfilling and financially rewarding profession. We will recap some of the more significant items that were mentioned throughout this writing, both positive and negative. There are many items on both viewpoints and hopefully, the good outweighs the bad. However, if being an OVER THE ROAD truck driver is ever to become a truly professional career, there is much work that needs to be done.

Trucking can be very good or it can be very bad. As in all professions, it eventually comes down to the money. Whether it is a pittance for doing something extra or industry-wide average earnings, the financial reward needs to be commensurate with effort, talent and time expended. Clearly, those that are most satisfied with this profession are those that are well paid and those that do the most complaining are those that are not. Complaints have been made and gone unheard or ignored, leaving the problems causing the complaints unresolved and also leaving many OVER THE ROAD truck drivers with few alternatives other than to leave the profession.

The present free-for-all system is not working for most drivers for the most part. OVER THE ROAD truck drivers are being fined horrendous amounts for simple violations. New drivers are trembling in their shoes when approaching weigh stations because they are unsure of the laws and requirements. Experienced drivers are also stressed because many times they are forced to run illegally just to earn a realistic paycheck. However, for the shippers and receivers, trucking companies and the government, everything is going their way. They have accomplished their mission beyond expectation, at the expense of millions of dedicated truck drivers. This crucial major labor group now has little or no representation.

There is no guarantee of being given even enough miles to generate a livable paycheck with which to make rent or mortgage payments or to buy groceries. When at company facilities, they are confined to those grounds unless they have a car, call a cab, or are fortunate enough to have a company shuttle available when it is needed. Using the truck to leave the premises is forbidden unless you are under a load. Having a voice in these matters is nonexistent. Of course, you can always leave and go to another company with the same or similar conditions or find a different career.

Changes are happening constantly and will continue until the profession comes to maturity in relation to pay and conditions. Chief among those are safety, which is directly affected by lack of fair and adequate income, so that drivers do not have to push themselves beyond endurance and capability to produce a living wage on a regular basis. Lives are definitely at stake!

Additionally, when a driver is committed to his job and/or company to the point of being continually on the job and away from his home and family for weeks or months at a time, he needs assurance that just compensation will be forthcoming regardless of any other circumstances that may develop, as it is in all other professions. His family requires this assurance also! Some kind of minimum wage would seem to be in order. Most normal people do not like to 'job hop' or even 'career hop'. Once a responsible individual has entered this profession and developed positive relationships, as well as medical coverage and other insurances and savings programs, it is difficult to simply pull up stakes and start over with another trucking company that may very well be a step backwards.

Everybody talks about the shortage of OVER THE ROAD truck drivers, driver fatigue and safety. If the pay and conditions were as they should be, these issues would self-correct. There is no shortage in other transportation related careers such as airline pilots, railroad engineers or longshoremen because even though their jobs are far less demanding, they have much higher pay and far better benefits. Most of them are no more intelligent or better educated than most truck drivers. If OVER THE ROAD truck driver pay improves to where it matches the demands required, there will no longer be a truck driver shortage either.

As it is now, all that is necessary to become an OVER THE ROAD truck driver is that you must be of average intelligence, in good health and willing to be away from home for long periods of time. You can expect to start out earning five or six hundred dollars a week and up to and beyond $1000 or more a week as a solo driver if you are successful. The hopeful expectation of these earnings has resulted in attracting not only the average American family man but also multitudes of misfits from our society and imported foreigners from other countries that barely speak English, adding to the safety problem.

The countless unprofessional driver training schools and questionable lease-operator and owner-operator programs have resulted in a tremendous amount of money being borrowed by individuals that are many times least able to afford it and /or continue on with OVER THE ROAD trucking as a career. Sadly, these schools are geared up to maximize enrollment and minimize training, knowing full well that only a small percentage of recruits will see it through.

It is important to locate a quality school that is more interested in you as a student than as a loan applicant. The longer and more thorough the initial training is, the better chance you will have of success. Examine all available schools thoroughly to be sure they provide everything you need to get started. Ask to speak with someone that has already completed their course. Leave no stone unturned.

Learning to become an OVER THE ROAD truck driver seems to be the most popular way for someone to gain the experience necessary to become a truck driver in any field, whether as an OVER THE ROAD driver, local driver, lease or owner-operator.

If you can get over all the many hurdles, this can be a stepping stone to a local driving job that will probably have less income but will get you home more often or even every night, in many cases. And a local job may not have less income after all. It may have more income in some cases.

Many large trucking companies have designed lease or owner-operator programs that appear to be very marginal in profitability. For those willing to make a full commitment of their time and effort to one of these programs, it may be possible to acquire the truck they drive after several years of intense OVER THE ROAD trucking. This requires that the driver and his family will be separated much of the time with only irregular visits home.

Very few succeed in accomplishing this. Do not be in a hurry to try this! In fact, do not even consider being an owner-operator unless you have three or four years of experience behind you. Everything is in favor of the companies with no guarantees of any kind for the drivers. They are capitalizing on the dreams, hopes and desires of individuals who should never attempt such a venture because, due to the many variables they are ultimately doomed to failure!

This includes becoming a company driver. Many times an OVER THE ROAD truck driver will find himself pleading with his dispatcher to get him more miles so he can pay his bills. It is not automatic that just because you are available for a load, you will get one. The truth and problems are buried by trucking companies in all the initial activity. The driver's plight seems to be of little concern to those in management, especially on the weekends. It is a well-known fact that dispatchers do not always tell the truth when dealing with drivers.

Sooner or later, new drivers realize they are underpaid and can do nothing about it. This is when they can become susceptible to getting involved in one of the many questionable lease or owner-operator programs. These plans are presented as the answer to all the problems. However, most owner-operator and lease-operator programs are marginal at best. You may be jumping from the frying pan into the fire.

Because of the industry-wide driver shortage caused by low pay and poor conditions, most OVER THE ROAD trucking companies seem to have looked the other way when it comes to logbooks and driver appearance. Some drivers look like they just got off a pirate's ship. Others look like Rip Van Winkle. Multiple rings and other metal piercing in the eyebrows, nose, ears and other body parts are commonplace along with ragged clothing, tattoos and muscle shirts. Some of them look like walking advertisements for a freak show!

Benefits and retirement programs cease to exist with many small companies operating by the seat of their pants. Working spouses seem to be expected to provide these things with their non-trucking employers. Having to depend on a working spouse to provide benefits should not be necessary in any profession. This results in more driver turnover and lack of respect by others.

The prevalent attitude toward OVER THE ROAD truckers is not as it should be by dispatch, customers or truck stop personnel. Deregulation has resulted in many of these drivers taking on the many duties previously performed routinely at truck terminals, such as fueling, scaling loads and maintenance and even warehouse sorting and segregating. Fuel islands are chaotic. Lack of parking space is a major issue that was not an issue before deregulation. Instead of being treated as valued business professionals and truck stop customers as the case may be, they are considered an interruption and many times ignored totally or worse, forgotten about. Tempers flair frequently.

Carrying piggyback trailers by rail on the train is becoming more and more prevalent. Trainload after trainload of this type of transportation can be observed every day, all across the country. Each of these trailers represents a driver's job. Additionally, many times the trailers that are transported by rail can become damaged en-route and it is up to the truck driver delivering the load on the other end to inspect each trailer and notice any such damage so that he will not be held responsible. With improved rail service, inter-modal transportation of piggyback trailers could increase dramatically, reducing much of the need for OVER THE ROAD truck drivers. This will not help increase driver pay.

Of course this results in the need for local drivers on each end but most railroad yards are a pain in the neck for drivers to deal with. Some of them are so large you can get lost in them and there is usually nobody to direct you or even adequate signs giving instructions. For experienced drivers it can be a real hassle; for first timers, overwhelming! Inter-modal is great for the companies but not for OVER THE ROAD truck drivers. If the hourly pay for handling these loads was higher, it might be more worthwhile. Unfortunately, local pay for most OVER THE ROAD trucking companies leaves much to be desired.

Most newcomers to truck owning or leasing are blindly getting involved in a very marginal business venture in high hopes of being successful in their new endeavor. Unfortunately, due to the many variables and circumstances beyond their control, the high cost of operating and amount of time demanded, not to mention the fluctuating cost of fuel, many of these well-meaning people eventually suffer financial disaster.

At the same time the moneylenders are reaping the harvest at the expense of those hard-working folks that have stuck their necks out, whether or not they succeed.

This is not to say that some of these truckers do not do well. Circumstances determine this. Some owner-operators are also driver trainers and therefore are earning well into six figures. They are obviously not home much.

Some lease and owner-operators that team up or become driver trainers at the same time to maximize their miles can do well if they make up their mind that their life belongs to their truck and the company they work with for a period of several years.

Husband/wife teams can do well if they have a strong relationship and can handle the constant togetherness. Many of these teams drive a combined total of 300,000 miles or more a year. When team income is kept under one roof, it is a definite advantage. You can be sure they do not have much time off for friends and family.

Some owner-operators find 'nitches' that are more profitable than the run of the mill trucking and become very successful. I know of no statistics to compare the successes and failures of these operations. I do know that they have to work hard to accomplish this.

All I can advise is that before getting too deeply involved in becoming an OVER THE ROAD truck driver of any kind you should check into it very thoroughly in every way possible. Understand that this can be very emotionally devastating for a family to be without one of their major players when he is most needed. Too many lives are being compromised or ruined. Preparation and planning are crucial!

The thing to ask yourself is, "Why do all these companies want drivers to own or lease the trucks that pull their loads rather than do it themselves?" The obvious short answer is, *"It saves them money and provides them with long-term drivers." Companies are profiting off each individual owner-operator or lease-operator, regardless of whether or not the individuals survive financially.*

*You must also ask yourself what makes you think you can operate more profitably than the company you are leased to, for about half the revenue?* You must take into consideration that at least 30 to 40 CPM must be set aside for your own pay. If this puts you into a break-even or negative cash flow, is it worth it? You will be reaching into your own pocket to support a truck. There are many owner-operators barely getting by. Your driver pay per mile can be reduced to ten or fifteen cents a mile after meeting all the other financial obligations. The price of fuel can make or break you.

For those that are determined to become an independent owner-operator, this is definitely an option after gaining the necessary knowledge and contacts. If this is the ultimate goal from the start, it is best to pursue an entry position with a company involved in the type hauling you are interested in right from the beginning such as autos, boats, machinery or whatever. It can take many years to gain the experience required to do this successfully. There is no reason to rush in too soon because a decent income can be earned as a company driver indefinitely. Then, when you and your family are ready to take the big step, you will have been properly prepared.

While it is true the compensation does not presently match the time and talents of an OVER THE ROAD trucker and the conditions are questionable, there are other things that might make this career purposeful. Touring this great land and experiencing the awesome sights constantly available is priceless. A trip through the Rocky Mountains can cause you to realize just how insignificant us mere mortals really are. These mountains have been here seemingly forever while we are present for an eye-blink in time. Attitude counts for a lot. Truly, today's OVER THE ROAD truck driver is a 'commercial tourist', getting paid to escape the boredom and stress of the eight to five segment of the population.

You will meet many interesting people from all walks of life from the shipping clerk to the CEO of a company. Some of these people recognize the importance of a truck driver and treat him with respect. They depend on movement of products and goods for their own livelihood. Plant tours and visits to various production and distribution facilities can be very interesting and educational. Much can be seen and learned on the road.

Basic requirements to become an OVER THE ROAD truck driver seem to be:

1. Excellent health.
2. Willingness to be away from home weeks/months at a time.
3. Driving skills with heavy equipment.
4. Able to maneuver oversized equipment in cities and places designed for much smaller equipment of the past.
5. Desire to travel/drive in 48 states and Canada in all kinds of weather and terrain.
6. Accept responsibility for the safety of your equipment and cargo.
7. Have excellent communication skills since most is done remotely via satellite in preference to direct voice methods.
8. Able to drive all night after waiting around all day for various reasons.
9. Ability to be punctual, dependable and courteous under difficult circumstances that are almost always uncompensated for.
10. Be prepared to eat out of a cooler and/or fast food restaurants because of the high cost of living on the road and limited income.
11. Be able to develop a positive attitude by accepting the negatives and making the best of the way things are because they are not going to change anytime soon.
12. You must be adventurous, flexible in your thinking and able to operate independently, using common sense quickly in a decision-making capacity, as needed.

Most long-time OVER THE ROAD truckers tolerate this profession by rationalizing. To some folks $30,000 a year is big money. Others cannot get by on less than $50,000 or more. This is why so many OVER THE ROAD truck drivers stick it out. Where else can someone earn $50,000 to $100,000 per year? Doing this might better than:

1. No job.
2. Working inside.
3. Poorer pay.

4. Having two or more jobs.
5. Regular hours, punching a time clock.

I have seen some OVER THE ROAD truck drivers tire of it and move inside to management as dispatchers, safety personnel or other positions, then go back on the road because it is solitary and pays better. Most eventually do go back inside for good because the stress out here is greater and the money just not worth the demands.

Nevertheless, at this time, you have to accept OVER THE ROAD trucking as it is or do not attempt to do it. You will be wasting your time and money. It is true that many from other careers can more easily accept the pay and conditions because of previously having had bad experiences in those prior positions. OVER THE ROAD trucking offers many different things to many different people. There is no one answer to most of the multitude of problems that exist. Since this aspect of transportation is still in it's infancy, many changes can be expected over the next several decades. One hundred years ago this profession did not exist. One hundred years from now, it will not be the same.

# 19.

# STARTER KIT

For those who would like to continue on and pursue OVER THE ROAD trucking as a career, I have put together a **STARTER KIT.** This kit is designed to make it as simple and easy as possible for anyone who is genuinely interested to get started in OVER THE ROAD trucking.

## STARTER KIT—A LIFETIME IN THE MAKING

There are many qualified tax advisors that advertise in the free monthly trucker magazines and newspapers that are far more qualified than someone unfamiliar with trucking. The important thing is to get someone who is knowledgeable and specializes in OVER THE ROAD truck drivers.

**DEDUCTIBLE EXPENSES:** This is a list of over 100 deductible expenses that are allowed by the IRS and can be entered onto the included spreadsheet.

**SPREAD SHEET & INCOME TAX ORGANIZER:** This form keeps a monthly recap of all your expenses and gives a running total for each column and grand total for the month and year. This makes doing your income tax a breeze and can save you thousands of dollars and many hours of time. This program can easily be reformatted for an owner-operator's expenses. Owner-operators who have seen it say it is better than what they acquired for several hundred dollars.

**INTRODUCTORY DRIVER TRAINER (TRAIN THE TRAINER) NOTES:** These notes are a compilation of decades of driver training experience and are designed to assist both trainer and trainee. They answer many of the questions a trainee has before he has a chance to ask them and relieve the trainer of having to wonder if he has covered this important material. When a trainee finishes reading them, he should feel prepared to finish his training in confidence. They can be modified to fit any individual's personality. These preparatory notes are immeasurably helpful to both trainer and trainee.

**TRIP ASSIGNMENT FORM:** This form is designed so that when you finish filling in the designated spaces, all the information for each trip assignment will be at your fingertips. In addition, it will cause you to be 100% efficient as you progress in each trip by requiring you to easily record all pertinent information regarding fuel ups, pickups and deliveries. When you finish each trip, it will provide complete information to fill out any payroll sheet for any company you choose to work for. It can serve as a permanent record of trip all activity.

**COMPARISON CHART TO CHOOSE A COMPANY TO WORK FOR:** This chart has many of the important items listed that need to be considered before choosing the company you may be with for the next several years. Changing jobs is never a pleasant experience so it is important to pick a company that best suits your needs the first time. Insurance, benefits and time off policies rank high on the list. A company close to your home location may be best, provided they meet your other demands. Then you can park your truck at the company yard on time off and not worry about security.

**CANADA LOGBOOK REQUIREMENTS:** If you get with a company that goes to Canada, and most of them do, you will want to keep this information handy. Canada has quite different logbook requirements than the United States and the fines are stiff.

**TRAINEE SELF-EVALUATION SHEET:** I developed this sheet so that the trainee himself can let the trainer know how good he thinks he is doing in all the different aspects of the training. It is amazing some of the answers and comments I get that I never would have realized without this questionnaire. It has been a big aid to me as a trainer to help me know what areas to concentrate on to help my trainees finish the training successfully.

**STEERING AXLE WEIGHT CHART (MAP):** This handy map shows all the different weight limits for the steering axle. This information is very important since it can be very difficult to get all the weights exactly legal for each state when grossing 80,000#. The entire STARTER KIT can be e-mailed to you and is only $19.95. It can be ordered by calling me 435-817-0545 during normal business hours. Or my e-mail address is *gordonknapp@ comcast.net*, facebook address is *gordonknapp68@yahoo.com*.

# 20.

# GLOSSARY OF CB AND TRUCKER TERMS

These is an incomplete list of some of the terms truckers use to identify things.

Air dryer—this is a unit that is attached inline to the air system that takes moisture from the system to prevent airline freeze-ups and other moisture problems.

Alligator—term for a tire recap lying in the road that has come loose from a tire because they have a look similar to an alligator's hide.

Back Door—when two or more trucks are traveling together, this is the last or rearmost position.

Bear—highway patrol. This name was derived from the forest fire prevention advertisement on TV many years ago that featured Smokey the Bear, a cartoon character that promoted safety when in and around wooded areas while camping and vacationing. His hat was similar to what some highway patrol wear.

Bear Bait—fast moving vehicle passing everybody else.

Bill of Lading (B/L)—document describing commodities being carried.

Black ice—clear ice formed by water freezing as temperature drops from non-freezing to freezing.

Blind spot—areas around the truck that are difficult or impossible for the driver to be able to see whether something may be near his vehicle.

Brake chamber—spring loaded, air-operated emergency brake canisters that function automatically on tractor and trailer so that the rig cannot roll away out of control should the air pressure bleed off.

Brake check—traffic ahead is slowing or stopping.

Bumper lane—right or slow lane on a multi-lane highway, indicating that the slower traffic travels bumper to bumper, sometimes like the bumper car ride in an amusement park.

Bumper sticker—term used to describe a small vehicle following a big rig too close, causing themselves to be an extreme annoyance to the truck driver.

Canned message—pre-installed messages on the sat-com for the most common messages used the most frequently.

Chicken coops—weigh station. These used to be small sheds that resembled the old 'chicken coops' of the past where country folks raised their own chickens. Modern weigh stations more closely resemble state of the art airport buildings, including towers, loudspeakers and large garages that are used as inspection bays.

City kitty—town police.

Chicken lights—multiple bright lights on the front of a truck that intimidate other traffic to 'get out of the way', thus being 'chicken' or intimidated by the large approaching vehicle from the rear.

Chicken truck—trucks that go faster than most and expect slower and smaller traffic to get out of their way. This term is also sometimes used to identify trucks that actually haul chickens.

COE—cab over engine.

Comedian strip—median strip in the center of a divided highway.

Coops—weigh station. Short version.

Coops closed—weigh station may have a full ramp or be checking out another truck but officers are still in there and may reopen momentarily.

Coops locked up—weigh station is closed and nobody there, music to a trucker's ears.

County Mounty—Sheriff or deputy sheriff.

Deadhead—running without a load.

Dedicated Run—some large shippers or manufacturers require regular drivers from a trucking company that haul their products exclusively.

Diesel Bear—Highway Patrol. /DOT inspector.

Disco Lights—emergency lights on police cars.

Doubles—two trailers pulled together.

Double clutch—letting the clutch out, then quickly depressing it again to allow the transmission gears to mesh properly, without grinding or jamming.

Eyeball out—headlight out.

Fifth wheel—this is the large, round plate attached behind the truck cab to the frame that connects to the king pin on the trailer. This term originates from the first trucks, which were four-wheelers. When it was decided to attach trailers to the truck to increase the payload capability, the connector appeared at that time as another wheel lying on the frame, thus the term, fifth wheel.

Fisheye mirrors—convex mirrors located on the tractor fenders to allow the driver to have more visibility in blind spots on both sides of the truck.

Floating gears—shifting a standard transmission without using the clutch. Requires foot/hand coordination in conjunction with timing of engine and transmission speed.

Four-wheeler—small vehicles.

Front door—when two or more trucks are traveling together, this is the lead or front position.

Full Grown Bear—State Police, Highway Patrol

Glad hand—the connector on the air hose that attaches the tractor air compressor line to the trailer air line.

Glad hand rubber grommet—this is the rubber ring in the glad hand that seals the connection between tractor and trailer. Sometimes they wear out and need to be replaced by the driver with a screwdriver or knife. Many times applying saliva to the rubber will cause an air leak to stop.

Hammer down—increase your speed

Hammer lane—passing or left lane on a multi-lane highway, derived from the expression 'hammer down' which means to go fast.

Hand—term used to identify a truck driver, shortened from 'hired hand'

Haz-mat—hazardous materials whereby specific handling, signing, placarding and routes must be adhered to. These routes are identified by signs with the letters HC encircled, nationwide

Headache Rack—protective barrier attached to the front of a flatbed trailer or behind the cab on the frame of a tractor that pulls flatbeds, to protect the driver in the event of a load shift when braking.

Hostler—Yardman that shuttles trailers into and out of loading docks with a yard horse at various shippers and receivers.

Horse—tractor

King Pin—this is the large pin underneath the nose of the trailer that connects to the 5th wheel of the tractor.

Jackknife—term used to describe when the trailer slides into the tractor in a folding jackknife position.

Jake Brake—engine retarder that causes additional compression on a diesel engine for braking assistance.

Jersey Barrier—concrete forms used as lane dividers.

Large Car—Big truck, refers to the power unit or tractor.

LTL—Less than Truckload.

Live load /unload—driver must be there.

Local—town police.

Lot lizard—prostitute that frequents truck stops or rest areas.

Macro—standard message form on a sat-com.

Mile stick—mile marker.

OS&D (over, short & damage)—discrepancies upon pickup or delivery.

Peek-a-boo Window—small window in the passenger door of a tractor near the floorboard to help the driver see traffic in the blind spot.

Pickle Park—rest area. Use your imagination on this one.

Piggyback—term used to describe trailers that are transported by rail.

Pigtail—electrical plug on the end of the tractor light cord that plugs into the trailer to supply power from the tractor to all the lights and signals on the trailer.

Port of Entry—another term for weigh station.

Pups—small or short trailers, used to be pulled as doubles or triples.

Radar detector—device used to warn drivers of nearby police using a radar gun to catch speeders.

Radar detector detectors—device used by police to let them know a driver has a radar detector, which is illegal for truckers to use nationwide but legal for the general population in private vehicles.

Regional—Confined to a particular area of the country.

Rocking Chair—when traveling in a group of trucks, this position is neither front nor rear but a middle location.

Roll with the flow—going the same speed as all other traffic regardless of the posted speed to prevent traffic backup and dangerous passing conditions.

Rubberneckers—People that slow to a crawl to gawk upon seeing an accident or other unusual event, thereby causing a traffic backup in their lane and unnecessarily increasing the possibility of another accident.

Salt and peppershaker—highway sand truck in winter.

Sandwich lane—center lane on a 3-lane highway going in the same direction.

Sat-com—satellite communicator installed in most fleet trucks.

Seal—security device designed to ensure that access or break-in to a loaded trailer

can be quickly detected and thereby investigated as to responsibility. Usually only one seal is assigned to each door on every load and on rear doors should be affixed to the right door since that door must be opened before the left door can be opened.

Shiny Hiney—stainless steel trailer doors.

Slack adjuster—brake adjustment part.

Smokey Bear—highway patrol. See bear.

Stage—prepare a load for shipping.

Stinger Rig—tractor with a trailer coupling other than a 5th wheel that connects low to the ground, giving it the impression of the stinger of a bee, usually an automobile or construction equipment hauler.

Snub braking—when in lower gears, to prevent brake loss/smoking going downhill, brake 5 mph to lower speed, then release brakes, regain speed and do it again until reaching the bottom of a long grade or mountain.

Split—junction or location where two highways come together.

Spot mirror—small, round convex mirror placed in various locations to help reduce blind spots.

Spread tandem—two axles on a trailer placed far enough apart to allow more weight distribution to be placed toward the rear of a trailer, to comply with weight distribution requirements.

Stab breaking—harsh, firm braking, then releasing until the vehicle stops in control.

Standard braking—steady even light pressure at low speed for descending a major mountain, to prevent over-heating or 'smoking' the brakes.

Stupid Ass—driver of any vehicle, truck or car, that passes promptly, then slows to your exact speed in your safety zone and stays there.

Tandem—two axles located close to each other to allow heavier weight to be carried safely.

TL—truckload.

Triples—three trailers hooked together.

Vehicle Onboard Radar—(VORAD)—greatest under-promoted safety invention since rumble strips on the shoulder of the road and engine brakes. All cars and trucks should have this.

Wagon—trailer

Weigh station—the most feared locations in various states for all truck drivers. It is at these locations that most local, state and federal officials perform unscheduled inspections of logbooks and equipment while at the same time checking to see that weight distribution is correct. Fines and 'out of service' orders can be very costly and/or time consuming for both the driver and the company he works for as a result of these inspections if things are not in order.

West coast mirrors—large mirrors located on both sides of a tractor for maximum rear visibility.

Wiggle-wagons—two or three small trailers hooked together.

Yard horse—small, very maneuverable tractors used to shuttle trailers into and away from the loading docks of various companies.

Yard stick—mile marker.

Zipper—dotted line painted on highway indicating that it is a passing area.

Owner-Operator James and Carol Warren

Author Gordon J. Knapp